Strindberg: Five Plays

AUGUST STRINDBERG

Strindberg: Five Plays

Translated, with an introduction, by

HARRY G. CARLSON

University of California Press

Berkeley • Los Angeles • London

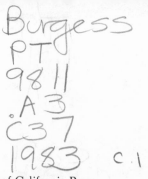

University of California Press
Berkeley and Los Angeles, California

University of California Press, Ltd.
London, England

© 1981, 1983 by Harry G. Carlson

Printed in the United States of America

1 2 3 4 5 6 7 8 9

Library of Congress Cataloging in Publication Data

Strindberg, August, 1849–1912.
   Strindberg, five plays.

   Contents: The father—Miss Julie—The dance of
death, pt. 1—[etc.]
   I. Title.
PT9811.A3C37   1983   839.7′26   82-15882
ISBN 0-520-04697-8
ISBN 0-520-04698-6 (pbk.)

For My Parents
Bertha A. and Harry C.

CONTENTS

INTRODUCTION

Probably no important figure in the history of drama provokes as varied reactions from critics as August Strindberg. On the one hand, he is respected for accomplishments in both realism and nonrealism, for his daring to experiment as few playwrights before or after him have done: aspiring to achieve in drama the immediacy of expression and fluidity of form possible in music and painting. Like Beethoven (whom he admired and identified with), he was equally adept at broad orchestral pieces like *A Dream Play* and intimate chamber works like *Miss Julie* and *The Dance of Death.* If Ibsen was the Rembrandt of modern drama, its master of the poetry of psychological portraiture, Strindberg was its Picasso, its restless, inventive spirit, prodigious and prolific, the progenitor of German expressionism and the theatre of the absurd, who taught vital lessons to as diverse talents as Artaud, O'Neill, O'Casey, Williams, Beckett, Pinter, and Albee.

On the other hand, Strindberg is criticized for lacking humor and for being too autobiographical. The reputation for gloominess, regrettably, is one he shares with fellow Scandinavians Ibsen,

1

Edvard Munch, and Ingmar Bergman. (I recall a friend who, after three hours at a Munch exhibit, said he felt an irresistible desire to rush out and catch an old Gene Kelly movie.) Certainly in the cases of Strindberg and Ibsen, the reputation is unjust and undeserved, probably the result of a heavy-handed interpretative approach that has long been traditional in the English-speaking theatre. Kenneth Tynan once described to me Laurence Olivier's shock at discovering that audiences found Strindberg's *The Dance of Death* wonderfully amusing when the play was produced with the lightness and wit it deserved. Contained in the play is the same metaphysical tension present in Beckett's *Waiting for Godot,* the same awareness of the great joke that destiny has played upon modern man: forcing him to go on, to try to find something to do to give him the feeling that he exists, while he waits in vain for a deity who has absconded with all meaning.

That Strindberg was autobiographical is indisputable. Like Goethe (another favorite), he proclaimed that his entire *oeuvre* could be read as a single, long confession, and several generations of scholars have taken him at his word, demonstrating convincingly how closely the artist drew upon the facts of his life for the substance of his art. Unfortunately, some critics have concluded from this evidence that his plays are coherent only when examined in the context of his life. At its best, biographical interpretation shows the brilliant alchemy he practiced, the transformation of the ordinary details of life into the gold of art. At its worst, the approach reduces the artist in stature by making him appear more subjective than he actually was. Certainly it fails to explain his continuing influence and popularity.

The fact is that there is not one Strindberg—the inveterate autobiographer—but many. In Sweden he is not only the national playwright, but novelist, poet, and pamphleteer as well, admired for his extraordinary capacity for synthesizing various gifts and insights. With the perspective and values of a classical scholar, he combined the sure instincts of a journalist who knows how to go straight for the jugular. He was at one time or another naturalist and symbolist, scientist and mystic, skeptic and true believer, aristocratic snob and proletarian stalwart, and, to be sure, misogynist—but also high priest and prophet of the Eternal Feminine.

Born in 1849 in Stockholm, he liked to romanticize his middle-class origin by making it appear more humble than it actually was. The title of his autobiography, *The Son of a Servant Woman* (1886–1887), emphasizes his proletarian roots, but the work itself reveals a man with deeply ambivalent feelings, as much an aristocrat of the intellect as a man of the people. After several desultory years at the University of Uppsala, he toyed with the idea of becoming a teacher, then a doctor, then an actor. But a few experiences years earlier presiding at Sunday church services had aroused in him an unquenchable desire to preach, to be a truthsayer. Innate skeptic that he was, he could never commit himself totally to a religious life; instead, he turned to writing with a strong sense of mission. The protagonists of his first plays, written in the early 1870s, are young men seeking earnestly to find callings that will give their lives meaning.

Several years of work as a reporter and editor, and then librarian, provided income to support more serious literary ambitions. By the early 1880s his promise as a novelist and poet was recognized not only in Sweden but throughout Scandinavia, and less than a decade later he had acquired an international reputation for the boldness of his plays. Not long after his death in 1912, it was evident that he was a major figure in modern drama, and perhaps in world drama as well.

To appreciate the full range of these achievements, it is necessary to adopt a new perspective, to complement the biographical approach with a less myopic view. E. H. Gombrich makes the telling point in his *Art and Illusion* that although we can perceive an object in two very different ways—now it is a duck, now a rabbit—"we cannot experience alternative readings at the same time." Perhaps this is why a biographical reading of Strindberg's work has tended to blind critics to other values.

The novel *Inferno* (1897) provides a good example of the multi-leveled meaning with which he was able to enrich his art. On the biographical level, the events depicted take place in the great watershed period in his life that scholars refer to as his "Inferno Crisis." For more than a half-decade between 1892 and 1897 he abandoned belles-lettres. At the same time his personal life and career were in shambles: his first marriage, to Swedish aristocrat and would-be actress Siri von Essen, had ended in 1891 after more than thirteen years, and a second marriage, to Austrian journalist Frida Uhl, broke up after less than two years. Living in exile on the Continent, he was a pariah in his homeland, his writings considered too radical politically and too candid sexually.

The story in the novel parallels the author's life fairly closely: an impoverished writer, grown unsure of his calling, is bereft of friends and family. Down and out in Paris, he plunges desperately into alchemical experiments and occult research, samples various drugs, and experiences a series of frightening hallucinatory episodes. Almost miraculously, he comes through the crisis infused with a new creative spirit, ready to begin a new life.

One view of *Inferno* sees in it clear evidence of Strindberg teetering on the edge of insanity. Another view holds that he was, like Hamlet, only mad north-by-northwest. His Inferno Crisis, after all, does not differ substantially from midlife crises suffered by other artists who enjoyed similar restorations of creative powers. Here was an artist testing new means of expression, using madness, as other artists have, to explore the boundaries of reality. However psychically wounded Strindberg was by his crisis—a matter of controversy among scholars—he recovered sufficiently to take on a full load of responsibilities, personal and professional, over the next decade. He married for the third time, albeit briefly (to Norwegian actress Harriet Bosse, almost thirty years his junior); wrote three dozen plays, seven novels, six essay collections, three collections of short stories, and a book of poetry; and finally achieved some of the recognition due him by his countrymen.

If, mindful of Gombrich's observation, we wrench our perspective on *Inferno,* forgetting for a moment the obvious biographical references, another level of meaning presents itself. The novel is filled with a host of literary, mythic, and occult allusions: to Dante, of course, but also, among other sources, to Balzac, Nietzsche, the Bible, Greco-Roman and Nordic mythology, Buddhism, Emanuel Swedenborg, and theosophy. The journey undertaken by the narrator resembles many another journey celebrated in Western literature: a pilgrimage in search of salvation, through "the dark night of the soul"—a journey as old and traditional as Odysseus's visit to the Underworld or Christ's Harrowing of Hell.

Nor is *Inferno* unique in this respect among Strindberg's works; whether it be in plays, novels, or poems, action and meaning often unfold on two levels, the first biographical, the second mythic or archetypal. Consequently, it is necessary to examine his work, so to speak, bifocally: both the near landscape of biography and the not-so-distant landscape of myth and fairy tale.

The historical setting for the biographical landscape in plays like *The Father* and *Miss Julie* is of course Europe in the late 1880s, and reflected in them are not only the author's personal problems and concerns—especially his marital squabbles—but a variety of political, psychological, and philosophical themes popular at the time. Strindberg's own divided sense of political allegiance—democratic on the one hand, elitist on the other—is present in *Miss Julie,* where his sympathies alternate between Jean, the servant, and Julie, the aristocrat. In both plays, echoing Schopenhauer as much as Darwin, Strindberg stresses the theme of life as a struggle for survival in which victory goes to the individual or the species best equipped by heredity to adapt to a changing environment. "I find the joy of life," he wrote in the Preface to *Miss Julie,* "in its cruel and powerful struggles, and my enjoyment comes from being able to know something, being able to learn something." In the same essay he goes on to enumerate the forces conspiring to bring about the heroine's destruction during the brief, tragic affair she has with her father's valet: weaknesses inherited from her mother, an improper upbringing, and the dangerously romantic atmosphere of a midsummer eve. Julie is unfit to wage the struggle successfully.

The basic conflict in *The Father* is between a man and wife for control of their daughter's future, but control of the future itself seems at stake as well. "We're not alike," the Captain says to Laura. "If it's true that we're descended from apes, it must be from different species." When Laura triumphs in the end, we sense it not only as the end of a battle between two individuals but as a turning point in a war in which the awesome powers of Nature have played a role. One of Strindberg's accomplishments in these plays was to suggest effectively that the dynamic interplay between heredity and environment in the survival of the fittest is a modern equivalent of the ancient Greek concept of fate.

Readings in the fledgling science of psychology (especially the Nancy school) confirmed Strindberg's own acute insights about the influence on behavior of the unconscious mind. The protagonists struggle not only with forces from without but with forces from within. Even as the Captain senses that a web is being spun around him, he lacks the ability to extricate himself from it. He knows that he is more dependent on his old nurse than he should be, but his need for her is so deep-rooted that he is unable to do without her. Julie too is a prisoner of forces beyond her understanding; she says she hates men but admits she cannot control the desires that erupt from time to time within her. The impression that psychological warfare is taking place is reinforced with numerous references to such popular phenomena of the day as hypnotism, the power of suggestion, and automatic writing. When the Captain's mind cracks under the strain of his battle with Laura, her brother, the Pastor, accuses her of an "unconscious crime."

Complementing the psychological dimension in the plays is a metaphysical dimension best examined by shifting our attention bifocally to the mythopoetic landscape. Present in almost all of Strindberg's plays, either explicitly or implicitly, is the metaphor of earthly life as a prison, a tomb of matter, in which man's spirit is trapped and seeks release. Inspired first by Schopenhauer and later by Gnosticism and Buddhism, the metaphor is most clearly developed in a short creation play, *Coram Populo,* that Strindberg wrote in 1877-1878 and then rewrote a decade later, after the Inferno Crisis. The central characters are God and Lucifer, vying for control over man's fate. God is an evil demiurge figure, a lower-order deity, who creates the earth in order to take pleasure in the sufferings of its inhabitants. Lucifer, furious over the injustice caused by his brother's cruel whim, works to counteract God's powers and to relieve the suffering. He teaches men resignation and that death is the only liberation from the earthly prison.

In Platonic terms the world that is the demiurge's creation is but a pale, false copy of the bright original. In Gnostic terms the liberation is to another realm of being, beyond the reach of the demiurge. The greatest cruelty, perhaps, is that men are permitted to dream of and long for the perfection of the original even as they struggle to survive in the imperfect copy. If the historical

setting for *The Father* and *Miss Julie* is the late nineteenth century, the mythic setting is After the Fall, where the harmony of
Eden has given way to the disharmony of the real world. In *Miss
Julie* a world of opposites prevails, producing inevitable, irrecon-
cilable conflict: between man and woman, servant and master,
class and class, and, by implication, man and God. Biblical imagery is used to particularize the metaphysical vision. Jean talks of
longing as a boy to enter Miss Julie's father's estate gardens, which
to him was the Garden of Eden; he speaks of the guards at the
gate as "angry angels with flaming swords." The most pervasive
biblical image in the play is that of St. John the Baptist, the har-
binger of redemption and reconciliation. Midsummer eve is St.
John's Eve, and Kristine, the cook, says that the gospel text to be
read in church will be about the beheading of the prophet. The
image of beheading foreshadows both the death of Julie's bird and
the action with which Julie takes her own life. In the Bible as well
as in the play, dancing* precedes tragedy—Salome's performance
with her seven veils and Julie's joining her servants in their midsummer eve festivities. When Herod is pleased with Salome's
dance, she asks for John's head as a prize; Julie at one point says to
Jean that she would like to see his brains on a chopping block. In
the play, however, unlike the biblical episode, it is the dancer who
becomes the victim.

Underscoring the tragic ironies evoked is the magical moment
Strindberg chose as the setting: midsummer eve, when for a brief
time servant and master are equal. But the hope of restoring the
lost harmony cannot be sustained, the differences are too great,
and with the coming of dawn the prisoners must return to their
shackles.

The Captain in *The Father* says that when he and Laura got
married, he felt as if he was becoming whole—opposites were
transcended. But the sensation was only fleeting, a dream that
vanished when he awoke to reality. In the Captain's description of
this awakening is a desolate, after-Eden landscape that could have
been rendered by Samuel Beckett: "We woke up, all right, but

---

* I am obliged to my student Michael Maggiar for pointing out in an essay on
the play the parallel images of dancing.

with our feet on the pillow. . . And . . . the dawn was sounded not by roosters, but capons, and the hens that answered didn't know the difference. When the sun should have been rising, we found ourselves in full moonlight, among the ruins, just like in the good old days. So, it wasn't an awakening after all—just a little morning nap, with wild dreams."

In Strindberg's post-Inferno Crisis plays are the same basic themes that concerned him earlier, but they have become denser and more evocative. Psychological warfare, for example, is internalized. In the 1880s he described conflicts like the one between the Captain and Laura as "battles of brains." In 1898, in the epochal dream play *To Damascus,* the Stranger's antagonists are his own doubles. In *Miss Julie* the heroine and her lover tell each other dreams that both reveal the past and foreshadow the future. In *A Dream Play* the lines between past, present, and future are blurred as life itself becomes a dream. To the metaphor of earth as prison, new implications are added, some mitigating the image's harshness, others making it more complex and comprehensive.

When Strindberg arrived in Paris in the mid-1890s, the city was the focal point of a revival of interest in arcane subjects that was reaching the climax of a half-century of development, with societies and journals devoted to alchemy, theosophy, astrology, and magic. Strindberg's exposure to these influences gave him new philosophic and poetic justifications for the resignation in the face of the terribleness of existence that he had Lucifer preach in the little creation play *Coram Populo.*

Earth as prison, as fallen Eden, often appears in Strindberg's works together with a particular sense of alienation. "At least once every century," he wrote in 1882, the hope of reconciliation with Nature "erupts in the form of revolution, or finds expression in the imaginative creations of seers. Rousseau's Emile, Voltaire's Candide, Schiller's [Karl] Moor [in *Die Räuber*], Defoe's Robinson Crusoe, Saint-Pierre's Paul and Virginie, are all sighs of longing . . . for the lost paradise—Nature—which can never be regained here on earth because civilization has laid waste to it.'"

The paradise had been lost for quite some time. Up until Strindberg's day, changing attitudes toward Nature had passed through two main historical phases: the first, from the time of Pythagoras to the late seventeenth century, organic or animate; and the second, from the late seventeenth to the middle of the nineteenth centuries, Newtonian mechanical. In the first phase, says Marjorie Nicolson in her *Breaking of the Circle,* the world "lived and flourished as did man, and like man was susceptible of decay, even of death." In the second phase the organic concept gave way to the image of a "world-machine, no longer animate, but mechanically responsive to the 'laws of Nature.'" Romanticism—an early enthusiasm for Strindberg and one to which he returned after the Inferno period—was an attempt to make the world organic again, to reunite man with Nature. "Great Pan is not dead," he wrote in 1896, "but he has been ill."

When Strindberg resumed writing fiction and drama in the late 1890s, he continued to rely on his own experiences for raw material, but he was now able to organize and enlarge these experiences in a significantly different way. Like many romantics, he cherished a nostalgia for the Middle Ages, a time when a hierarchy of meaning was still intact and man knew his place in Nature's scheme of things. Every element and creature was a link in the great chain of being and related to every other through the principle of universal analogy or correspondence. A king, for example, was related vertically to his subjects and horizontally to the sun, fire, gold, the lion, and the rose. When, during the Enlightenment, the old world died, so did analogy, to be revived in the nineteenth century by the discovery, or, perhaps, more accurately, the rediscovery, of symbols and correspondences. For a number of writers attracted to this rediscovery—especially Balzac, Baudelaire, Emerson, Strindberg, Yeats, and Joyce—the most stimulating and inspiring theory of correspondences was that of Emanuel Swedenborg, the eighteenth-century mystic and theologian. At a time when Strindberg's psychic anguish was most intense, his sense of alienation most profound, he found his way back through Swedenborg's correspondences, which provided a philosophy of life and philosophy of art at the same time. In the great chaos of existence he was now able to see endless coherence. Nature was whole again and man once more the microcosm that faithfully reflected the macrocosm of the universe.

Inventories of correspondences appear in *A Dream Play* and

The Ghost Sonata. In the first play Indra's Daughter takes the Poet to the massive, seashell-shaped Fingal's Grotto, the cave in the Hebrides much celebrated by romantic artists. She tells him that if as a child he had ever heard wonderful things in a seashell, "imagine what you'll hear in one this big!" There, she sings the lamentations of the elements, and the "Song of the Winds"— "Men breathed us in / and taught us / these songs of pain ..."— evokes echoes of the seventeenth-century metaphysical poets, suggesting the same kinds of correspondences between the elements and human passions present in Andrew Marvell's "The Unfortunate Lover": "And from the Winds the Sighs he bore, / Which through his surging Breast do roar. ..." In *The Ghost Sonata* the brief love between the Student and the Young Lady is exchanged in a cascade of analogies: six-pointed hyacinths are compared to six-pointed stars, which in turn are compared to six-pointed snowflakes. "As above," the mystics say, "so below."

Strindberg found solace in other correspondence systems as well. Two of his favorite sources were Eliphas Lévi's *The Key of the Mysteries* and Bernhardin de Saint-Pierre's *Harmonies of Nature.* In an essay in 1896 he wrote that he had read in Saint-Pierre "that the death's-head moth is called *Haïe* in French because of the sound it makes. What sound? 'Aï!': the universal human cry of pain; the scream with which the tree sloth laments the drudgery of existence; the expression of loss uttered by Apollo at the death of his friend Hyacinthus, and imprinted on the flower bearing his name." Through correspondences Nature and the gods echo man's lament over the pain of existence. In *A Dream Play* the god Indra resents that complaining is mankind's mother tongue; his daughter descends to earth and learns that the lamentations of men are indeed justified: "Human beings are to be pitied." In *The Ghost Sonata* the Young Lady, the hyacinth girl, droops and dies like Hyacinthus, and the Student is left to lament her loss.

If the pain of existing in this prison of a world is more moving and poignant in Strindberg's later plays than in the earlier ones, it is because he was able, using occult sources, to draw on a broader register of expressive imagery. This is not to say that he abandoned old idols. A quotation from Schopenhauer appears in an 1896 essay: "The world—with its endless space, in which everything is enclosed, with its endless time, in which everything moves, and with its wonderful, manifold variety of things, which fill up both [time and space]—is only a cerebral phenomenon." Similarly, Indra's Daughter says that the world is only an illusion, a phantom, a dream image. The concept of the illusoriness of reality was drawn, as were many images in *A Dream Play*, from Indic mythology, which provided Strindberg with still another correspondence system to use in his art.

The Sanskrit word for the illusory sphere of time and space is *māyā*, personified as earth mother, the great weaver of the fabric of life. In a note he made for *A Dream Play*, Strindberg refers to "life's motley, unmanageable canvas, woven by the 'World Weaveress,' who sets up the 'warp' of human destinies and then constructs the 'woof' from our intersecting interest and variable passions." The Doorkeeper in the play is a "World Weaveress" figure as she sits crocheting her giant star-patterned comforter. At the end of the play a mysterious door is opened to reveal: nothing. Everyone assembled for the opening is confused except Indra's Daughter, who understands that this is the key to the riddle of the world, that this is exactly what is concealed behind māyā, the veil of illusion. She later explains that "in the dawn of time . . . Brahman, the divine primal force, allowed itself to be seduced by Māyā, the world mother, into propagating . . . And so the world, life, and human beings are only an illusion, a phantom . . ."—nothing. The inhabitants of the house in *The Ghost Sonata* are also ignorant of the secret of the riddle. Strindberg wrote in a 1907 letter to his German translator that for the Colonel "illusion (māyā) has become reality."

The renewal of Strindberg's interest in romanticism at the turn of the century was in a way a return to something he had never left: the spirit of fairy tales and of the age of chivalry. Early and late he wrote fairy tale plays (for example, *Lucky Per's Journey* in 1881–1882 and *Swanwhite* in 1901), and one cluster of chivalric images is either implied or expressed directly in both realistic and nonrealistic plays: a princess held captive in a tower and hoping to be rescued by a knight in shining armor. In *Miss Julie* the heroine dreams of being trapped in a high place and longing to get down; Jean, who has been attracted to her ever since they were both children, dreams of climbing a high tree to find a treasure. In *The Dance of Death* tower and earth-as-prison images are fused. Alice feels trapped living with her husband, the Captain, in a military fortifications tower that once served as a prison, on an island called by its inhabitants "Little Hell." The Captain sarcastically describes their situation as "Sir Bluebeard and the maiden in the tower." *A Dream Play* contains two variations on the theme. Indra's Daughter tries in vain to free a prisoner, the Officer, from a castle; later the Officer waits outside a theatre for his beloved, Victoria, who is upstairs dressing and for some strange reason has not left the theatre for seven years. At one point, he asks permission to go and fetch her but is rebuffed by the Doorkeeper, and so goes on waiting, day after day, year after year. In *The Ghost Sonata* the Student falls in love with the Young Lady, whom he sees at the window of a beautiful house, and feels encouraged when she seems to signal to him by dropping her bracelet.

In each instance Strindberg has the image cluster serve ironic purposes. Jean cannot free the princess, and Julie, as much as she longs to come down, fears that the descent will lead to her destruction. In *The Dance of Death* when Alice's cousin Kurt arrives at the prison tower, she sees him as her liberator. "Oh!" she exults, "the tower will open its portals." At the end, however, it is Kurt who escapes the prison, and Alice and the Captain are back together again. In the Foulport scene in *A Dream Play* the Officer spots Victoria with another man but does nothing about it. "He has his Victoria," he says, "and I have mine. And mine no one may see!" And the Student in *The Ghost Sonata* learns that he can never win the Young Lady because she is sick and dying. The dropping of the bracelet was not a signal; it fell off because her hand had grown thin.

These are not simple or conventional fairy tales in which expectations of danger, rescue, and requited love are raised and satisfied. These are fairy tales *manqués,* fairy tales with some of the ambiguous and tragic implications ordinarily associated with myths. Not that Strindberg was unaware of the positive psychological purposes fairy tales serve. In 1896 he wrote that they "let the child in his imagination undergo his phylogenesis, in other words: to experience the earlier stages of his existence, just as the foetus in the womb passes through the whole line of its evolution as an animal." The evolutionary phases are expressed comprehensively in the image cluster of maiden, tower, and rescuer because it can be interpreted from several points of view: the maiden's, the rescuer's, or both, in the sense that they are one and the same. We wait for the rescuer until finally we discover that he is us. As Strindberg develops the image cluster in different contexts, various meanings are suggested, psychological and metaphysical. Psychologically, the prison is childhood. One is liberated by overcoming childish fears and accepting grown-up responsibilities, the most important of which is to give and accept love. Put another way, the prisoner must want to be set free to love, just as the rescuer must have the courage to set love free in himself. In the cases of Julie and Jean, neither prisoner nor rescuer measures up to the task. The Officer in *A Dream Play* has the opportunity to play both roles and fails each time. He can accept neither the challenge of the Daughter's attempt to rescue him nor the challenge of his own to fetch and free Victoria.

Metaphysically, the prison is the world of māyā, and in all the plays mentioned only Indra's Daughter succeeds at the complex task: to awaken from the dream of life. Like a bodhisattva, she learns first that "Human beings are to be pitied" (in Sanskrit the lesson is *karuṇa,* compassion for all living beings), then that all is nothing (*śūnya* or "void"), and finally that the only liberation is release from delusion (*mokṣa*).

Out of the contradiction implied—between the necessity to break free of the psychological prison and the necessity to accept that only death brings liberation from the metaphysical prison—Strindberg shaped a marvelous poetic tension that informs his best work. Like other great artists, he recognized the obligation not to formulate answers to the great mysteries but expressive metaphors for them. Perhaps this is why his plays remain both contemporary and timeless.

TRANSLATOR'S NOTE

AND ACKNOWLEDGMENTS

Every translation is an interpretation that implies the making of choices, and the reader has the right, I think, to know the criteria used by the translator to arrive at his choices. Two influences were crucial for me: a special interest in the way Strindberg used imagery in general and mythic imagery in particular—see the Introduction and my book *Strindberg and the Poetry of Myth*—and long experience in the theatre as actor and director. Consequently, two goals were foremost: first, to attempt to render his images into English with something approximating the impact they have (or had) in Swedish, even if it meant totally recasting certain metaphors to make them more meaningful to an audience with very different expectations than the one Strindberg wrote for; and, second, to render his dialogue as playable as possible, even if that meant excising certain forms of social address that were common in Strindberg's day but seem unnecessarily formal or stilted today, or altering stage directions to conform to changing conventions, such as allowing a little more time to elapse between the moment a servant is summoned and the moment he or she appears. How-

14

ever acceptable it was in the late nineteenth-century continental theatre for someone to appear the instant a bell was rung, the jack-in-the-box effect suggested is likely to seem undesirably ludicrous to a modern audience accustomed to more realistically motivated action.

Two Swedish editions were used for the translations: the standard collected works, *Samlade skrifter,* ed. John Landquist, 55 vols. (Stockholm: Bonniers, 1912–1919); for *The Dance of Death, A Dream Play,* and *The Ghost Sonata* (vols. 34, 36, and 45, respectively); and *August Strindberg's dramer,* ed. Carl Reinhold Smedmark, 3 vols. (Stockholm: Bonniers, 1962–1964) for *The Father* and *Miss Julie* (vol. 3). The latter edition is particularly useful because it includes in the case of *The Father* excerpts from Strindberg's own French translation of the play, and in the case of *Miss Julie* a revised version of the original Swedish edition, which had been censored in part by Strindberg's publisher, Joseph Seligmann. Incorporated into the present translations are several changes made by Strindberg in the French version of *The Father* and almost all the revisions made by editor Smedmark in the Preface and play text of *Miss Julie.*

Regarding the goal of playability, I was very fortunate to have opportunities to temper the translations of four of the five plays that follow in the incalculably valuable forge of live rehearsals. I am especially grateful to the many people, professional and amateur, onstage and behind the scenes, whose encouragement and many helpful suggestions made the translator's task easier and more rewarding: at Broadway's Circle in the Square (for which the translation of *The Father* was commissioned for a spring 1981 production)—artistic director Theodore Mann, managing director Paul Libin, guest director Göran Graffman, production associate Marita Lindholm Gochman, and actors Jessica Allen, W. B. Brydon, Peter Crombie, David Faulkner, Pauline Flanagan, Kate Purwin, Frances Sternhagen, Ralph Waite, and Richard Woods; at the Lincoln Center Institute (for whose workshop the translation of *Miss Julie* was commissioned for a summer 1981 production at TOMI Theater)—Institute Associate Director June Dunbar, guest director Thomas Bullard and actors Kate McGregor-Stewart, Jill O'Hara, William Russ, and Diane Venora; and at Queens College (where *The Ghost Sonata* and *A Dream Play* were mounted in 1980 and 1982 respectively)—my colleague, designer Jay Keene, and actors Gabrielle Angieri, Robert Brownstein, Joseph Costanza, Gloria Criscuolo, Deborah Dotson, Peter Harrison, Pedro Jimenez, John Napolitano, Eugene Paceleo, Michelle Ricca, Maurice Schlafer, and Frank Stellato.

Special thanks to Elinor Fuchs, Francesca Mantani, and Judith Moffett.

And of course my greatest thanks to that tireless listener, Carolyn.

Landfall   H.G.C.
East Hampton, New York
July 1982

Strindberg: Five Plays

The Father

(1887)

Characters

CAPTAIN ADOLF, *a cavalry officer*
LAURA, *his wife*
BERTHA, *their daughter*
MARGRET, *his old nurse*
DOCTOR OESTERMARK
PASTOR JONAS, *Laura's half-brother*
CORPORAL NOYD,* *an orderly*
SVAIRD, *another orderly*

Act I

(The CAPTAIN'*s living room. A door upstage right to the entrance hall. A large, round table in the center of the room with magazines and newspapers. To the right a leather sofa and a*

---

*"Noyd" is an approximate phonetic pronunciation of the Corporal's name, Nöjd, which means "satisfied" (translator).

table. At extreme right, in a corner, a wallpaper-covered door. To the left, a desk with a clock, and a door leading to the rest of the house. Hunting equipment and various weapons are mounted on the walls. Uniform coats hang on a rack by the door. A lamp is lit on the table.

    The CAPTAIN *and the* PASTOR *are sitting on the sofa. The* CAPTAIN *is dressed in a fatigue uniform, with riding boots and spurs. The* PASTOR *is in clerical garb and is smoking a pipe. The* CAPTAIN *rings.)*

SVAIRD (*enters*): Yes, sir?

CAPTAIN: Is Noyd out there?

SVAIRD: Corporal Noyd's in the kitchen, waiting for orders.

CAPTAIN: So, he's in the kitchen again! Tell him I want to see him, at once!

SVAIRD: Yes, sir! (*leaves*)

PASTOR: Something wrong?

CAPTAIN: Oh, there's talk he's responsible for getting the maid in trouble. The rascal's a damned nuisance.

PASTOR: Wasn't he up on the same kind of charge last year?

CAPTAIN: That's right—you remember. Maybe if you say something to him, he'll listen. I've sworn at him, and I've had him thrashed. Nothing seems to work.

PASTOR: And you want me to preach to him. What effect do you think God's word will have on a cavalry trooper?

CAPTAIN: You have a point. It has no effect on me, you know that . . .

PASTOR: That I know!

CAPTAIN: But perhaps it will on him. Anyway, it's worth a try. (NOYD *enters.*) What have you been up to now, Noyd?

NOYD: God save you, Captain, I can't tell you that with the Pastor here.

PASTOR: Don't be embarrassed, my boy!

CAPTAIN: I want the truth now, no stories.

NOYD: Well, you see, sir, it was like this. We were at a dance at Gabriel's, and, uh, so Ludvig said . . .

CAPTAIN: What does Ludvig have to do with this? Stick to the point.

NOYD: Well, so then, uh, . . . Emma said, "Let's go to the barn."

CAPTAIN: So it was Emma who seduced you, eh?

NOYD: Not far from it. What I mean is—if the girl doesn't want to, nothing happens.

CAPTAIN: Once and for all: are you the father of the child or not?

NOYD: How can I be sure of that?

CAPTAIN: What do you mean? You can't be sure?

NOYD: No, sir, that's something you can never be sure of.

CAPTAIN: Are you saying you weren't the only one?

NOYD: Yes, I was, that time, but that doesn't prove I was the only one.

CAPTAIN: So, you're trying to blame Ludvig? Is that it?

NOYD: It's not easy to know who to blame.

CAPTAIN: But you told Emma you wanted to marry her.

NOYD: Well, you always have to tell them that . . .

CAPTAIN (*to the* PASTOR): This is disgraceful!

PASTOR: It's an old story. Now listen, Noyd, you're man enough to know whether you're the father, aren't you?

NOYD: All right, I had the girl, but Pastor, you know yourself that doesn't mean something has to come of it.

PASTOR: We're talking about you now, my boy. Certainly, you don't want to leave her alone with a child. No one can force you to marry her, but you have to take care of the child! That you have to do!

NOYD: Then so does Ludvig.

CAPTAIN: This'll have to go to a civil court. I can't settle it. And it doesn't amuse me, either. Dismissed!

PASTOR: Please Adolf! Just a moment, Noyd. Don't you think it's dishonorable to leave a girl like that—with a child? Don't you think so? Eh? Don't you consider behavior like that as, as . . . well . . .?

NOYD: I would, if I knew I was the father. But you see, Pastor, that's something you never know. And to have to slave away your whole life for somebody else's child—would that be fair? Surely, you and the Captain can understand that yourselves, can't you?

CAPTAIN: Dismissed!

NOYD: God bless you, Captain! (*leaves*)

CAPTAIN: And stay out of the kitchen, damn you! (*to the* PASTOR) Why did you let him off so easily?

PASTOR: What do you mean? Wasn't I hard on him?

CAPTAIN: You just sat there muttering to yourself.

PASTOR: To be honest, I really didn't know what to say. I feel sorry for the girl, of course, but I also feel sorry for the boy. Suppose he isn't the father? If the girl wet nurses in a children's home for four months, the home will take care of the child for good. The boy can't be a wet nurse. Afterwards, she can find a good job in a respectable home. But his future could be ruined if he's thrown out of the regiment.

CAPTAIN: I wouldn't want to be the judge in this case. The boy is scarcely as innocent as he claims, but it's hard to tell. We know one thing, though: if anyone's to blame, it's the girl.

PASTOR: Oh, well, I won't pass judgment. What were we discussing when we were interrupted by this unpleasant business? It was Bertha's confirmation, wasn't it?

CAPTAIN: Not just her confirmation—her whole upbringing. Everyone in this house full of women wants to decide how my child should be raised. Your stepmother wants to make her a spiritualist; the governess a Methodist; old Margret wants her to be a Baptist; the serving girls want her to join the Salvation Army; and Laura wants her to be an artist. How can the girl grow up to be a whole person when she's being pulled in different directions like that? Meanwhile I, who should be making the decisions, am opposed at every turn. That's why I have to get her away from this place, before it's too late.

PASTOR: You have too many women running your house.

CAPTAIN: Yes, don't I? It's like walking into a cage of tigers. If I didn't hold a red-hot poker under their noses, they'd tear me to pieces in a minute. (*The* PASTOR *laughs.*) Yes, you laugh, you scoundrel. It wasn't enough that I married your sister, you had to palm off your stepmother on me as well.

PASTOR: Well, good Lord, a stepmother isn't someone you have living with you.

CAPTAIN: No, you'd rather have her living with me.

PASTOR: Oh, each of us has his own burdens to bear.

CAPTAIN: Yes, but I have more than my share. I even have my old nurse, who treats me as if I still wore a bib. Margret's kind and good, God knows, but she doesn't belong here.

PASTOR: You don't keep your womenfolk in line, Adolf. They have entirely too much to say.

CAPTAIN: And would you, dear friend, kindly tell me how to keep women in line?

PASTOR: I must admit—even if Laura is my own sister, she was never easy to get along with.

CAPTAIN: Ah, Laura's got her faults, but they're not so bad.

PASTOR: Listen, you can be frank with me—I know her.

CAPTAIN: She was brought up with a lot of romantic ideas and found it a little hard to adjust. When all is said and done, she is my wife . . .

PASTOR: And because she's your wife, she's perfect. No, my friend, she's the one who plagues you most.

CAPTAIN: Well . . . Oh, it's this whole place—there's something wrong here. Laura won't let Bertha go, and I can't let her stay in this madhouse.

PASTOR: So, Laura won't let her go . . . then I'm afraid there's going to be trouble. She's always been fierce about getting her own way. I remember that when we were children, she'd hold her breath until she got what she wanted.

CAPTAIN: I'm not surprised. Sometime she gets so emotional I'm worried she's going to be sick.

PASTOR: But what is it you want for Bertha that creates such conflict? Can't you compromise?

CAPTAIN: Don't think I want to make her into some sort of prodigy or copy of myself. The fact is, I don't want to be a pimp for my own daughter by raising her to be fit for nothing but marriage. And then if she doesn't get married, there's only bitterness ahead. On the other hand, I don't want to push her into some masculine career requiring long training that would be wasted if she did marry.

PASTOR: But then what do you want?

CAPTAIN: I want her to be a teacher. If she stays single, she can take care of herself and be no worse off than the poor schoolmasters who have whole families to support. If she does get married, she can use her training to help raise her own children. Doesn't that sound reasonable?

PASTOR: It is reasonable. But what about the talent she's shown for painting? Wouldn't it be a crime to suppress that?

CAPTAIN: No. I showed her work to a prominent painter who said it was just art school stuff. But then last summer some young ass turned up who knew better and said she had a colossal talent, and that settled the matter as far as Laura was concerned.

PASTOR: Was he infatuated with Bertha?

CAPTAIN: I took that for granted.

PASTOR: Then God help you, my friend, I don't see any way out. This is serious, and of course Laura gets support . . . in there.

CAPTAIN: Yes, you can bet on it. I run into skirmishes everywhere, and between you and me, when it comes to war, women have their own rules.

PASTOR: Don't you think I know what it's like?

CAPTAIN: You, too?

PASTOR: Are you surprised?

CAPTAIN: But the worst thing is, they seem to be deciding Bertha's future in there out of sheer spite. (*The* PASTOR *rises.*) There are constant nasty comments about how men will find out that women can do this or that. It's man versus woman, all day long, endlessly. Are you going? No, stay for supper. I don't know what there is, but do stay. I'm expecting the new doctor, you know. Have you seen him yet?

PASTOR: Just in passing. He seems like a decent, respectable sort.

CAPTAIN: Really? That's good. Do you think he'll be my ally?

PASTOR: Who knows? It depends on how much experience he's had with women.

CAPTAIN: Won't you stay?

PASTOR: No thanks, my friend. I promised to be home for supper, and my wife gets anxious if I'm late.

CAPTAIN: Anxious? Angry, you mean. Well, as you wish. Let me help you with your coat.

PASTOR: It's very cold tonight. Thanks. Adolf, take care of yourself. You seem on edge.

CAPTAIN: Me, on edge?

PASTOR: Yes, are you feeling all right?

CAPTAIN: You've been talking to Laura.

PASTOR: Laura?

CAPTAIN: Yes, for twenty years she's treated me as if I had one foot in the grave.

PASTOR: No. I'm concerned about you. Take care of yourself, that's my advice. Good-bye, my friend—but you wanted to talk about Bertha's confirmation.

CAPTAIN: Not at all! I don't care one way or the other, I promise you. I don't believe in it, but I have no intention of being a martyr for the sake of truth. I'm past all that. Good-bye. Regards to your wife.

PASTOR: And mine to Laura. Good-bye. (*He leaves. The* CAPTAIN *unlocks the desk and begins working on his accounts.*)

CAPTAIN: Thirty-four—nine, forty-three—seven, eight, fifty-six. (LAURA *enters.*)

LAURA: Could you please . . .

CAPTAIN: In a minute! ——— Sixty-six, seventy-one, eighty-four, eighty-nine, ninety-two, one hundred. What is it?

LAURA: Am I disturbing you?

CAPTAIN: Not at all! You want the housekeeping allowance, I suppose.

LAURA: Yes, the housekeeping allowance.

CAPTAIN: Put your receipts there, and I'll go through them.

LAURA: Receipts?

CAPTAIN: Yes!

LAURA: Now you want receipts?

CAPTAIN: Naturally, I want receipts. With our finances as shaky as they are, I've got to try to straighten out the accounts, or there'll be trouble.

LAURA: If our finances are bad, it's not my fault.

CAPTAIN: That's precisely what we'll determine by going through the receipts.

LAURA: If the tenant farmer doesn't pay his rent, it's not my fault.

CAPTAIN: And who recommended the tenant so warmly? You! Why did you recommend such a . . . misfit?

LAURA: Why did you take on such a "misfit" then?

CAPTAIN: Because I couldn't eat, sleep, or work in peace until you got him here. You wanted him because your brother wanted to get rid of him; your mother wanted him because I didn't want him; the governess wanted him because he was a Methodist; and old Margret because, as a child, she had known his grandmother. That's why he was taken on, and if I hadn't taken him on, I'd be in the madhouse now or in my grave. However, here's the housekeeping allowance and your pin money. I'll get the receipts later.

LAURA (*curtseying*): Thank you so much. ——— And do you keep receipts too for your outside expenses?

CAPTAIN: That doesn't concern you.

LAURA: No, that's true, just as my child's upbringing doesn't concern me. And did you gentlemen reach a decision after this evening's session?

CAPTAIN: I had already reached a decision and was simply sharing it with the only friend this family and I have in common. Bertha will be boarded in town, and she'll move in two weeks from now.

LAURA: Where will she be boarded, if I may ask?

CAPTAIN: At Sayvberg's,* the judge advocate.

LAURA: That atheist who calls himself a freethinker!

CAPTAIN: According to the law, children will be raised in the father's faith.

LAURA: And the mother has nothing to say about it?

CAPTAIN: Nothing at all. She sells her rights when she marries. In return her husband supports her and her children.

LAURA: So she has no rights over her own child?

CAPTAIN: None whatever. Once you've sold your goods, you can't get them back and still keep the money.

LAURA: But if the father and mother decide together . . .

CAPTAIN: How could we do that? I want her to live in town, you want her to live at home. The arithmetic mean would have her staying somewhere in the middle—at the railway station. This is a problem that can't be solved by compromise.

LAURA: Then it has to be solved by other means! ———— What was Noyd doing here?

CAPTAIN: That's a confidential military matter.

LAURA: Which everyone in the kitchen knows about.

CAPTAIN: Fine, then you should know about it, too.

LAURA: I do.

CAPTAIN: And are ready to pronounce sentence?

LAURA: It's written in the law.

CAPTAIN: The law doesn't say who the child's father is.

LAURA: No, but you usually know.

CAPTAIN: Some people say that's something you can never be sure of.

*An approximate phonetic pronunciation of "Sävberg's" (translator).

LAURA: That's strange! Can't you be sure of who a child's father is?

CAPTAIN: No, so they say.

LAURA: That's strange! Then, why does a father have more rights over a child than a mother?

CAPTAIN: He has them only when he assumes the responsibility or has it forced on him. And of course in a marriage the matter of paternity is not in doubt.

LAURA: Never?

CAPTAIN: I should hope not.

LAURA: What if the wife was unfaithful?

CAPTAIN: That's not relevant here. Was there something else you wanted?

LAURA: No, nothing!

CAPTAIN: Then I'm going up to my room. Let me know when the Doctor comes. (*He locks the desk and rises.*)

LAURA: I will.

CAPTAIN (*crossing to the wallpaper-covered door right*): As soon as he comes. I don't want to keep him waiting. Do you understand? (*leaves*)

LAURA: I understand. (*Alone, she examines the money.*)

MOTHER-IN-LAW'S VOICE (*offstage*): Laura!

LAURA: Yes, mother!

MOTHER-IN-LAW'S VOICE: Is my tea ready?

LAURA (*at the doorway*): In a minute, mother. (*She starts toward the upstage door as* SVAIRD *enters.*)

SVAIRD: Doctor Oestermark is here, ma'am.

DOCTOR (*entering*): How do you do.

LAURA (*crossing, offering her hand*): Welcome, Doctor! We're all so happy you've come. The Captain is out, but he'll be back shortly.

DOCTOR: I apologize for coming so late, but I've already been out on calls.

LAURA: Please sit down! Please!

DOCTOR: Thank you very much.

LAURA: Yes, there's a lot of illness in the district just now, but I hope you'll soon feel at home. It's very important for us, so isolated out here in the country, to find a doctor who's really interested in his patients. I've heard so many good things about you, I hope we'll be friends.

DOCTOR: You're too kind, ma'am. I hope for your sake that I won't have to call here professionally too often. Your family is generally healthy, I presume, and . . .

LAURA: Fortunately, we haven't had any serious illnesses, but things aren't entirely what they should be.

DOCTOR: Is that so?

LAURA: They aren't the way we would like them to be, God knows.

DOCTOR: Oh? That's too bad.

LAURA: In a family there are things which honor and conscience force us to hide from the world . . .

DOCTOR: But not from your doctor.

LAURA: No. That's why it's my painful duty to tell you the whole truth right from the start.

DOCTOR: Can't we postpone this conversation until I've had the pleasure of meeting the Captain?

LAURA: No! You must hear what I have to say first, before you see him.

DOCTOR: So, it's about him?

LAURA: About him, my poor husband.

DOCTOR: That's very upsetting. You have my sympathy, believe me.

LAURA (*taking out a handkerchief*): My husband is sick in his mind. Now you know everything, and you can judge for yourself later.

DOCTOR: I'm shocked to hear that. I've read and admired the Captain's splendid monographs on mineralogy and always thought him to have a clear and strong intelligence.

LAURA: Oh? I'd be so happy if all of us close to him were mistaken.

DOCTOR: Of course, it's possible that his mind is affected in other ways. Tell me . . .

LAURA: That's what we're afraid of, too. You see, sometimes he has the most bizarre ideas. I know that's not unusual for a scholar, but they disturb the whole family. For example, he has a mania for buying things.

DOCTOR: Oh? What does he buy?

LAURA: Books. Whole crates of them, which he never reads.

DOCTOR: Ah, well, buying books is hardly a dangerous sign in a scholar.

LAURA: You don't believe what I'm saying.

DOCTOR: Oh, I'm convinced, ma'am, that you believe what you're saying.

LAURA: But is it reasonable for a person to believe that he can see in a microscope what's happening on another planet?

DOCTOR: Does he say he can do that?

LAURA: Yes, that's what he says.

DOCTOR: In a microscope?

LAURA: In a microscope, yes!

DOCTOR: Perhaps you misunderstood him, perhaps . . .

LAURA: You don't believe me, Doctor. And here I am telling you our family's secret . . .

DOCTOR: Please, I'm honored by your confidence in me, but as a doctor I must observe for myself and test before making a judgment. Has the Captain shown any signs of capriciousness or lack of will?

LAURA: Has he? We've been married for twenty years and he has yet to make one decision that he hasn't reversed.

DOCTOR: Is he obstinate?

LAURA: He always has to have his way, but do you know what happens, Doctor, when he gets it? He gives in and begs me to decide.

DOCTOR: Yes, this could be serious. I'll have to look into it. The will, you see, is the driving force of the mind. If it's injured, the mind falls to pieces.

LAURA: And God knows I've had to learn to give in to his every wish all these years. Oh, if you knew what I've been through with him, if you knew!

MOTHER-IN-LAW'S VOICE: Laura!

LAURA: Yes!

DOCTOR: I understand your concern. Please trust me. But I must ask you one thing. Avoid discussing ideas that provoke strong reactions from the Captain—in a susceptible mind such things grow quickly into obsessions or fixed ideas. Do you understand?

LAURA: In other words, avoid arousing his suspicions.

DOCTOR: Exactly! A sick person can start imagining all sorts of things.

LAURA: I see! I understand! Yes, yes. Excuse me, Doctor, I have to see what my mother wants. I'll only be a moment . . . Oh, here's Adolf . . . (*leaves*)

CAPTAIN (*entering through the wallpaper-covered door*): Oh, you here already, Doctor? Welcome!

DOCTOR: Captain! It's a pleasure to meet such a distinguished man of science.

CAPTAIN: Oh, please. My military duties don't allow much time for research. All the same, I think I am close to an important discovery.

DOCTOR: Really?

CAPTAIN: You see, I've been analyzing meteorite samples and found carbon—evidence of organic life! What do you say to that?

DOCTOR: And you saw this through a microscope?

CAPTAIN: For God's sake, no! Through a spectroscope!

DOCTOR: A spectroscope! Excuse me! Then you'll soon be able to tell us what's happening on Jupiter!

CAPTAIN: Not what's happening, but what has happened. If only that damned bookdealer in Paris would send my books. I think all the bookdealers in the world are conspiring against me. Would you believe that for two months I haven't had a single reply—not to orders, letters, or even insulting telegrams? I don't know what to do—it doesn't make any sense!

DOCTOR: It's probably just ordinary incompetence. You shouldn't take it so seriously.

CAPTAIN: But dammit, I can't get my monograph ready in time, and I know they're working on the same thing in Berlin. But we're supposed to be talking about you now, not me. You can stay here with us, if you like—we have a little apartment in the wing—or you can live in the old doctor's residence.

DOCTOR: Just as you please.

CAPTAIN: No, as you please. Tell me.

DOCTOR: It's up to you to decide.

CAPTAIN: It's not up to me to decide. You're the one who has to say what you want. I don't care one way or the other.

DOCTOR: Well, it's hard to decide, I . . .

CAPTAIN: For Christ's sake, man, make a choice! I have no prefer-
ence in the matter, no opinion, no desire. Are you so spineless
that you don't know what you want? Make up your mind, or I'll
lose my temper!

DOCTOR: All right, if it's up to me, I'll stay here.

CAPTAIN: Good! ——— Thank you! (*rings*) ——— Ah! ———
I'm sorry, Doctor, but nothing annoys me more than people
who can't make up their minds. (MARGRET *enters.*) Oh, it's you,
Margret. Listen, dear, do you know if the wing apartment is
ready for the Doctor?

MARGRET: Yes, Captain, it is.

CAPTAIN: Fine. Then I won't keep you, Doctor, you must be tired.
Once again, you're welcome. Good night. We'll see you in the
morning.

DOCTOR: Good night, Captain.

CAPTAIN: And I assume that my wife has told you enough to help
you find your way around.

DOCTOR: Your wife was very helpful and told me things a new-
comer should know. Good night. (*leaves*)

CAPTAIN: What is it, dear? Did you want something?

MARGRET: Master Adolf, I want you to listen to your old Margret.

CAPTAIN: Of course. You're the only one I can listen to without
getting convulsions.

MARGRET: Master Adolf, don't you think you could meet Miss
Laura halfway on this business about Bertha. Think how a
mother feels . . .

CAPTAIN: Think how a father feels, Margret!

MARGRET: Yes, yes, yes. But a father has other things besides his
child. That's all a mother has.

CAPTAIN: Precisely. She has only one burden; I have three, and I
bear hers as well. Don't you think I would have amounted to
more in life than an old soldier if it hadn't been for her and her
child.

MARGRET: Yes, but that's not what I wanted to talk about.

CAPTAIN: Oh, I'm sure it wasn't. You want me to admit I'm in the
wrong.

MARGRET: Don't you think I want what's best for you?

CAPTAIN: Of course, dear, I believe that. It's just that you don't know what's best for me. You see, it's not enough that I've given my child life; I want to give her my soul, too.

MARGRET: That's beyond me. Still, I think you ought to be able to come to some agreement.

CAPTAIN: You're not my friend, Margret!

MARGRET: Me? Lord, what are you saying, Master Adolf? Do you think I can forget that you were my baby when you were little?

CAPTAIN: No, dear, and have I forgotten that? You've been like a mother to me, giving me support when everyone else was against me. But now, when it's most important, you're deserting me and going over to the enemy.

MARGRET: The enemy?

CAPTAIN: Yes, the enemy! You know very well how it's been in this house—you, who's seen everything, from beginning to end.

MARGRET: Yes, I've seen! But my God, must two people torture the life out of each other this way, two people who otherwise are so kind and want only what's best for everyone? Miss Laura is never that way with me or the others . . .

CAPTAIN: No, only with me, I know that. But I tell you, Margret, if you abandon me now, you'll be committing a sin. There's a web being spun around me here and that doctor is not my friend!

MARGRET: Oh, Master Adolf, you believe only the worst of people. But that's what comes of not having the true faith. That's what's the matter.

CAPTAIN: And you and the Baptists have found the only true faith. How happy you must be!

MARGRET: Yes, I'm not as unhappy as you, Master Adolf. Turn your heart to God, and you'll see how happy He'll make you in love for your neighbor.

CAPTAIN: It's strange, but the moment you talk about God and love, your voice gets hard and your eyes so hateful. No, Margret, I doubt that you have the true faith.

MARGRET: Yes, be proud and stern in your book learning, but it won't take you far when it comes to the test.

CAPTAIN: How arrogantly you speak, oh humble heart! I know

perfectly well that learning means nothing to creatures like you!

MARGRET: Shame on you! But old Margret is still fond of her great big boy. He'll return to her, like a good child, when a storm comes up.

CAPTAIN: Margret! Forgive me. You must believe me, you're the only one here who wishes me well. Help me. I feel something's about to happen. I don't know what, but it isn't right, whatever it is. (*a scream from within the house*) What was that? Who screamed?

BERTHA (*rushing in*): Poppa, poppa, help me! Save me!

CAPTAIN: Bertha, my darling, what is it? What is it?

BERTHA: Help me! I think she wants to hurt me!

CAPTAIN: Who wants to hurt you? Tell me, tell me!

BERTHA: Grandma! But it was my own fault. I tried to trick her!

CAPTAIN: Tell me about it!

BERTHA: Yes, but promise you won't say anything! Do you hear? Promise!

CAPTAIN: All right, but what happened? (BERTHA *looks at* MAR-GRET.) You can go, Margret. (MARGRET *leaves.*)

BERTHA: Well, you see, in the evenings she turns down her lamp and has me sit at her table with a piece of paper and a pen. And then she says the spirits are going to write.

CAPTAIN: What's that? Why haven't you told me about this before?

BERTHA: Forgive me, I didn't dare to. Grandma says the spirits get revenge if you tell. And then the pen writes, and I don't know if it's me doing it or not. Sometimes it goes fine, but sometimes not at all. And when I'm tired, it won't work, but it has to work anyway. And tonight I thought I was writing well, but then Grandma said I got it out of a book, and that I had tricked her. And then she got so terribly angry.

CAPTAIN: Do you believe in spirits?

BERTHA: I don't know!

CAPTAIN: But I know they don't exist!

BERTHA: But Grandma says you don't understand and that you have bad things that can see on other planets.

CAPTAIN: Is that right? What else does she say?

BERTHA: She says you can't work miracles!

CAPTAIN: I never said I could. Do you know what meteorites are? They're bits of rock that fall from other heavenly bodies. By examining them, I can tell whether they contain the same substances that our earth does. That's all I can see.

BERTHA: But Grandma says there are things she can see and you can't.

CAPTAIN: Well, she's lying.

BERTHA: Grandma doesn't lie!

CAPTAIN: How do you know?

BERTHA: Then Momma lies, too.

CAPTAIN: Oh.

BERTHA: And if you say Momma lies, I'll never believe you again!

CAPTAIN: I didn't say that, and so you have to believe me when I tell you that for your own good, for the sake of your future, you must leave home. Do you understand? Wouldn't you like to move to town and learn something useful?

BERTHA: Oh, yes! I want so much to move to town—anywhere, away from here! As long as I can see you sometimes—often! Oh, in there it's so gloomy, so horrible, like a winter night. But when you come home, Poppa, it's like a morning in spring!

CAPTAIN: My beloved child! My dear child!

BERTHA: But Poppa, you have to be nice to Momma, do you hear? She cries so much.

CAPTAIN: Hm! ——— Then you want to live in town?

BERTHA: Yes, yes!

CAPTAIN: But what if Momma doesn't want it?

BERTHA: But she must want it!

CAPTAIN: But if she doesn't?

BERTHA: Then I don't know what'll happen. But she will, she will!

CAPTAIN: Will you ask her?

BERTHA: You ask her, nicely. She doesn't listen to me.

CAPTAIN: Hm! ——— Well, if you want it and I want it, but she doesn't want it, what then?

BERTHA: Oh, then things will be so difficult again! Why can't you both . . .

LAURA (*entering*): So, Bertha is here! Then maybe we can hear her opinion on how her future is to be decided.

CAPTAIN: The child can hardly be expected to have any well-

founded opinions about what to do with her life. You and I
should be able to determine that because we know the problems
of young girls growing up.

LAURA: But since we two differ, why not let Bertha decide?

CAPTAIN: No, I won't let anyone interfere with my rights, neither
woman nor child. Bertha, please leave us alone. (BERTHA *hesitates.*)

LAURA: Bertha, stay for a moment! (*The girl, uncertain, does not
move.*) Do you want to move to town, or do you want to stay
here at home?

BERTHA: I don't know . . .

LAURA: What you want, of course, is not the important thing. But
it would be interesting to hear what you have to say . . . Well?
(*The* CAPTAIN *takes* BERTHA's *arm and leads her gently, but
firmly, to the door left.*)

CAPTAIN: I said for you to go. (BERTHA *leaves.*)

LAURA: You were afraid to let her speak because you knew she'd
agree with me.

CAPTAIN: As a matter of fact, I know she wants to leave home. But
I also know that you can make her change her mind.

LAURA: Oh, am I so powerful?

CAPTAIN: Yes, you have a satanic power when it comes to getting
what you want. But that's the way it is for people who aren't
scrupulous about the means they use. For instance, how did you
get rid of old Dr. Norling, and how did you get the new one
here?

LAURA: Yes, how did I?

CAPTAIN: You insulted Dr. Norling, so he left. Then you got your
brother to fix this new one's appointment.

LAURA: So, Bertha's leaving?

CAPTAIN: Yes, in two weeks.

LAURA: And that's final?

CAPTAIN: Yes!

LAURA: Have you talked to Bertha about this?

CAPTAIN: Yes!

LAURA: Then I'll have to try to prevent it!

CAPTAIN: You can't.

LAURA: Can't I? Do you think that as a mother I'd let my child loose among atheists, to learn that everything I taught her was nonsense, so that she'd despise me for the rest of my life?

CAPTAIN: Do you think that as a father I'd permit ignorant and conceited women to teach my daughter that I'm a charlatan?

LAURA: It's less important for a father.

CAPTAIN: Why is that?

LAURA: Because a mother is closer to a child. Haven't we discovered that no one can really know who a child's father is?

CAPTAIN: What has that to do with us?

LAURA: You can't be sure you're Bertha's father.

CAPTAIN: I can't?

LAURA: Since no one can be sure, how can you be?

CAPTAIN: Are you joking?

LAURA: No, I'm just repeating what you taught me. Besides, how do you know I haven't been unfaithful to you?

CAPTAIN: I believe you capable of a great deal, but not that. And I don't think you'd talk about it if it were true.

LAURA: Suppose I was prepared to endure anything, to be driven out, despised, anything, in order to hold onto my child. And suppose I'm telling the truth right now when I say: Bertha is my child, but not yours. Suppose . . .

CAPTAIN: Stop it!

LAURA: Just suppose—your power would be finished.

CAPTAIN: You'd have to prove that I wasn't the father.

LAURA: That wouldn't be difficult. Do you want me to?

CAPTAIN: Stop it!

LAURA: For instance, I'd only have to name the real father—and the time and place, of course. ——— Let's see—when was Bertha born? ——— Three years after we were married . . .

CAPTAIN: Stop it, I said! Or . . .

LAURA: Or what? All right, we'll stop. But think carefully about what you do and what you decide. Don't make yourself ridiculous.

CAPTAIN: I find all this very sad.

LAURA: Then you *are* ridiculous!

CAPTAIN: But not you?

LAURA: No, not as a woman, not as a mother!

CAPTAIN: That's why I can't fight you.

LAURA: Why try to fight an enemy who's so superior?

CAPTAIN: Superior?

LAURA: Yes! It's curious, but I've yet to meet a man I didn't feel superior to.

CAPTAIN: Well, for once you've met your match, and you won't forget it!

LAURA: That'll be interesting.

MARGRET (*enters*): Supper's on the table. Are you ready to eat?

LAURA: Yes, I'm famished! (*The* CAPTAIN *stays behind and sits in an armchair by the table.*) Aren't you coming?

CAPTAIN: No, thanks, I don't want anything.

LAURA: Why not? Are you upset?

CAPTAIN: No, I'm just not hungry.

LAURA: Come on, otherwise there'll be such—unnecessary questions! ——— Be sensible! ——— Oh, very well, sit there then! (*leaves*)

MARGRET: Master Adolf! What's the matter now?

CAPTAIN: I don't know. Explain to me how women can treat a grown man as if he were a child.

MARGRET: Maybe it's because all men, big and small, are born of woman . . .

CAPTAIN: And no woman is born of man. Margret, I am Bertha's father. You believe that, don't you?

MARGRET: Lord, how childish you are! Of course you're your own child's father. Come and eat now and don't sit there sulking! Come on now, come on!

CAPTAIN (*rising*): Get out, woman! Go to hell, you witches! (*at the door*) Svaird! Svaird!

MARGRET: But Captain! Listen to me . . .

CAPTAIN: Get out, woman! Get out!

MARGRET: God preserve us, what'll happen now?

SVAIRD (*enters*): Yes sir!

CAPTAIN: Hitch up the racing sleigh, immediately!

SVAIRD: Yes sir! (*leaves*)

CAPTAIN (*putting on his hat and preparing to go*): Don't expect me home before midnight! (*leaves*)

MARGRET: Oh, Jesus, help us!

Act II

(The same setting as Act I. A lamp is lit on the table: it is night. The DOCTOR *and* LAURA)

DOCTOR: After talking with your husband, I'm not at all convinced your fears are justified. First of all, you were mistaken when you said he used a microscope to make his findings. Now that I know it was a spectroscope, I'm more inclined to regard his work as a contribution to science than a sign of mental illness.

LAURA: But I never said that.

DOCTOR: Madam, I remember specifically asking about this point because I thought I hadn't heard you correctly. We must be very careful before making charges that could lead to a man being committed to an asylum.

LAURA: Committed?

DOCTOR: Yes. Under those circumstances, he loses all his civil and family rights.

LAURA: I didn't know that.

DOCTOR: There's another thing that disturbs me. He said his letters to bookdealers went unanswered. Can I ask if you—with the best of intentions—intercepted them?

LAURA: Yes, I did. I had to protect the family interests. I couldn't stand by and let him ruin us all.

DOCTOR: Forgive me, but I don't think you realize the consequences of what you did. If he discovers that you've been secretly interfering in his affairs, his suspicions will be confirmed, and they'll grow like an avalanche. Surely you must know yourself how painful it is to have your most fervent desires frustrated, to have your will thwarted.

LAURA: If only you knew.

DOCTOR: Try to judge, then, how he must have felt.

LAURA *(rising)*: It's midnight, and he's not home yet. I'm afraid I fear the worst.

DOCTOR: Please, tell me what happened this evening after I left. It's vital that I know everything.

LAURA: He had all sorts of fantasies and curious ideas. Can you imagine, he raved about not being the father of his own child?

DOCTOR: That is strange. How did he hit upon that?

LAURA: I have no idea. Unless it was because he had one of the orderlies brought up on charges involving child support. When I took the girl's side, he got very excited and said that no one could know for sure who a child's father was. God knows I did everything I could to calm him down, but now I think he's past help. (*She cries.*)

DOCTOR: This mustn't be allowed to go on. Something must be done. Has the Captain ever had such strange ideas before?

LAURA: A similar thing happened six years ago. And he admitted as much himself—yes, and even wrote about it in a letter to the doctor—that he was afraid of losing his sanity.

DOCTOR: I see . . . The roots of this case are deep and personal. These are things I can't comment on. I can only go by what I see. What's done can't be undone, unfortunately. Steps should have been taken earlier. ———— Where do you think he is now?

LAURA: I can't imagine. He gets such crazy notions.

DOCTOR: Do you want me to stay until he returns?

LAURA: Yes.

DOCTOR: But we mustn't arouse his suspicions. I could say that I looked in on your mother because she wasn't feeling well.

LAURA: That's a good idea. Don't leave us, Doctor. I'm so worried! But wouldn't it be better to come right out and tell him what you think of his condition?

DOCTOR: Not necessarily. It depends on how the case develops. But we mustn't stay in here. Perhaps I should go into another room, to make it look more convincing.

LAURA: Yes, that would be better. Then Margret can sit in here. She always waits up for him when he's out. (*She goes to the door.*) Margret! Margret! She's the only one who has any power over him.

MARGRET (*entering*): Yes, ma'am. Is the master home?

LAURA: No, but you can sit in here and wait for him. When he comes, tell him my mother is sick and that's why the Doctor is here.

MARGRET: Yes, ma'am. I'll take care of everything.

LAURA (*opening the door*): Right this way, Doctor.

DOCTOR: Thank you. (*They leave.* MARGRET *has her glasses on and carries a book of psalms. Sounds of strong winds*)

MARGRET: Yes, yes, yes. (*reads aloud*)

> "A mournful and a wretched thing
> is life and soon 'tis done,
> the shadow of death's angel's wing
> no man has yet outrun.
> 'Tis vanity, all vanity!"

Amen, amen.

> "Each on earth who has a soul
> to earth's demands is slave
> and only sorrow survives whole
> to carve upon the open grave:
> 'Tis vanity, all vanity!"

Amen, amen. (BERTHA *enters carrying a tray with a coffee pot and some embroidery.*)

BERTHA (*softly*): Margret, can I sit in here with you? It's so terrible up there!

MARGRET: My Lord, child, what are you doing up?

BERTHA: I have to finish Poppa's Christmas present. (*Holding up the coffee pot*) And look what I brought you!

MARGRET: But, sweetheart, this won't do. You've got to get up early in the morning, and it's past midnight.

BERTHA: I don't care. I don't dare sit up there alone. I think it's haunted.

MARGRET: I knew it! I knew it! Yes, take my word for it, it's not Christmas elves that are watching over this house. What happened? Did you see something?

BERTHA: No, but I heard someone singing up in the attic.

MARGRET: In the attic? At this time of night?

BERTHA: Yes, and it was so sad, the saddest song I ever heard. It sounded like it came from the store room, you know, to the left, where the cradle is . . .

MARGRET: Lord save us! And such a terrible storm tonight— enough to blow the chimney down!

> "Wo, how do we pass this life on earth?
> In work and pain from the time of birth.
> It's hardship even when life is best

And the most to hope for is to stand the test."

Amen, amen! Yes, dear child, God grant us a happy Christmas!

BERTHA: Margret, is it true that Poppa's sick?

MARGRET: I'm afraid he is.

BERTHA: Then we can't have a real Christmas Eve. But why isn't he in bed, if he's sick?

MARGRET: Well, child, with his kind of illness you don't have to stay in bed. Shh, there's someone in the entry. Take the coffee pot with you and go to bed, or your father will be angry.

BERTHA (*leaving with the tray*): Good night, Margret.

MARGRET: Good night. God bless you.

CAPTAIN (*taking off his coat as he enters*): Are you still up? Go to bed!

MARGRET: Oh, I just wanted to wait until . . . (*The* CAPTAIN *lights a candle. Opening his desk, he sits down and takes out letters and newspapers from his pocket.*) Master Adolf!

CAPTAIN: What is it?

MARGRET: The old mistress is sick, and the Doctor's here.

CAPTAIN: Anything serious?

MARGRET: No, I don't think so. Just a cold.

CAPTAIN (*rising*): Who was the father of your child, Margret?

MARGRET: Oh, I've told you so many times. It was that rascal Johansson.

CAPTAIN: Are you sure it was he?

MARGRET: Don't be childish, of course I'm sure. He was the only one.

CAPTAIN: Yes, but was he sure he was the only one? No, he couldn't be; only you could be sure of that. That's the difference, you see.

MARGRET: I don't see any difference.

CAPTAIN: No, you can't see it, but it's there, all the same. (*Leafing through a photograph album on the table.*) Do you think Bertha looks like me? (*He stops at a picture in the album.*)

MARGRET: Like two peas in a pod.

CAPTAIN: Did Johansson admit he was the father?

MARGRET: Oh well . . . he had no choice—he was forced to.

CAPTAIN: How awful! ——— (*The* DOCTOR *enters.*) Good evening, Doctor. How is my mother-in-law?

DOCTOR: Oh, nothing serious. Just a slight sprain in her left ankle.

CAPTAIN: I thought Margret said it was a cold. Apparently we have different diagnoses. Go to bed, Margret! (*She leaves; pause*) Won't you sit down, Doctor?

DOCTOR (*sitting*): Thank you.

CAPTAIN: Is it true that if you cross a mare with a zebra, you get striped foals?

DOCTOR (*surprised*): That's absolutely right!

CAPTAIN: And isn't it true too that you'll continue to get striped foals in the next generation, even if the new sire is a horse?

DOCTOR: Yes, that's also true.

CAPTAIN: And so, under certain circumstances, a stallion can sire both striped and unstriped foals.

DOCTOR: Yes, it would seem so.

CAPTAIN: In other words, the offspring's resemblance to the father proves nothing.

DOCTOR: Well . . .

CAPTAIN: In other words, paternity can never be proved.

DOCTOR: I see . . .

CAPTAIN: You're a widower, aren't you, with children?

DOCTOR: Er . . . Yes . . .

CAPTAIN: Don't you feel ridiculous sometimes as a father? Nothing is more ludicrous than a man walking with a child and talking about *his* children. "My *wife's* children," he should say. Didn't you ever feel something false about your position? Were there no twinges of doubt? I won't say "suspicions," because I assume that for a man like you, your wife was above suspicion.

DOCTOR: No, there weren't—ever. Wasn't it Goethe who said that a man must take his children on trust?

CAPTAIN: Trust, where a woman's concerned? That's risky.

DOCTOR: There are all kinds of women.

CAPTAIN: Recent research shows there's only one kind! ——— When I was young, I was strong and—if I do say so myself— handsome. Two experiences were enough to make me wary. The first was on a steamer. I was sitting with some friends in the lounge when the young woman who ran the restaurant sat down beside me in tears and related that her fiancé had been lost at sea. We felt sorry for her, and I ordered champagne.

After the second glass, I patted her foot; after the fourth, her knee, and before morning I had consoled her.

DOCTOR: One swallow doesn't make a summer.

CAPTAIN: The second experience, in fact, involved a summer swallow. It was at a resort and she was a young married woman, alone with her children while her husband stayed in town. She was religious, with very strict principles, and preached morality to me. She was completely honorable—as far as I know. I lent her a book, two books. When the time came for her to leave, I was surprised when she returned them. Three months later, I found a calling card in one of the books with a fairly outspoken declaration of affection. It was innocent, as innocent as such a declaration from a married woman could be—to a stranger who had never made any advances to her. Moral: never take too much on trust!

DOCTOR: Or too little, either!

CAPTAIN: No, no more than is prudent! But you see, Doctor, this woman was so unaware of her own motives that she told her husband of her infatuation for me. That's where the danger is: women are unaware that they are instinctively wicked. This explains their behavior, but it doesn't excuse it.

DOCTOR: Captain, your thoughts are taking a morbid direction. Be careful!

CAPTAIN: What do you mean, morbid? You know that all boilers explode when the pressure gauge reaches the limit. It's just that the limit isn't the same for each one. Have you got that down? After all, you are here to observe me. If I weren't a man now, I could blame someone else or ask for sympathy. I might be able to give you a complete diagnosis of my illness—even its history. But unfortunately, I am a man, and so I must fold my arms like an ancient Roman and hold my breath till I die. Good night!

DOCTOR: Captain, if you're ill, it's no reflection on your manhood to tell me everything. I have to hear your side, too.

CAPTAIN: You've heard enough listening to one side, I suspect.

DOCTOR: No, Captain. Do you know, when I sat in the theatre the other night and heard Mrs. Alving in *Ghosts* talking about her dead husband, I thought to myself: what a damn shame the man isn't alive to speak for himself.

CAPTAIN: Do you think he'd have spoken up, even then? And if any man came back from the grave, do you think he'd be believed? Good night, Doctor. As you can see, I'm perfectly calm, so you can sleep in peace.

DOCTOR: Good night, Captain. I won't trouble you any more about this.

CAPTAIN: Are we enemies?

DOCTOR: Of course not. It's just too bad we can't be friends. Good night. (*The* CAPTAIN *follows the* DOCTOR *to the door upstage: then he goes to the door left and opens it slightly.*)

CAPTAIN: Come in, so we can talk. I heard you listening at the door. (LAURA *enters, embarrassed. The* CAPTAIN *sits at the desk.*) It's late, but we must have this out. Sit down. (*pause*) I went to the post office this evening and picked up some letters. It's evident from them that you've been intercepting both my outgoing and incoming mail. The consequence is that time has been lost and my research probably made useless.

LAURA: I only meant well. You were neglecting your duties for this other business.

CAPTAIN: You didn't mean well at all. You must have guessed that one day my research would bring me more honor than my military career, and you couldn't stand that because it would only emphasize your own insignificance. Now I've intercepted letters addressed to you.

LAURA: How chivalrous of you.

CAPTAIN: In keeping with the high opinion you have of me! From these letters it's clear that for a long time you've been turning my friends against me by spreading rumors about my mental condition. And your efforts have been so successful that there isn't a single person, from the Colonel to the cook, who believes I'm sane. Since you're so interested in my condition, here it is. My reason, as you know, is undisturbed, so I can handle my responsibilities both as a soldier and a father. As for my feelings, I can control them as long as my will is intact. But you've gnawed and gnawed away at my will until it's ready to slip its gears and spin out of control. I won't appeal to your feelings, because you don't have any—that's your strength—but I do appeal to your own interests.

LAURA: My interests?

CAPTAIN: You've succeeded in so filling my mind with doubt that my reason is getting cloudy and my thoughts starting to wander. This is the first sign of the madness you've been waiting for, and it can come at any moment. You have a choice: which is in your best interest—to have me sane or insane? Think carefully! If I go to pieces, I'll lose my job. Then where will you be? If I die, you'll get the insurance. But if I kill myself, you'll get nothing. So, you see, your best interest dictates that you let me live out my life.

LAURA: Is this a trap?

CAPTAIN: It's your trap. You can avoid it or stick your head in it.

LAURA: You say you'll kill yourself, but you never would.

CAPTAIN: Are you sure? Do you think a man can go on living when he has nothing and no one to live for?

LAURA: Then you surrender?

CAPTAIN: No, I'm offering an armistice.

LAURA: On what terms?

CAPTAIN: That I can keep my reason. Free me from my doubts and I'll retreat from the field.

LAURA: What doubts?

CAPTAIN: As to whether I'm Bertha's father.

LAURA: Do you have doubts about that?

CAPTAIN: Yes, and you've aroused them.

LAURA: I?

CAPTAIN: Yes, you've dripped them in my ear like poison, and circumstances have made them grow. Free me from uncertainty! Tell me straight out that it's true and I'll forgive you in advance.

LAURA: How can I admit to something I'm not guilty of?

CAPTAIN: What does it matter? You know I won't reveal it. Do you think a man goes around trumpeting his shame?

LAURA: If I say it's true, you'll have certainty; if I said it isn't, you won't. It seems you'd rather have it true.

CAPTAIN: Yes, however strange that sounds, because then at least I'll be certain.

LAURA: Do you have any grounds for your suspicions?

CAPTAIN: Yes and no!

LAURA: I know what you're after: you're trying to blame me so you can get rid of me and keep the child yourself. You won't catch me in a trap like that.

CAPTAIN: Do you think I'd want to keep another man's child if I knew you were guilty?

LAURA: No, I'm sure you wouldn't. That's why I realize you were lying just now when you said you'd forgive me in advance.

CAPTAIN (*rising*): Laura, save me and my sanity. You don't understand what I'm saying. If the child isn't mine, I have no rights over her, and want none. Isn't that what you're after? Or maybe that isn't enough. You want both me here to support you and power over the child.

LAURA: Power, yes. What has this whole life-and-death struggle been for if not for power?

CAPTAIN: The child was my life to come. She was my immortality—the only kind that's valid, perhaps. If you take that away, you've cut off my life.

LAURA: Why didn't we separate—before it was too late?

CAPTAIN: Because the child bound us together, but that bond has become a chain. How could that be? How? I never thought about it before, but now memories come flooding back, accusing, condemning. We had been married two years and were childless—you know best why. I became ill and lay close to death. One day, between attacks of fever, I heard voices outside my room. It was you and the lawyer, talking about my inheritance, which I still had then. He was explaining that you wouldn't inherit anything, since we had no children, and he asked if you were pregnant. I couldn't hear what your answer was. I recovered and we had a child. Who is the father?

LAURA: You are!

CAPTAIN: No, I'm not! It's becoming clear that there's a crime buried here. And what a fiendish crime! You women were so tender-hearted about freeing black slaves—what about white ones? I've worked and slaved for you, your child, your mother, your servants. I sacrificed a career and advancement. I've gone sleepless. I've been tortured. And anxiety over your welfare has turned my hair grey. All this so you could live a life free from worry and when you were old, relive it in your child. And all this I've stood without complaining because I thought I was father to this child. This is the lowest form of theft, the cruellest slavery. I've had seventeen years of hard labor and I was innocent. What can you possibly do to make amends?

LAURA: Now you really are crazy!

CAPTAIN (*sits*): That's what you hope! And all the while I've been watching you conceal your crime. You were unhappy, and I felt sorry for you because I didn't know why. And when I caressed you, thinking I was chasing away morbid ideas, I was only soothing your guilty conscience. When you cried out in your sleep, I tried not to listen. But now I remember—the night before last, on Bertha's birthday. It was between two and three in the morning and I was sitting up reading. You screamed as if someone was trying to smother you: "Don't touch me, don't touch me!" I pounded on the wall, because—I didn't want to hear any more. I've had suspicions for so long and I didn't want to hear them confirmed. This is what I've suffered for you. What will you do for me?

LAURA: What should I do? I can only swear before God and everything that's sacred to me that you are Bertha's father.

CAPTAIN: What good is that? You've already said that a mother can and should commit any crime for the sake of her child. I beg you in token of the past, I beg you as someone wounded who wants to be put out of his misery—tell me everything. Can't you see that I'm as helpless as a child crying out to its mother? Won't you forget that I'm a man, that I'm a soldier who gives orders? I ask only the pity you'd show a sick person. I surrender my weapon and beg for mercy.

LAURA (*has come up to him and put her hand on his forehead*): What! A grown man, crying?

CAPTAIN: Yes, I'm crying, although I'm a man. Doesn't a man have eyes? Doesn't a man have hands, limbs, senses, opinions, passions? Isn't he nourished by the same food as a woman, wounded by the same weapons, warmed and cooled by the same winter and summer? If you prick us, do we not bleed? If you tickle us, do we not laugh? If you poison us, do we not die? Why shouldn't a man be able to complain, a soldier be able to cry? Because it's unmanly? Why is it unmanly?

LAURA: Yes, cry, my child, then you have your mother with you again. Do you remember it was as your second mother that I came into your life? You were big and strong, but so innocent. You were a child, a great child who was either born too soon or came unwanted.

CAPTAIN: Yes, that's the way it was. My parents didn't want me, so I was born without a will. When you and I became one, I thought I would become whole. That's where you got your strength. In the barracks I commanded; with you I obeyed. I grew up at your side, looked up to you as to a higher being, listened to you as if I were your foolish child.

LAURA: That's true, and so at first, I loved you as though you were my child. But you saw, I'm sure, that each time your feelings changed and you came to me as a lover, I felt strange. Our love-making was a joy, but it was followed by the sense that my very blood was ashamed. The mother became the mistress—ugh!

CAPTAIN: I saw, but misunderstood. I thought you despised my lack of virility, and so I wanted to win you as a woman by proving myself as a man.

LAURA: That's where you made your mistake. The mother was your friend, you see, but the woman was your enemy. Love between a man and woman is war. And don't imagine that I gave myself. I didn't give. I took—whatever it was I wanted. But you always kept the upper hand—I made sure of that.

CAPTAIN: No, you always had the upper hand. You could hypnotize me when I was wide awake, so that I neither saw nor heard, only obeyed. You could have given me a raw potato and made me believe it was a peach. You could force me to admire your silly ideas as strokes of genius. You could have made me commit crimes—even serious ones. When I finally realized that you lacked any real intelligence and acted only out of instinct, and that I had followed you so blindly, I woke up to find my honor gone. I wanted to blot out my humiliation through some heroic gesture: a brave deed, a discovery—even a respectable suicide. I wanted to go to war, but couldn't. That's when I turned all my energies to science. And now, just as I reach out to gather the fruit, you chop off my arm. With all hope of honor gone, I'm finished. A man can't live without honor.

LAURA: But a woman can?

CAPTAIN: Yes, because she has her children, and he has none. —— And so we lived our lives like everyone else, as unconsciously as children—filled with fantasies, ideals, and illusions. Then we woke up. We woke up, all right, but with our feet on the pillow, and the one who woke us was himself a sleepwalker. When women grow old and stop being women, they get beards on their chins. I wonder what men get when they grow old and stop being men. And so, the dawn was sounded not by roosters but capons, and the hens that answered didn't know the difference. When the sun should have been rising, we found ourselves in full moonlight, among the ruins, just like in the good old days. So, it wasn't an awakening after all—just a little morning nap, with wild dreams.

LAURA: You should have been a poet, you know.

CAPTAIN: Perhaps.

LAURA: Well, I'm sleepy. If you have any more fantasies, save them till morning.

CAPTAIN: One last word about reality. Do you hate me?

LAURA: Yes, sometimes. When you behave like a man.

CAPTAIN: This is like race hatred. If it's true that we're descended from apes, it must be from different species. We're not like each other, are we?

LAURA: What are you trying to say?

CAPTAIN: In this struggle for survival one of us must go under.

LAURA: Which one?

CAPTAIN: The weaker, naturally.

LAURA: And the stronger is in the right?

CAPTAIN: No question about it—since he has the power!

LAURA: Then I am in the right.

CAPTAIN: You think you have the power?

LAURA: Yes. And tomorrow I'll have it legally when I have you committed.

CAPTAIN: Committed?

LAURA: Yes! Then I'll be able to raise my child myself and not have to listen to your hallucinations.

CAPTAIN: And what will you live on?

LAURA: Your pension!

CAPTAIN (*advances threateningly*): How can you have me committed?

LAURA (*taking out a letter*): With this letter. The authorities already have a certified copy.

CAPTAIN: What letter?

LAURA (*backing out toward the door left*): Yours. The one you wrote to the doctor years ago, telling him you were crazy. (*The* CAPTAIN *is unable to speak.*) Now that you've fulfilled your unfortunately necessary function as father and breadwinner, you're not needed any more, so you can go. You can go, because although you realize that my intelligence is as strong as my will, you don't have the courage to admit it! (*The* CAPTAIN *crosses to the table. As* LAURA *disappears through the door, he picks up the lighted lamp and throws it after her.*)

Act III

(*The same setting as the last act. The lamp has been replaced. The wallpaper-covered door has been barricaded with a chair.* LAURA *and* MARGRET *enter.*)

LAURA: Did you get the keys?

MARGRET: Get them? No, may God forgive me, I took them out of his pocket. They were in the clothes Noyd had left hanging to brush.

LAURA: Then Noyd is still on duty?

MARGRET: Yes.

LAURA: Give them to me!

MARGRET: Yes, ma'am. This is just like stealing! Listen to him pacing up there, ma'am—back and forth, back and forth.

LAURA: Is his door safely locked?

MARGRET: Oh, yes, it's locked.

LAURA (*opens the desk and sits down*): Pull yourself together, Margret. If we're all going to get through this, we've got to remain calm. (*a knock at the door*) See who that is.

MARGRET (*opening the door to the hall*): It's Noyd.

LAURA: Let him in.

NOYD (*enters*): There's a dispatch from the Colonel, ma'am.

LAURA: Let me have it! (*reads*) Ha! Report! ——— Noyd, have you emptied all the cartridges from the guns and pouches?

NOYD: As you ordered, ma'am.

LAURA: Then wait outside, while I answer the Colonel's letter. (*He leaves. She writes.*)

MARGRET: Listen to that, ma'am, what's he doing now up there?

LAURA: Quiet, while I'm writing. (*The sounds of someone sawing are heard from above.*)

MARGRET (*half to herself*): Oh, God help us all! Where's this going to end?

LAURA (*finishing*): There. Give this to Noyd. And my mother must know nothing about all this for now! Do you hear? (MARGRET *exits.* LAURA *opens the drawers in the desk and takes out some papers. The* PASTOR *enters, takes a chair, and sits down next to* LAURA.)

PASTOR: Good evening, Laura. I'm sorry I couldn't get here sooner. This is a difficult business.

LAURA: Yes, Jonas. I've never had such a night and day in my whole life.

PASTOR: Thank God you weren't hurt.

LAURA: Yes, thank God, but just think what could have happened!

PASTOR: Tell me, what started it? I've heard such different stories.

LAURA: It started with his wild fantasies about not being Bertha's father, and ended with him throwing a lighted lamp in my face.

PASTOR: This is terrible! He's gone completely insane. What'll we do?

LAURA: Try to prevent more violence. The Doctor's sent for a strait jacket from the asylum. In the meantime, I've sent a message to the Colonel and begun trying to make sense of the mess Adolf's made of the family finances.

PASTOR: How awful! But I've always expected something like this. When you mix fire and water there's bound to be an explosion. What's that stuff in the drawer?

LAURA (*taking a drawer out of the desk*): Things he's been saving, I suppose.

PASTOR (*rummaging through the drawer*): Oh, my God! That's your doll—and there's your christening cap—and Bertha's rat-

tle—and your letters—and that locket. ———— (*choking up*)
Whatever has happened, he must have loved you very much,
Laura. Saving such things! I never did that.

LAURA: I guess he did love me once, but . . . time changes so many
things.

PASTOR: What's this? ———— Why, it's a deed for a cemetery
plot! ———— Yes, better the grave than the asylum! Laura! Tell
me—how much are you to blame for all this?

LAURA: I? How can I be blamed for a person going mad?

PASTOR: Yes, yes! . . . I won't say anything! Blood is thicker than
water, after all.

LAURA: Just what do you mean by that?

PASTOR (*staring at her*): Now, listen Laura . . .

LAURA: What is it?

PASTOR: You can't deny that all this fits in with your plans to
bring up the child yourself.

LAURA: I don't understand.

PASTOR: I can't help admiring you!

LAURA: Do you?

PASTOR: And he'll end up my ward! Guardian to an atheist! Do
you know, I've always considered him to be a weed in our garden! (LAURA *gives a short, stifled laugh, then quickly turns serious.*)

LAURA: How dare you to say that to me, his wife?

PASTOR: Oh, you're too strong for me, Laura! Incredibly strong!
Like a fox in a trap—you'd rather bite off your own leg than let
yourself be caught! ———— Like a master thief: with no accomplice, not even a conscience! ———— Can you look at yourself in
a mirror?

LAURA: I never use mirrors!

PASTOR: No, you don't dare to! ———— Let me see your hand!
———— Not one incriminating spot of blood, not a sign of the
subtle poison! One little innocent murder that the law can't
touch; an unconscious crime; unconscious? What a brilliant
idea! Listen to him working up there! ———— Be careful: if that
man gets loose, he'll saw you in two!

LAURA: You're talking too much—like someone with a bad conscience. ———— Have me arrested, if you can!

PASTOR: I can't.

LAURA: You see! You can't, because I'm innocent! ——— Now you look after your ward and I'll look after mine! ——— Here's the Doctor! (*The* DOCTOR *enters.* LAURA *rises.*) Welcome, Doctor. At least you'll help me, won't you? Though I'm afraid there's not much that anyone can do. Do you hear how he's carrying on up there? Are you finally convinced?

DOCTOR: I'm convinced there was an act of violence. The question is whether we should consider it a result of anger or insanity.

PASTOR: But even disregarding this incident, you'll have to admit he has fixed ideas.

DOCTOR: I think your own ideas are even more fixed, Pastor.

PASTOR: If you're referring to my deeply held convictions . . .

DOCTOR: Let's leave that for now. ——— Madam, the decision of whether your husband is fined and imprisoned or committed to an asylum depends on you. How would you describe his behavior?

LAURA: I can't answer that now!

DOCTOR: Then you have no "deeply held conviction" about what would be best for the family? What do you think, Pastor?

PASTOR: Well, it's not easy to say . . . it'll be a scandal either way.

LAURA: But if he's only fined for assault, the same thing could happen again.

DOCTOR: And if he's put in prison, he'd be out again in a short while. So, it seems the best thing for everyone, then, would be for us to agree that he's insane. ——— Where is his old nurse?

LAURA: Margret? Why?

DOCTOR: She'll be the one who'll put the strait jacket on him— but only after I've talked to him and given the order, not before! I have the—garment outside. (*goes out into the entrance hall and returns with a large bundle*) Please have her come in. (LAURA *rings.*)

PASTOR: This is dreadful, dreadful! (MARGRET *enters.*)

DOCTOR (*taking out the strait jacket*): Margret, do you see this jacket? When I think it's necessary, in order to prevent violence, I want you to slip it on the Captain from behind. As you can see, it has unusually long sleeves, to restrain his movement.

And these are tied behind the back. Then you fasten these
straps and buckles to the nearest arm of a chair or sofa or whatever. Will you do it?

MARGRET: No, Doctor, I can't, I can't do it.

LAURA: Why don't you do it yourself, Doctor?

DOCTOR: Because the patient doesn't trust me. Actually, you
would be the logical person, but I'm afraid he doesn't trust you,
either. (LAURA *shudders.*) Perhaps, you, Pastor . . .

PASTOR: No, please—not me! (NOYD *enters.*)

LAURA: Did you deliver the letter?

NOYD: As ordered, ma'am.

DOCTOR: Ah, Noyd! You know the circumstances here and you
know the Captain's ill. You'll help us with the patient, won't
you?

NOYD: I'll do anything I can for the Captain.

DOCTOR: I want you to put this jacket on him . . .

MARGRET: No! He mustn't touch him! Noyd mustn't hurt him.
It's better if I do it, but gently, so gently. Noyd can stand outside, ready to help, if necessary. ———— Yes, he can do that. (*a
pounding on the wallpaper-covered door*)

DOCTOR: There he is! Hide the jacket under your shawl on that
chair! Everyone out for now! The Pastor and I will wait for him
here—that door can't hold much longer! ———— All right, out!

MARGRET (*exiting left*): Lord Jesus, help us!

(LAURA *closes the desk and exits left.* NOYD *exits upstage.
The lock on the wallpaper-covered door bursts open, throwing
the chair to the floor. The* CAPTAIN *enters carrying an armload
of books.*)

CAPTAIN (*putting the books on the table*): It's all down in black
and white in these books. So, I wasn't crazy, after all. Here, in
Book One, line 215, of *The Odyssey,* Telemachus is talking to
the goddess Athene: "My mother says I am his (that is, Odysseus's) son; I know not / surely. Who can know from whom he
springs?" And this doubt Telemachus has about Penelope—the
most virtuous of women! That's beautiful! Isn't it? And here's
the prophet Ezekiel: "The fool saith, behold my father, but who
can tell whose loins have begotten him?" That's clear enough!
Now, what's this? *The History of Russian Literature* by Merz-

lyakov. Alexander Pushkin, Russia's greatest poet—he died after a duel, but it wasn't a bullet that killed him, it was the tormenting rumor of his wife's unfaithfulness. On his deathbed he swore she was innocent! What an ass! How could he swear to that? You see, I do read my books! ——— Oh, so you're here, Jonas! And the Doctor, of course. Did I ever tell you what I said to the English woman who complained that Irishmen throw lighted kerosene lamps in their wives' faces? ——— "God, what women," I said. ——— "Women?" she minced! ——— "Yes, of course," I replied. When things have reached the point that a man, a man who has loved and worshipped a woman, picks up a lighted lamp and throws it in her face ... then ... finally, you can be sure.

PASTOR: Sure of what?

CAPTAIN: Nothing! You're never sure of anything. The only thing you can do is have faith, isn't that right, Jonas? Have faith and you'll be saved! Oh, yes! But I know that faith can damn you! That I know!

DOCTOR: But Captain ...

CAPTAIN: Shut up! I'm not talking to you! I don't want to listen to you mouthing what they say in there! *In there!* And you know very well what I mean! ——— Listen, Jonas, do you believe you're the father of your children? I seem to remember you had a tutor in your house—handsome devil everybody talked about.

PASTOR: Adolf! Take care!

CAPTAIN: Feel around under your wig and see if you don't find two little bumps there. Look at him—he's turning pale! Yes, yes, it was only talk, but how they talked! Well, we're all targets for that kind of ridicule, we husbands. Isn't that right, Doctor? By the way, how was your marriage bed? Wasn't there a certain lieutenant staying with you? Wait, let me guess. Wasn't he ... (*whispers in the* DOCTOR'S *ear*) ——— Look, he's getting pale, too! Well, don't feel bad. She's dead and buried and what's done is done. As a matter of fact, though, I know the man and he's now—look at me, Doctor! ——— No, look me right in the eye!—he's now a major in the dragoons! By God, I think you have horns, too!

DOCTOR (*pained*): Captain, let's change the subject.

CAPTAIN: Ha! I want to talk about horns and he wants to change the subject!

PASTOR: Adolf, my friend, do you know that your mind is sick?

CAPTAIN: Yes, of course, I know that. But if I were to keep yanking on your horns a while longer, they'd have to look you up, too. I am insane, but how did I get that way? You don't care. Nobody cares. Now *I* want to change the subject. (*He picks up the photograph album from the table.*) Dear God, there's my child! Mine? Oh, no, we can't be sure of that, can we? But there must be some way we can make sure. Of course, I know! First, to be socially respectable, you get married. Immediately afterward, you get divorced and become lovers. When a child comes, you adopt it. Then you say, "This is my *adopted* child"—at least you could be sure of that. Right? But what good is all this to me? What good is anything now that you've taken away my hope of immortality? How can science and philosophy help me when I have nothing to live for? Of what use is life without honor? I grafted my right arm, half my brain, half my spinal cord onto another stem, because I believed they would grow together and unite into a single, more perfect tree. Then someone came along with a knife and cut below the graft. Now I'm only half a tree, and the other part continues to grow with my arm and half my brain, while I wither and die, because I gave away the best parts of myself. Now I want to die. Do what you want with me. I no longer exist.

(*The* DOCTOR *whispers to the* PASTOR, *and they exit left.* BERTHA *enters. The* CAPTAIN *sinks down at the table.* BERTHA *crosses to him.*)

BERTHA: Are you sick, Poppa?

CAPTAIN (*looks up dully*): Me?

BERTHA: Do you know what you did? Do you know you threw a lamp at Momma?

CAPTAIN: Did I?

BERTHA: Yes, you did! Think if she'd been hurt!

CAPTAIN: What difference would that have made?

BERTHA: You're not my father when you talk like that.

CAPTAIN: What did you say? I'm not your father? How do you know that? Who told you? And who is your father then? Who?

BERTHA: Well, not you, anyway!

CAPTAIN: Still not me! Who, then? Who? You seem well-informed. Who told you? To think that I'd live to see my own child tell me to my face I'm not her father! Don't you realize you're insulting your mother when you say that? Don't you understand it's her shame, if it's true?

BERTHA: Don't say anything bad about Momma, you hear?

CAPTAIN: No, you stick together, all of you—against me! That's the way it's been, the whole time.

BERTHA: Poppa!

CAPTAIN: Don't ever call me that again!

BERTHA: Poppa, Poppa!

CAPTAIN (*draws her to him*): Bertha, my beloved child, you are my child! Yes, yes. How could it be otherwise? It must be so! The other was just a sick idea, carried on the wind like fever or plague. Look at me, so that I can see my soul in your eyes! —————— But I see her soul, too! You have two souls, and you love me with one and hate me with the other. But you must love only me. You must only have one soul, or you'll never have any peace, and neither will I. You must only have one thought, the child of my thought, and you must only have one will, mine.

BERTHA: I don't want that! I want to be myself.

CAPTAIN: I won't have it! You see, I'm a cannibal, and I want to devour you. Your mother wanted to devour me, but couldn't. I am Saturn, the god who swallowed up his own children because it had been prophesied that otherwise they would swallow him. To eat or be eaten! Yes, that is the question! If I don't devour you, you'll devour me, and you've already bared your teeth! But don't be afraid, my darling child, I won't hurt you. (*He goes to the weapon collection and takes down a revolver.*)

BERTHA (*tries to escape*): Momma, Momma, help! He wants to kill me!

MARGRET (*enters*): Master Adolf, is something the matter?

CAPTAIN (*examining the revolver*): Have you taken the cartridges?

MARGRET: Oh, yes, when I was tidying up, but if you sit over here and calm yourself, I'll get them for you! (*She takes him by the arm and guides him over to the chair where he sits, dully. Then she picks up the strait jacket and stands behind his chair.* BER-

THA *sneaks out left.*) Master Adolf, do you remember when you were my dearest little boy and I tucked you in at night and said your prayers with you? "Now I lay me down to sleep." And do you remember how I used to light a candle and tell you wonderful fairy tales when you had bad dreams and couldn't sleep? Do you remember?

CAPTAIN: Tell me more, Margret, it makes my head feel better. Tell me more.

MARGRET: All right, but you have to listen! Do you remember once how you took the big kitchen knife and wanted to carve wooden boats and how I came in and had to play a trick to get it away from you? You were such a silly boy, and we had to trick you because you didn't understand that we only wanted what was best for you. And so I said, "Give me that snake, or it'll bite you!" And then you dropped the knife. (*takes the revolver out of his hand*)

And then there were the times you didn't want to get dressed. And I had to coax you by saying you were getting a golden coat and would look like a prince. And then I'd take your little green jacket, which was just ordinary wool, and hold it out in front of you like this and say: "In with your arms, both of them!" And then I'd say: "Sit nice and still now, while I button up the back." (*He is in the strait jacket.*) And then I'd say: "Stand up now, like a good boy, and walk across the floor so I can see how it fits..." (*She guides him to the sofa.*) And then I'd say: "Now it's time for bed!"

CAPTAIN: What's that? Why do I have to got to bed now, when I just got dressed? Damn! What have you done to me? (*tries to free himself*) Oh, you devilishly cunning woman! Who would have thought you were so clever! (*He lies down on the sofa.*) Outwitted, trapped, shorn, and not even allowed to die!

MARGRET: Forgive me, Master Adolf, forgive me, but I had to stop you from killing the child!

CAPTAIN: Why didn't you let me kill her? Life is hell and death a heaven, and children belong to heaven.

MARGRET: What do you know about what comes after death?

CAPTAIN: That's all we do know—it's life we don't know anything about. Oh, if only we'd known that from the beginning!

MARGRET: Master Adolf! Humble your stubborn heart and pray to God for mercy! It's still not too late. It wasn't too late for the thief on the cross when our Saviour said: "Today thou shalt be with me in Paradise."

CAPTAIN: Are you croaking over the corpse already, you old crow? (MARGRET *takes a book of psalms from her pocket. The* CAPTAIN *shouts.*) Noyd! Is Noyd there? (NOYD *enters.*) Throw this woman out! She wants to suffocate me with her psalm book. Throw her out the window or up the chimney! Anywhere!

NOYD (*looking at* MARGRET): God bless you, Captain, but . . . but I can't do that! I just can't. If there were six men, yes, but a woman . . .

CAPTAIN: Can't you manage a woman?

NOYD: I could manage her all right, but there's something special about a woman that stops you from laying a hand on her.

CAPTAIN: What do you mean, "special"? Haven't they laid hands on me?

NOYD: Yes, but I can't do it, Captain! It's the same as if you asked me to hit the Pastor. It's something inside me, like religion! I can't! (LAURA *enters and signals to* NOYD *to leave; he does so.*)

CAPTAIN: Omphale! It's Queen Omphale herself! Now you play with Hercules's club while he spins your wool!

LAURA (*crossing to the sofa*): Adolf! Look at me! Do you think I'm your enemy?

CAPTAIN: Yes, I do. I think you're all my enemies. First, there was my mother, who didn't want me because my birth would cause her pain, and so she starved herself and I was born half crippled. My sister was my enemy when she made me her lackey. The first woman I slept with was my enemy when she gave me ten years of illness in return for the love I gave her. My daughter became my enemy when she had to choose between you and me. And you, my wife, were my mortal enemy, because you wouldn't leave me alone until you had me lying here dead!

LAURA: I don't know that I've ever thought about or intended what you think I've done. I may have had a vague desire to get rid of you, like some obstacle, and if you can see some plan in my actions, it's possible there was one, but I wasn't aware of it. I've never given a thought to the things that happened—they simply skimmed along on the rails you yourself laid down. Before God and my conscience I feel innocent, even if I'm not. You were always like a stone on my heart, pressing and pressing down until my heart tried to shake off its awful burden. That's how it's been and if I've unintentionally hurt you, I ask your forgiveness.

CAPTAIN: Even if all that is true, how can it help me? And who is to blame? Maybe the whole idea of marriage. There was a time a man married a wife. Now he either enters into a spiritual partnership with a business woman or moves in with a friend! Then he fornicates with the partner or violates the friend! And what happens to love—healthy, sensual love? It dies in the process. And what about the offspring of this business transaction—the interest on this joint bank account where there's no joint responsibility? Who keeps the bank book when the crash comes? Who is the physical father to the spiritual child?

LAURA: Those suspicions of yours about the child are completely unfounded.

CAPTAIN: That's just what's so horrible. At least if they were real, there would be something to take hold of, to grab onto. Now there are only shadows, hiding in the bushes and sticking out their heads to laugh. It's like grappling with thin air, fighting with blank cartridges. A painful truth would have been a challenge, rousing body and soul to action, but now . . . my thoughts dissolve into mist, and my brain grinds emptiness until it catches fire! Put a pillow under my head. And throw something over me, I'm cold! I'm so terribly cold! (LAURA *takes her shawl and spreads it over him.* MARGRET *leaves to fetch a pillow.*)

LAURA: Give me your hand, dear.

CAPTAIN: Ha! My hand? Which you've tied behind my back . . . Omphale! Omphale! But I can feel your soft shawl against my mouth. It's warm and smooth like your arm, and it smells of vanilla as your hair did when you were young, Laura—when you were young—and we walked in the birch woods, surrounded by primroses and thrushes! Lovely, lovely! Think how beautiful life was then, and what it's become. You didn't want it to turn out like this any more than I did. Yet it has. What power rules over our lives?

LAURA: God alone rules . . .

CAPTAIN: The God of strife then—or nowadays the Goddess! Take away this cat that's lying on me! Take it away! (MARGRET *enters with a pillow and takes away the shawl.*) Give me my tunic! Throw it over me. (MARGRET *fetches the tunic from the clothes rack and spreads it over him.*) Ah, my tough lion's skin you wanted to take from me. Omphale! Omphale! You cunning woman who so loved peace you invented disarmament. Wake up, Hercules, before they take away your club! You wanted to lure us out of our armor, calling it nothing but decoration. But it was iron, *iron,* before it was decoration! That was when the blacksmith made the battle dress; now it's the seamstress! Omphale! Omphale! Brute strength brought down by treacherous weakness. Curse you, damned woman, and your whole sex! (*He raises himself to spit, but falls back on the sofa.*) What sort of pillow have you given me, Margret? It's so hard and so cold, so cold! Come and sit beside me here on the chair. That's it! Let me lay my head in your lap! Like that. ——— You're so warm! Lean over so I can feel your breast. ——— Oh, it's so sweet to sleep at a woman's breast, be she mother or mistress. But sweetest of all a mother's!

LAURA: Do you want to see your child, Adolf? Tell me!

CAPTAIN: My child? A man has no children. Only women have children, and so the future is theirs, while we die childless. "Now I lay me down to sleep!"

MARGRET: Listen, he's praying to God!

CAPTAIN: No, to you, to get me to sleep, for I'm tired, so tired! Good night, Margret; blessed art thou amongst women! (*He raises himself, but falls back with a cry into* MARGRET's *lap.*)

LAURA (*crosses to left and calls*): Help! Doctor! Doctor! (*The* DOCTOR *enters, followed by the* PASTOR.) Help us, if it isn't too late. I think he's stopped breathing! (*The* DOCTOR *examines the* CAPTAIN's *pulse.*)

DOCTOR: He's had a stroke!

PASTOR: Is he dead?

DOCTOR: No, he might regain consciousness, but in what state, it's hard to tell.

PASTOR: Once to die and after this the judgment . . .

DOCTOR: No judgment! And no recriminations! You who believe
   a God guides the destinies of men can refer the matter to Him.

MARGRET: Oh, Pastor, he prayed to God at the last!

PASTOR (*to* LAURA): Is that true?

LAURA: It's true.

DOCTOR: If it is—and I can no more judge of that than I can of the
   cause of his illness—then my work is done. It's up to you now,
   Pastor.

LAURA: Is that all you have to say at this deathbed, Doctor?

DOCTOR: That's all. It's all I know. He who knows more, let him
   speak.

BERTHA (*enters and rushes to her mother*): Momma, Momma!

LAURA: My child! My own child!

PASTOR: Amen!

Miss Julie

(1888)

Author's Preface

The theatre has long seemed to me to be, like art in general, a *Biblia pauperum,* a Bible in pictures for those who can't read what is written or printed, and the playwright a lay preacher hawking the ideas of the day in popular form, so popular that the middle classes, the theatre's primary audience, can understand the basic questions without too much effort. And so the theatre has always been a public school for the young, the half-educated, and women, who still possess that primitive capacity for deceiving themselves or letting themselves be deceived, that is to say, are receptive to the illusion, to the playwright's power of suggestion. It seems to me, therefore, in our time, when rudimentary, undeveloped, and fanciful ways of thinking seem to be evolving toward reflection, investigation, and analysis, that the theatre, like religion, is dying out, a form for whose enjoyment we lack the necessary preconditions. Supporting this assertion is the serious theatre crisis now prevailing throughout Europe, especially in those bastions of culture that produced the greatest thinkers of the age, England and Germany, where the art of drama, like most of the other fine arts, is dead.

In other countries people have believed it possible to create a new drama by filling old forms with new contents. For a number of reasons, however, this has failed: in part because there has not been sufficient time to popularize the new ideas, so that the public does not understand the basic questions; in part because partisan politics has stirred up emotions, making dispassionate enjoyment impossible—how can people be objective when their innermost beliefs are offended or when they are subjected in the confines of a theatre to the public pressure of an applauding or hissing audience?; and in part because new forms have not been found for the new contents, so that the new wine has burst the old bottles.

In the following play, instead of trying to do anything new— which is impossible—I have simply modernized the form in accordance with demands I think contemporary audiences make upon this art. Toward this end, I have chosen, or let myself be moved by, a theme that can be said to lie outside partisan politics since the problem of social climbing or falling, of higher or lower, better or worse, man or woman, are, have been, and will be of lasting interest. When I took this theme from a true story I heard told some years ago, which made a strong impression on me, I found it appropriate for tragedy, for it still seems tragic to see someone favored by fortune go under, much more to see a family die out. Perhaps the time will come when we will be so advanced, so enlightened, that we can witness with indifference what now seem the coarse, cynical, heartless dramas life has to offer, when we have closed down those lower, unreliable mechanisms of thought called feelings, because better developed organs of judgment will have found them superfluous and harmful. The fact that the heroine arouses compassion is because we are too weak to resist the fear that the same fate could overtake us. A hypersensitive spectator may not be satisfied with compassion alone, while a man with faith in the future may demand some positive proposals to remedy the evil, in other words, a program of some kind. But for one thing there is no absolute evil. The fall of one family can mean a chance for another family to rise, and the alternation of rising and falling fortunes is one of life's greatest delights since happiness lies only in comparison. And to the man who wants a program to remedy the unpleasant fact that the bird of prey eats the dove and the louse eats the bird of prey I ask: why should it be remedied? Life is not so idiotically mathematical that only the great eat the small; it is just as common for a bee to kill a lion or at least drive it mad.

If my tragedy depresses many people, it is their own fault. When we become as strong as the first French revolutionaries, it will afford nothing but pleasure and relief to witness the thinning out in royal parks of overage, decaying trees that have long stood in the way of others equally entitled to their time in the sun, the kind of relief we feel when we see someone incurably ill die!

Recently, my tragedy *The Father* was criticized for being too sad, as if one should expect cheerful tragedies. People clamor pretentiously for "the joy of life," and theatre managers call for farces, as if the joy of life lay in being silly and depicting people as if they were all afflicted with St. Vitus's dance or imbecility. I find the joy of life in its cruel and powerful struggles, and my enjoyment comes from being able to know something, being able to learn something. That is why I have chosen an unusual case, but one from which we can learn much—in a word an exception, but an important exception which proves the rule—though this will probably offend those who love the conventional and predictable. What will next shock simple minds is that I have not motivated the action in a simple way, nor is there a single point of view. Every event in life—and this is a rather new discovery!—is ordinarily the result of a whole series of more or less deep-lying motives. The spectator, however, usually singles out the one that is either easiest for him to understand or is most advantageous to him personally. Take the case of a suicide. "Financial problems," says a businessman. "Unrequited love," says a woman. "Physical illness," says an invalid. "Dashed hopes," says a shipwrecked man. It might be that all or none of these were motives and that the deceased concealed the real motive by advancing a totally different one that would bring the most credit to his memory!

I have motivated Miss Julie's tragic fate by a great number of circumstances: her mother's primary instincts, her father raising her incorrectly, her own nature, and the influence of her fiancé on her weak and degenerate brain. Also, more particularly: the festive

Pull out animal doll

2)

Flowers

atmosphere of midsummer night, her father's absence, her monthly indisposition, her preoccupation with animals, the provocative effect of the dancing, the magical midsummer twilight, the powerfully aphrodisiac influence of flowers, and, finally, the chance that drives the couple together into a room alone—plus the boldness of the aroused man.

My treatment of the subject has thus been neither one-sidedly physiological nor exclusively psychological. I have not put the entire blame on what she inherited from her mother, nor on her monthly indisposition, nor on immorality. I have not even preached morality—this I left to the cook in the absence of a minister.

This multiplicity of motives, it pleases me to assert, is in keeping with the times. And if others have done it before me, then it pleases me that I have not been alone in my "paradoxes," as all discoveries are called.

As for characterization, I have made my people rather "characterless" for the following reasons:

The word *character* has come to mean many things over the course of time. Originally, it must have meant the dominant trait in the soul-complex and was confused with temperament. Later it became the middle-class expression for the automaton, one whose disposition was fixed once and for all or had adapted himself to a particular role in life. In a word, someone who had stopped growing was called a character. In contrast the person who continued to develop, the skillful navigator on the river of life, sailing not with sheets belayed, but veering before the wind to luff again, was called characterless—in a derogatory sense, of course—because he was so difficult to understand, classify, and keep track of. This bourgeois concept of the immobility of the soul was transferred to the stage, which the bourgeoisie has always dominated. There a character became a man who was ready-made; whenever he appeared, he was drunk or comical or sad. The only thing necessary to characterize him was to give him a physical defect—a clubfoot, a wooden leg, a red nose—or have him repeat an expression, such as "that was splendid" or "Barkis is willin'." This simplified view of human character still survives in the great Molière. Harpagon is nothing but a miser although he could have been not only a miser but an excellent financier, or splendid father and good citizen. What is worse is that his "defect" is very advantageous to his son-in-law and daughter, who are his heirs and therefore should not criticize him, even if they have to wait a bit before climbing into bed together. Therefore, I do not believe in simple theatrical characters. And an author's summary judgments of people—this one is stupid, that one brutal, this one jealous, that one stingy—should be challenged by naturalists, who know how rich the soul-complex is and realize that "vice" has a reverse side closely resembling virtue.

As modern characters living in an age of transition more compulsively hysterical than the one that preceded it at least, I have depicted my people as more vacillating and disintegrating than their predecessors, a mixture of the old and the new. If the valet belches something modern from the depths of his ancient slave's soul, it is because I think it not improbable that through newspapers and conversations modern ideas filter down even to the level a servant lives on. There are those who find it wrong in modern drama for characters to speak Darwinism. At the same time they hold up Shakespeare as a model. I would like to remind these critics that the gravedigger in *Hamlet* speaks the fashionable philosophy of the day—Giordano Bruno's (Bacon's)—which is more improbable since there were fewer means then for the spread of ideas than there are now. Besides, "Darwinism" has existed in every age, ever since the description in Genesis of the steps in creation from lower animals to man. It is just that only now have we discovered and formulated it.

My souls (characters) are conglomerates of past and present cultural phases, bits from books and newspapers, scraps of humanity, pieces torn from fine clothes and become rags, patched together as is the human soul. I have also added a little evolutionary history by having the weaker mind steal and repeat words from the stronger. Ideas are induced through the power of suggestion: from other people, from the surroundings (the blood of the greenfinch), and from attributes (the straight razor); and I have inanimate objects (the Count's boots, the bell) serve as agents for *Gedankenübertragung* ["thought transference"]. Finally, I have used "open suggestion," a variation of sleeplike hypnosis, which is now so well known and popularized that it cannot arouse the kind of ridicule or skepticism it would have done in Mesmer's time.

Miss Julie is a modern character. Not that the man-hating half-woman has not existed in all ages but because now that she has been discovered, she has come out in the open to make herself heard. The half-woman is a type who pushes her way ahead, selling herself nowadays for power, decorations, honors, and diplomas, as formerly she used to do for money. The type implies a retrogressive step in evolution, an inferior species who cannot endure. Unfortunately, they are able to pass on their wretchedness; degenerate men seem unconsciously to choose their mates from among them. And so they breed, producing an indeterminate sex for whom life is a torture. Fortunately, the offspring go under either because they are out of harmony with reality or because their repressed instincts break out uncontrollably or because their hopes of achieving equality with men are crushed. The type is tragic, revealing the drama of a desperate struggle against Nature, tragic as the romantic heritage now being dissipated by naturalism, which has a contrary aim: happiness, and happiness belongs only to the strong and skillful species.

But Miss Julie is also: a relic of the old warrior nobility now giving way to a new nobility of nerve and intellect, a victim of her own flawed constitution, a victim of the discord caused in a family by a mother's "crime," a victim of the delusions and conditions of her age—and together these are the equivalent of the concept of Destiny, or Universal Law, of antiquity. Guilt has been abolished by the naturalist, along with God, but the consequences of an action—punishment, imprisonment or the fear of it—that he cannot erase, for the simple reason that they remain, whether he pronounces acquittal or not. Those who have been injured are not as kind and understanding as an unscathed outsider can afford to be. Even if her father felt constrained not to seek revenge, his daughter would wreak vengeance upon herself, as she does here, out of an innate or acquired sense of honor, which the upper classes inherit—from where? From barbarism, from the ancient Aryan home of the race, from medieval chivalry. It is a beautiful thing, but nowadays a hindrance to the survival of the race. It is the nobleman's harikari, which compels him to slit open his own stomach when someone insults him and which survives in a modified form in the duel, that privilege of the nobility. That is why Jean, the servant, lives, while Miss Julie cannot live without honor. The slave's advantage over the nobleman is that he lacks this fatal preoccupation with honor. But in all of us Aryans there is something of the nobleman, or a Don Quixote. And so we sympathize with the suicide, whose act means a loss of honor. We are noblemen enough to be pained when we see the mighty fallen and as superfluous as a corpse, yes, even if the fallen should rise again and make amends through an honorable act. The servant Jean is a race-founder, someone in whom the process of differentiation can be detected. Born the son of a tenant farmer, he has educated himself in the things a gentleman should know. He has been quick to learn, has finely developed senses (smell, taste, sight) and a feeling for what is beautiful. He is already moving up in the world and is not embarrassed about using other people's help. He is alienated from his fellow servants, despising them as parts of a past he has already put behind him. He fears and flees them because they know his secrets, pry into his intentions, envy his rise, and look forward eagerly to his fall. Hence his dual, indecisive nature, vacillating between sympathy for people in high social positions and hatred for those who currently occupy those positions. He is an aristocrat, as he himself says, has learned the secrets of good society, is polished on the surface but coarse beneath, wears a frock coat tastefully but without any guarantee that his body is clean.

He has respect for Miss Julie, but is afraid of Kristine because she knows his dangerous secrets. He is sufficiently callous not to let the night's events disturb his plans for the future. With both a slave's brutality and a master's lack of squeamishness, he can see blood without fainting and shake off misfortune easily. Consequently, he comes through the struggle unscathed and will probably end up an innkeeper. And even if *he* does not become a Rumanian count, his son will become a university student and possibly a county police commissioner.

In any case he has important things to say about the lower classes' view of life—when he is telling the truth, that is, which he often does not do, for he is more interested in saying what is favorable to himself than in telling the truth. When Miss Julie says she assumes the lower classes feel oppressed from above, Jean natural-ly agrees since it is his intention to win sympathy, but he quickly changes his attitude when he realizes that it is more to his advan-tage to distance himself from the "rabble."

Apart from the fact that Jean is rising in the world, he is superi-or to Miss Julie because he is a man. Sexually, he is an aristocrat because of his masculine strength, his more keenly developed senses, and his capacity for taking the initiative. His sense of infe-riority is mostly due to the social circumstances in which he hap-pens to be living, and he can probably shed it along with his va-let's jacket.

His slave mentality expresses itself in the fearful respect he has for the Count (the boots) and his religious superstition; but he respects the Count mainly as the occupant of the kind of high position to which he himself aspires; and the respect remains even after he has conquered the daughter of the house and seen how empty the lovely shell was.

I do not believe that love in any "higher" sense can exist be-tween two people of such different natures, and so I have Miss Julie's love as something she fabricates in order to protect and excuse herself; and I have Jean suppose himself capable of loving her under other social circumstances. I think it is the same with love as with the hyacinth, which must take root in darkness *before* it can produce a sturdy flower. Here a flower shoots up, blooms, and goes to seed all at once, and that is why it dies so quickly.

Kristine, finally, is a female slave. Years standing over the stove have made her conventional and lethargic; instinctively hypocriti-cal, she uses morality and religion as cloaks and scapegoats. A strong person would not need these because he can either bear his guilt or reason it away. Kristine goes to church as a quick and easy way to unload her household thefts on Jesus and to take on a new charge of innocence. Furthermore, she is a minor character, and I purposely simply sketched her in, as I did the minister and the doctor in *The Father*, because I wanted ordinary people, as coun-try ministers and provincial doctors usually are. If my minor char-acters seem abstract to some people, it is because ordinary people are abstract to some extent in their occupations. As they carry out their duties, they lose their individuality, showing only one side of themselves, and as long as the spectator has no need to see them from several sides, my abstract depiction of them is probably correct.

As for the dialogue, I have broken with tradition somewhat by not making my characters catechists who ask stupid questions in order to elicit clever replies. I have avoided the symmetrical, mathematical, constructed dialogue of French drama and let characters' minds function irregularly, as they do in a real-life conversation, where no topic of discussion is exhausted entirely and one mind by chance finds a cog in another mind in which to engage. Consequently, the dialogue also wanders, presenting material in the opening scenes that is later taken up, reworked, repeated, expanded, and developed, like the theme in a musical composition.

The plot is serviceable enough, and since it really concerns only two people, I have concentrated on them, including only one minor character, the cook, and having the father's unhappy spirit hover over and behind the action. I have done this because I believe that people of today are most interested in the psychological process. Our inquisitive souls are not satisfied just to see something happen; we want to know how it happened. We want to see the strings, the machinery, examine the double-bottomed box, feel for the seam in the magic ring, look at the cards to see how they are marked.

In this regard I have kept in mind the monographic novels of the brothers Goncourt, which I find more appealing than anything else in contemporary literature.

As for the technical aspects of composition, I have experimented with eliminating act divisions. The reason is that I believe our dwindling capacity for accepting illusion is possibly further disturbed by intermissions, during which the spectator has time to reflect and thereby escape the suggestive influence of the author-hypnotist. My play will probably run an hour and a half, and since people can listen to a lecture, sermon, or conference discussion for just as long or longer, I imagine that a ninety-minute theatre piece will not be too tiring. I tested this concentrated form in 1872 in one of my first plays, *The Outlaw*, although with little success. The first draft was in five acts, and when I noticed the disjointed,

restless effect it produced, I burned it. From the ashes rose a single, long, coherent act of fifty pages in print, with a playing time
of one hour. And so the form is not new, and I seem to have a feel
for it; changing tastes may make it timely. My hope for the future
is to so educate audiences that they can sit through a one-act play
that lasts an entire evening. But this will require experimentation.
Meanwhile, in order to relax tension for the audience and the actors, without breaking the illusion for the audience, I have used
three art forms traditionally associated with drama: monologue,
mime, and ballet. The original association was with the tragedy of
antiquity, monody having become monologue, and chorus, ballet.

Our realists today condemn the monologue as implausible, but
if I motivate it, I can make it plausible and use it to advantage. It
is perfectly plausible for an orator to pace the floor alone and practice his speech aloud, plausible for an actor to rehearse his lines
aloud, for a servant girl to talk to her cat, a mother babble to her
baby, an old maid jabber to her parrot, a sleeper talk in his sleep.
And in order to give the actor a chance, for once, to work indepen-
dently, free for a moment of the author's authority, I have
sketched in the monologues rather than worked them out in detail.
Since it is irrelevant what someone says in his sleep or to a parrot
or to a cat, for this has no influence on the action, a talented actor,
absorbed in the mood and the situation, perhaps can improvise the
monologue more effectively than the author, who cannot determine in advance how much may be spoken, and for how long,
before an audience senses that the illusion is broken.

As we know, some Italian theatres have returned to improvisa-
tion, producing actors who are creative in their own right, although in accordance with the author's intentions. This could be
the beginning of a fertile new art form, something worthy of the
name *creative*.

In places where a monologue would be implausible, I have re-
sorted to mime, and here I leave the actor even greater freedom to
be creative—and to win independent acclaim. But in order not to
try the audience beyond its limits, I have let music—coming from
the midsummer dance, and thus believably motivated—exercise
its illusion-evoking power during the sections of dumb show. I beg
the music director to consider carefully his choice of pieces; the

wrong mood may be produced if there are familiar selections from popular dances or operettas, or unusual folk melodies, no matter how ethnographically correct.

The ballet I have indicated cannot be replaced by a so-called "crowd scene" because crowd scenes are always badly acted, with a mob of grimacing idiots trying to use the occasion to appear clever and so disturb the illusion. And since uneducated people do not improvise when they wish to poke fun maliciously but use ready-made material that can take on a double meaning, I did not compose the taunting song they sing. Instead, I used a little-known dance song* I discovered myself in the Stockholm area. The words are only approximately appropriate, but this is intentional, for the slyness (weakness) of the slave does not permit him to make a direct attack. And so the seriousness of the action forbids clowning; there must be no coarse sneering in a situation which closes the lid on a family coffin.

As for the scenery, I have borrowed from impressionist painting the device of making a setting appear cut off and asymmetrical, thus strengthening the illusion. When we see only part of a room and a portion of the furniture, we are left to conjecture, that is to say, our imagination goes to work and complements what is seen. I have also profited by doing away with those tiresome exits through doors because scenery doors, made of canvas, wobble at the slightest touch; they cannot even allow a father to express his anger after a bad dinner by going out and slamming the door behind him "so that the whole house shakes." (In the theatre it wobbles.) I have also confined the action to one setting, both to allow the characters more time to interact with their environment and to break with the tradition of expensive scenery. With only one setting we should be able to demand that it be realistic, but nothing is more difficult than to get a room on stage to look like a room, however easily the scene painter can produce flaming volcanoes and waterfalls. Even if the walls must be of canvas, it is surely time to stop painting shelves and kitchen utensils on them. We have so many other stage conventions in which we are asked to

*The version of the song as it appears in this translation of the play is a free interpretation of the playwright's intention rather than a literal rendering of the actual song he chose (translator).

believe, we should not have to strain ourselves trying to believe in
painted pots and pans.

16   I have placed the upstage wall and the table diagonally so that
the actors can play facing the audience or in half-profile when
they sit opposite each other at the table. I saw a diagonal backdrop
in a production of *Aïda*; it led the eye out into unknown vistas and
did not look simply like a defiant reaction to the boredom of
straight lines.

17   Another perhaps necessary innovation is the removal of footlights. The purpose of this lighting from below is said to be to
make the actors' faces fatter, but I ask: why must all actors have
fat faces? Does not this lighting obliterate many subtleties in the
lower part of the face, especially the jaws, distort the shape of the
nose, and cast shadows up over the eyes? Even if this were not so,
one thing is certain: actors find it so painful for their eyes that
they are unable to use them with full expressiveness. Footlights
strike the retina in places usually protected (except in the case of
seamen, who have to look at the sun's reflection in the water), and
so we seldom see anything but a crude rolling of the eyes, either to
the side or up toward the balconies, exposing the whites. Perhaps
this also accounts for the tedious habit, especially common among
actresses, of blinking eyelashes. And when anyone on stage wants
to speak with his eyes, he must resort to staring straight out, thus
breaking the wall of the curtain line and coming into direct contact with the audience. Justly or unjustly, this unfortunate practice
is called "greeting your friends."

19   Would not sufficiently strong side lighting (using parabolic re-
flectors, for example) provide the actor with a new advantage: the
strengthening of mime effects through the most expressive asset
in his face—the play of his eyes?

I have no illusions about getting the actor to play for the audience rather than with it, although this would be desirable. I cannot
hope to see an actor play with his back to the audience throughout
an entire important scene, though I wish very much that crucial
scenes were staged, not next to the prompter's box, like duets intended to evoke applause, but in places more appropriate to the
action. In other words, I call for no revolution, just small modifica-
tions, for to really transform the stage into a room where the

fourth wall is removed, and consequently a portion of the furniture faces away from the audience, would probably, for the present, produce a disturbing effect.

When it comes to makeup, I dare not hope to be listened to by the ladies, who would rather be beautiful than believable. But the actor might consider whether it is really to his advantage when putting on makeup to fix an abstract character, like a mask, on his face. Picture an actor who has put the sharp, charcoal lines of anger of an old man between his eyes and then, with that incensed look, has to smile in response to someone else's line. What a terrible grimace there would be as a result! And how would the false forehead attached to his wig, bald as a billiard ball, wrinkle when the old man got angry?

In a modern psychological drama, where the subtlest movements of the soul must be revealed more through the face than through gesture and sound, it would probably be best to experiment with strong side lighting on a small stage, and with actors wearing no makeup, or at least a minimum of it.

If, in addition, we could avoid having the orchestra visible, its lights disturbing, and the musicians' faces turned toward the audience; if the seating in the auditorium were raised so that eye level for the spectator was higher than the hollow of the actor's knee; if we could get rid of stage boxes (behind bull's-eye openings), with their grinning late arrivals from dinners and supper parties; if we could have complete darkness during performances; and, finally, and most importantly, a *small* stage and a *small* auditorium, then perhaps we might see a new drama arise, or at the very least a theatre that was once again a place of entertainment for educated people. While waiting for this theatre, we will just have to go on writing, preparing the repertoire that will one day be needed.

Here is an attempt! If it fails, there is surely time enough for another!

Characters

MISS JULIE, *25 years old*
JEAN, *her father's valet, 30 years old*
KRISTINE, *her father's cook, 35 years old*

(*The action takes place in the count's kitchen on midsummer eve.*)

Setting

(*A large kitchen, the ceiling and side walls of which are hidden by draperies. The rear wall runs diagonally from down left to up right. On the wall down left are two shelves with copper, iron, and pewter utensils; the shelves are lined with scalloped paper. Visible to the right is most of a set of large, arched glass doors, through which can be seen a fountain with a statue of Cupid, lilac bushes in bloom, and the tops of some Lombardy poplars. At down left is the corner of a large tiled stove; a portion of its hood is showing. At right, one end of the servants' white pine dining table juts out; several chairs stand around it. The stove is decorated with birch branches; juniper twigs are strewn on the floor. On the end of the table stands a large Japanese spice jar, filled with lilac blossoms. An ice-box, a sink, and a washstand. Above the door is an old-fashioned bell on a spring; to the left of the door, the mouthpiece of a speaking tube is visible.*

(KRISTINE *is frying something on the stove. She is wearing a light-colored cotton dress and an apron.* JEAN *enters. He is wearing livery and carries a pair of high riding-boots with spurs, which he puts down on the floor where they can be seen by the audience.*)

JEAN: Miss Julie's crazy again tonight; absolutely crazy!

KRISTINE: So you finally came back?

JEAN: I took the Count to the station and when I returned past the barn I stopped in for a dance. Who do I see but Miss Julie leading off the dance with the gamekeeper! But as soon as she saw me she rushed over to ask me for the next waltz. And she's been waltzing ever since—I've never seen anything like it. She's crazy!

KRISTINE: She always has been, but never as bad as the last two weeks since her engagement was broken off.

JEAN: Yes, I wonder what the real story was there. He was a gentleman, even if he wasn't rich. Ah! These people have such romantic ideas. (*sits at the end of the table*) Still, it's strange, isn't it? I mean that she'd rather stay home with the servants on midsummer eve instead of going with her father to visit relatives?

KRISTINE: She's probably embarrassed after that row with her fiancé.

JEAN: Probably! He gave a good account of himself, though. Do you know how it happened, Kristine? I saw it, you know, though I didn't let on I had.

KRISTINE: No! You saw it?

JEAN: Yes, I did. ——— That evening they were out near the stable, and she was "training" him—as she called it. Do you know what she did? She made him jump over her riding crop, the way you'd teach a dog to jump. He jumped twice and she hit him each time. But the third time he grabbed the crop out of her hand, hit her with it across the cheek, and broke it in pieces. Then he left.

KRISTINE: So, that's what happened! I can't believe it!

JEAN: Yes, that's the way it went! ——— What have you got for me that's tasty, Kristine?

KRISTINE (*serving him from the pan*): Oh, it's only a piece of kidney I cut from the veal roast.

JEAN (*smelling the food*): Beautiful! That's my favorite *délice*. (*feeling the plate*) But you could have warmed the plate!

KRISTINE: You're fussier than the Count himself, once you start! (*She pulls his hair affectionately.*)

JEAN (*angry*): Stop it, leave my hair alone! You know I'm touchy about that.

KRISTINE: Now, now, it's only love, you know that. (JEAN *eats.* KRISTINE *opens a bottle of beer.*)

JEAN: Beer? On midsummer eve? No thank you! I can do better than that. (*opens a drawer in the table and takes out a bottle of red wine with yellow sealing wax*) See that? Yellow seal! Give me a glass! A wine glass! I'm drinking this *pur.*

KRISTINE (*returns to the stove and puts on a small saucepan*): God help the woman who gets you for a husband! What a fuss-budget.

JEAN: Nonsense! You'd be damned lucky to get a man like me. It certainly hasn't done you any harm to have people call me your sweetheart. (*tastes the wine*) Good! Very good! Just needs a little warming. (*warms the glass between his hands*) We bought this in Dijon. Four francs a liter, not counting the cost of the bottle, or the customs duty. ———— What are you cooking now? It stinks like hell!

KRISTINE: Oh, some slop Miss Julie wants to give Diana.

JEAN: Watch your language, Kristine. But why should you have to cook for that damn mutt on midsummer eve? Is she sick?

KRISTINE: Yes, she's sick! She sneaked out with the gatekeeper's dog—and now there's hell to pay. Miss Julie won't have it!

JEAN: Miss Julie has too much pride about some things and not enough about others, just like her mother was. The Countess was most at home in the kitchen and the cowsheds, but a *one*-horse carriage wasn't elegant enough for her. The cuffs of her blouse were dirty, but she had to have her coat of arms on her cufflinks. ———— And Miss Julie won't take proper care of herself either. If you ask me, she just isn't refined. Just now, when she was dancing in the barn, she pulled the gamekeeper away from Anna and made him dance with her. *We* wouldn't behave like that, but that's what happens when aristocrats pretend they're common people—they get *common!* ———— But she is quite a woman! Magnificent! What shoulders, and what—et cetera!

KRISTINE: Oh, don't overdo it! I've heard what Clara says, and she dresses her.

JEAN: Ha, Clara! You're all jealous of each other! I've been out riding with her ... And the way she dances!

KRISTINE: Listen, Jean! You've going to dance with me, when I'm finished here, aren't you?

JEAN: Of course I will.

KRISTINE: Promise?

JEAN: Promise? When I say I'll do something, I do it! By the way, the kidney was very good. (*corks the bottle*)

JULIE (*in the doorway to someone outside*): I'll be right back! You go ahead for now! (JEAN *sneaks the bottle back into the table drawer and gets up respectfully.* MISS JULIE *enters and crosses to* KRISTINE *by the stove.*) Well? Is it ready? (KRISTINE *indicates that* JEAN *is present.*)

JEAN (*gallantly*): Are you ladies up to something secret?

JULIE (*flicking her handerkchief in his face*): None of your business!

JEAN: Hmm! I like the smell of violets!

JULIE (*coquettishly*): Shame on you! So you know about perfumes, too? You certainly know how to dance. Ah, ah! No peeking! Go away.

JEAN (*boldly but respectfully*): Are you brewing up a magic potion for midsummer eve? Something to prophecy by under a lucky star, so you'll catch a glimpse of your future husband!

JULIE (*caustically*): You'd need sharp eyes to see him! (to KRISTINE) Pour out half a bottle and cork it well. ———— Come and dance a schottische with me, Jean . . .

JEAN (*hesitating*): I don't want to be impolite to anyone, and I've already promised this dance to Kristine . . .

JULIE: Oh, she can have another one—can't you Kristine? Won't you lend me Jean?

KRISTINE: It's not up to me, ma'am. (*to* JEAN) If the mistress is so generous, it wouldn't do for you to say no. Go on, Jean, and thank her for the honor.

JEAN: To be honest, and no offense intended, I wonder whether it's wise for you to dance twice running with the same partner, especially since these people are quick to jump to conclusions . . .

JULIE (*flaring up*): What's that? What sort of conclusions? What do you mean?

JEAN (*submissively*): If you don't understand, ma'am, I must speak more plainly. It doesn't look good to play favorites with your servants. . . .

JULIE: Play favorites! What an idea! I'm astonished! As mistress of the house, I honor your dance with my presence. And when I dance, I want to dance with someone who can lead, so I won't look ridiculous.

JEAN: As you order, ma'am! I'm at your service!

JULIE (*gently*): Don't take it as an order! On a night like this we're all just ordinary people having fun, so we'll forget about rank. Now, take my arm! ——— Don't worry, Kristine! I won't steal your sweetheart! (JEAN *offers his arm and leads* MISS JULIE *out.*)

Mime

(The following should be played as if the actress playing KRISTINE *were really alone. When she has to, she turns her back to the audience. She does not look toward them, nor does she hurry as if she were afraid they would grow impatient. Schottische music played on a fiddle sounds in the distance.* KRISTINE *hums along with the music. She clears the table, washes the dishes, dries them, and puts them away. She takes off her apron. From a table drawer she removes a small mirror and leans it against the bowl of lilacs on the table. She lights a candle, heats a hairpin over the flame, and uses it to set a curl on her forehead. She crosses to the door and listens, then returns to the table. She finds the handkerchief* MISS JULIE *left behind, picks it up, and smells it. Then, preoccupied, she spreads it out, stretches it, smoothes out the wrinkles, and folds it into quarters, and so forth.)*

JEAN (*enters alone*): God, she really *is* crazy! What a way to dance! Everybody's laughing at her behind her back. What do you make of it, Kristine?

KRISTINE: Ah! It's that time of the month for her, and she always gets peculiar like that. Are you going to dance with me now?

JEAN: You're not mad at me, are you, for leaving . . . ?

KRISTINE: Of course not! ——— Why should I be, for a little thing like that? Besides, I know my place . . .

JEAN (*puts his arm around her waist*): You're a sensible girl, Kristine, and you'd make a good wife . . .

JULIE (*entering; uncomfortably surprised; with forced good humor*): What a charming escort—running away from his partner.

JEAN: On the contrary, Miss Julie. Don't you see how I rushed back to the partner I abandoned!

JULIE (*changing her tone*): You know, you're a superb dancer! ——— But why are you wearing livery on a holiday? Take it off at once!

JEAN: Then I must ask you to go outside for a moment. You see, my black coat is hanging over here...(*gestures and crosses right*)

JULIE: Are you embarrassed about changing your coat in front of me? Well, go in your room then. Either that or stay and I'll turn my back.

JEAN: With your permission, ma'am! (*He crosses right. His arm is visible as he changes his jacket.*)

JULIE (*to* KRISTINE): Tell me, Kristine—you two are so close—. Is Jean your fiancé?

KRISTINE: Fiancé? Yes, if you wish. We can call him that.

JULIE: What do you mean?

KRISTINE: You had a fiancé yourself, didn't you? So...

JULIE: Well, we were properly engaged...

KRISTINE: But nothing came of it, did it? (JEAN *returns dressed in a frock coat and bowler hat.*)

JULIE: *Très gentil, monsieur Jean! Très gentil!*

JEAN: *Vous voulez plaisanter, madame!*

JULIE: *Et vous voulez parler français!* Where did you learn that?

JEAN: In Switzerland, when I was wine steward in one of the biggest hotels in Lucerne!

JULIE: You look like a real gentleman in that coat! *Charmant!* (*sits at the table*)

JEAN: Oh, you're flattering me!

JULIE (*offended*): Flattering you?

JEAN: My natural modesty forbids me to believe that you would really compliment someone like me, and so I took the liberty of assuming that you were exaggerating, which polite people call flattering.

JULIE: Where did you learn to talk like that? You must have been to the theatre often.

JEAN: Of course. And I've done a lot of traveling.

JULIE: But you come from here, don't you?

JEAN: My father was a farm hand on the district attorney's estate nearby. I used to see you when you were little, but you never noticed me.

JULIE: No! Really?   No, indeed.

JEAN: Sure. I remember one time especially...but I can't talk about that.

JULIE: Oh, come now! Why not? Just this once!

JEAN: No, I really couldn't, not now. Some other time, perhaps.

JULIE: Why some other time? What's so dangerous about now?

JEAN: It's not dangerous, but there are obstacles. ———— Her, for example. (*indicating* KRISTINE, *who has fallen asleep in a chair by the stove*)

JULIE: What a pleasant wife she'll make! She probably snores, too.

JEAN: No, she doesn't, but she talks in her sleep.

JULIE (*cynically*): How do *you* know?

JEAN (*audaciously*): I've heard her! (*pause, during which they stare at each other*)

JULIE: Why don't you sit down?

JEAN: I couldn't do that in your presence.

JULIE: But if I order you to?

JEAN: Then I'd obey.

JULIE: Sit down, then. ———— No, wait. Can you get me something to drink first?

JEAN: I don't know what we have in the ice box. I think there's only beer.

JULIE: Why do you say "only"? My tastes are so simple I prefer beer to wine. (JEAN *takes a bottle of beer from the ice box and opens it. He looks for a glass and a plate in the cupboard and serves her.*)

JEAN: Here you are, ma'am.

JULIE: Thank you. Won't you have something yourself?

JEAN: I'm not partial to beer, but if it's an order ...

JULIE: An order? ———— Surely a gentleman can keep his lady company.

JEAN: You're right, of course. (*opens a bottle and gets a glass*)

JULIE: Now, drink to my health! (*He hesitates.*) What? A man of the world—and shy?

JEAN (*In mock romantic fashion, he kneels and raises his glass.*): Skål to my mistress!

JULIE: Bravo! ———— Now kiss my shoe, to finish it properly. (JEAN *hesitates, then boldly seizes her foot and kisses it lightly.*) Perfect! You should have been an actor.

JEAN (*rising*): That's enough now, Miss Julie! Someone might come in and see us.

JULIE: What of it?

JEAN: People talk, that's what! If you knew how their tongues were wagging just now at the dance, you'd . . .

JULIE: What were they saying? Tell me! ——— Sit down!

JEAN (*sits*): I don't want hurt you, but they were sayings things ——— suggestive things, that, that . . . well, you can figure it out for yourself! You're not a child. If a woman is seen drinking alone with a man—let alone a servant—at night—then . . .

JULIE: Then what? Besides, we're not alone. Kristine is here.

JEAN: Asleep!

JULIE: Then I'll wake her up. (*rising*) Kristine! Are you asleep? (KRISTINE *mumbles in her sleep.*)

JULIE: Kristine! ——— She certainly can sleep!

KRISTINE (*in her sleep*): The Count's boots are brushed—put the coffee on—right away, right away—uh, huh—oh!

JULIE (*grabbing* KRISTINE'S *nose*): Will you wake up!

JEAN (*severely*): Leave her alone—let her sleep!

JULIE (*sharply*): What?

JEAN: Someone who's been standing over a stove all day has a right to be tired by now. Sleep should be respected . . .

JULIE (*changing her tone*): What a considerate thought—it does you credit—thank you! (*offering her hand*) Come outside and pick some lilacs for me! (*During the following*, KRISTINE *awakens and shambles sleepily off right to bed.*)

JEAN: Go with you?

JULIE: With me!

JEAN: We couldn't do that! Absolutely not!

JULIE: I don't understand. Surely you don't imagine . . .

JEAN: No, I don't, but the others might.

JULIE: What? That I've fallen in love with a servant?

JEAN: I'm not a conceited man, but such things happen—and for these people, nothing is sacred.

JULIE: I do believe you're an aristocrat!

JEAN: Yes, I am.

JULIE: And I'm stepping down . . .

JEAN: Don't step down, Miss Julie, take my advice. No one'll believe you stepped down voluntarily. People will always say you fell.

JULIE: I have a higher opinion of people than you. Come and see! —— Come! (*She stares at him broodingly.*)

JEAN: You're very strange, do you know that?

JULIE: Perhaps! But so are you! —— For that matter, everything is strange. Life, people, everything. Like floating scum, drifting on and on across the water, until it sinks down and down! That reminds me of a dream I have now and then. I've climbed up on top of a pillar. I sit there and see no way of getting down. I get dizzy when I look down, and I must get down, but I don't have the courage to jump. I can't hold on firmly, and I long to be able to fall, but I don't fall. And yet I'll have no peace until I get down, no rest unless I get down, down on the ground! And if I did get down to the ground, I'd want to be under the earth ... Have you ever felt anything like that?

JEAN: No. I dream that I'm lying under a high tree in a dark forest. I want to get up, up on top, and look out over the bright landscape, where the sun is shining, and plunder the bird's nest up there, where the golden eggs lie. And I climb and climb, but the trunk's so thick and smooth, and it's so far to the first branch. But I know if I just reached that first branch, I'd go right to the top, like up a ladder. I haven't reached it yet, but I will, even if it's only in a dream!

JULIE: Here I am chattering with you about dreams. Come, let's go out! Just into the park! (*She offers him her arm, and they start to leave.*)

JEAN: We'll have to sleep on nine midsummer flowers, Miss Julie, to make our dreams come true! (*They turn at the door.* JEAN *puts his hand to his eye.*)

JULIE: Did you get something in your eye?

JEAN: It's nothing—just a speck—it'll be gone in a minute.

JULIE: My sleeve must have brushed against you. Sit down and let me help you. (*She takes him by the arm and seats him. She tilts his head back and with the tip of a handkerchief tries to remove the speck.*) Sit still, absolutely still! (*She slaps his hand.*) Didn't you hear me? —— Why, you're trembling; the big, strong man is trembling! (*feels his biceps*) What muscles you have!

JEAN (*warning*): Miss Julie!

JULIE: Yes, *monsieur* Jean.

JEAN: *Attention! Je ne suis qu'un homme!*

JULIE: Will you sit still! ——— There! Now it's gone! Kiss my hand and thank me.

JEAN (*rising*): Miss Julie, listen to me! ——— Kristine has gone to bed! ——— Will you listen to me!

JULIE: Kiss my hand first!

JEAN: Listen to me!

JULIE: Kiss my hand first!

JEAN: All right, but you've only yourself to blame!

JULIE: For what?

JEAN: For what? Are you still a child at twenty-five? Don't you know that's it's dangerous to play with fire?

JULIE: Not for me. I'm insured.

JEAN (*boldly*): No, you're not! But even if you were, there's combustible material close by.

JULIE: Meaning you?

JEAN: Yes! Not because it's me, but because I'm young ———

JULIE: And handsome—what incredible conceit! A Don Juan perhaps! Or a Joseph! Yes, that's it, I do believe you're a Joseph!

JEAN: Do you?

JULIE: I'm almost afraid so. (JEAN *boldly tries to put his arm around her waist and kiss her. She slaps his face.*) How dare you?

JEAN: Are you serious or joking?

JULIE: Serious.

JEAN: Then so was what just happened. You play games too seriously, and that's dangerous. Well, I'm tired of games. You'll excuse me if I get back to work. I haven't done the Count's boots yet and it's long past midnight.

JULIE: Put the boots down!

JEAN: No! It's the work I have to do. I never agreed to be your playmate, and never will. It's beneath me.

JULIE: You're proud.

JEAN: In certain ways, but not in others.

JULIE: Have you ever been in love?

JEAN: We don't use that word, but I've been fond of many girls, and once I was sick because I couldn't have the one I wanted. That's right, sick, like those princes in the Arabian Nights— who couldn't eat or drink because of love.

JULIE: Who was she? (JEAN *is silent.*) Who was she?

JEAN: You can't force me to tell you that.

JULIE: But if I ask you as an equal, as a—friend! Who was she?

JEAN: You!

JULIE (*sits*): How amusing . . .

JEAN: Yes, if you like! It was ridiculous! ——— You see, that was the story I didn't want to tell you earlier. Maybe I will now. Do you know how the world looks from down below? ——— Of course you don't. Neither do hawks and falcons, whose backs we can't see because they're usually soaring up there above us. I grew up in a shack with seven brothers and sisters and a pig, in the middle of a wasteland, where there wasn't a single tree. But from our window I could see the tops of apple trees above the wall of your father's garden. That was the Garden of Eden, guarded by angry angels with flaming swords. All the same, the other boys and I managed to find our way to the Tree of Life. ——— Now you think I'm contemptible, I suppose.

JULIE: Oh, all boys steal apples.

JEAN: You say that, but you think I'm contemptible anyway. Oh well! One day I went into the Garden of Eden with my mother, to weed the onion beds. Near the vegetable garden was a small Turkish pavilion in the shadow of jasmine bushes and overgrown with honeysuckle. I had no idea what it was used for, but I'd never seen such a beautiful building. People went in and came out again, and one day the door was left open. I sneaked close and saw walls covered with pictures of kings and emperors, and red curtains with fringes at the windows—now you know the place I mean. I ——— (*breaks off a sprig of lilac and holds it in front of* MISS JULIE's *nose*) ——— I'd never been inside the manor house, never seen anything except the church—but this was more beautiful. From then on, no matter where my thoughts wandered, they returned—there. And gradually I got a longing to experience, just once, the full pleasure of—*enfin,* I sneaked in, saw, and marveled! But then I heard someone coming! There was only one exit for ladies and gentlemen, but for me there was another, and I had no choice but to take it! (MISS JULIE, *who has taken the lilac sprig, lets it fall on the table.*) Afterwards, I started running. I crashed through a raspberry bush, flew over a strawberry patch, and came up onto the rose terrace. There I caught sight of a pink dress and a pair of white stockings—it was you. I crawled under a pile of weeds, and I mean under—under thistles that pricked me and wet dirt that stank. And I looked at you as you walked among the roses, and I thought: if it's true that a thief can enter heaven and be with the angels, then why can't a farmhand's son here on God's earth enter the manor house garden and play with the Count's daughter?

JULIE (*romantically*): Do you think all poor children would have thought the way you did?

JEAN (*at first hesitant, then with conviction*): If *all* poor—yes—of course. Of course!

JULIE: It must be terrible to be poor!

JEAN (*with exaggerated suffering*): Oh, Miss Julie! Oh! —————— A dog can lie on the Countess's sofa, a horse can have his nose patted by a young lady's hand, but a servant ————— (*changing his tone*) ————— oh, I know—now and then you find one with enough stuff in him to get ahead in the world, but how often? ————— Anyhow, do you know what I did then? ————— I jumped in the millstream with my clothes on, was pulled out, and got a beating. But the following Sunday, when my father and all the others went to my grandmother's, I arranged to stay home. I scrubbed myself with soap and water, put on my best clothes, and went to church so that I could see you! I saw you and returned home, determined to die. But I wanted to die beautifully and pleasantly, without pain. And then I remembered that it was dangerous to sleep under an elder bush. We had a big one, and it was in full flower. I plundered its treasures and bedded down under them in the oat bin. Have you ever noticed how smooth oats are?—and soft to the touch, like human skin . . . ! Well, I shut the lid and closed my eyes. I fell asleep and woke up feeling very sick. But I didn't die, as you can see. What was I after? ————— I don't know. There was no hope of winning you, of course. ————— You were a symbol of the hopelessness of ever rising out of the class in which I was born.

JULIE: You're a charming storyteller. Did you ever go to school?

JEAN: A bit, but I've read lots of novels and been to the theatre often. And then I've listened to people like you talk—that's where I learned most.

JULIE: Do you listen to what we say?

JEAN: Naturally! And I've heard plenty, too, driving the carriage or rowing the boat. Once I heard you and a friend . . .

JULIE: Oh? ——— What did you hear?

JEAN: I'd better not say. But I was surprised a little. I couldn't imagine where you learned such words. Maybe at bottom there isn't such a great difference between people as we think.

JULIE: Shame on you! We don't act like you when we're engaged.

JEAN (*staring at her*): Is that true? ——— You don't have to play innocent with me, Miss . . .

JULIE: The man I gave my love to was a swine.

JEAN: That's what you all say—afterwards.

JULIE: All?

JEAN: I think so. I know I've heard that phrase before, on similar occasions.

JULIE: What occasions?

JEAN: Like the one I'm talking about. The last time . . .

JULIE (*rising*): Quiet! I don't want to hear any more!

JEAN: That's interesting—that's what *she* said, too. Well, if you'll excuse me, I'm going to bed.

JULIE (*gently*): To bed? On midsummer eve?

JEAN: Yes! Dancing with the rabble out there doesn't amuse me much.

JULIE: Get the key to the boat and row me out on the lake. I want to see the sun come up.

JEAN: Is that wise?

JULIE: Are you worried about your reputation?

JEAN: Why not? Why should I risk looking ridiculous and getting fired without a reference, just when I'm trying to establish myself. Besides, I think I owe something to Kristine.

JULIE: So, now it's Kristine . . .

JEAN: Yes, but you, too. ——— Take my advice, go up and go to bed!

JULIE: Am I to obey you?

JEAN: Just this once—for your own good! Please! It's very late. Drowsiness makes people giddy and liable to lose their heads! Go to bed! Besides—unless I'm mistaken—I hear the others coming to look for me. And if they find us together, you'll be lost!

(*The* CHORUS *approaches, singing:*)

   The swineherd found his true love

a pretty girl so fair,
The swineherd found his true love
but let the girl beware.

For then he saw the princess
the princess on the golden hill,
but then saw the princess,
so much fairer still.

So the swineherd and the princess
they danced the whole night through,
and he forgot his first love,
to her he was untrue.

And when the long night ended,
and in the light of day, of day,
the dancing too was ended,
and the princess could not stay.

Then the swineherd lost his true love,
and the princess grieves him still,
and never more she'll wander
from atop the golden hill.

JULIE: I know all these people and I love them, just as they love
me. Let them come in and you'll see.

JEAN: No, Miss Julie, they don't love you. They take your food,
but they spit on it! Believe me! Listen to them, listen to what
they're singing! ——— No, don't listen to them!

JULIE (*listening*): What are they singing?

JEAN: It's a dirty song! About you and me!

JULIE: Disgusting! Oh! How deceitful! ———

JEAN: The rabble is always cowardly! And in a battle like this, you
don't fight; you can only run away!

JULIE: Run away? But where? We can't go out—or into Kristine's
room.

JEAN: True. But there's my room. Necessity knows no rules. Besides, you can trust me. I'm your friend and I respect you.

JULIE: But suppose—suppose they look for you in there?

JEAN: I'll bolt the door, and if anyone tries to break in, I'll shoot!
——— Come! (*on his knees*) Come!

JULIE (*urgently*): Promise me . . .?

JEAN: I swear! (MISS JULIE *runs off right.* JEAN *hastens after her.*)

Ballet

(*Led by a fiddler, the servants and farm people enter, dressed festively, with flowers in their hats. On the table they place a small barrel of beer and a keg of schnapps, both garlanded. Glasses are brought out, and the drinking starts. A dance circle is formed and "The Swineherd and the Princess" is sung. When the dance is finished, everyone leaves, singing.*)

(MISS JULIE *enters alone. She notices the mess in the kitchen, wrings her hands, then takes out her powder puff and powders her nose.*)

JEAN (*enters, agitated*): There, you see? And you heard them. We can't possibly stay here now, you know that.

JULIE: Yes, I know. But what can we do?

JEAN: Leave, travel, far away from here.

JULIE: Travel? Yes, but where?

JEAN: To Switzerland, to the Italian lakes. Have you ever been there?

JULIE: No. Is it beautiful?

JEAN: Oh, an eternal summer—oranges growing everywhere, laurel trees, always green . . .

JULIE: But what'll we do there?

JEAN: I'll open a hotel—with first-class service for first-class people.

JULIE: Hotel?

JEAN: That's the life, you know. Always new faces, new languages. No time to worry or be nervous. No hunting for something to do—there's always work to be done: bells ringing night and day, train whistles blowing, carriages coming and going, and all the while gold rolling into the till! That's the life!

JULIE: Yes, it sounds wonderful. But what'll I do?

JEAN: You'll be mistress of the house: the jewel in our crown! With your looks . . . and your manner—oh—success is guaranteed! It'll be wonderful! You'll sit in your office like a queen and push an electric button to set your slaves in motion. The guests will file past your throne and timidly lay their treasures before you. —— You have no idea how people tremble when they

get their bill. ——— I'll salt the bills and you'll sweeten them
with your prettiest smile. ——— Let's get away from here
——— (*takes a timetable out of his pocket*) ——— Right away,
on the next train! ——— We'll be in Malmö six-thirty tomorrow morning, Hamburg at eight-forty; from Frankfort to Basel
will take a day, then on to Como by way of the St. Gotthard
Tunnel, in, let's see, three days. Three days!

JULIE: That's all very well! But Jean—you must give me courage!
——— Tell me you love me! Put your arms around me!

JEAN (*hesitating*): I want to—but I don't dare. Not in this house,
not again. I love you—never doubt that—you don't doubt it, do
you, Miss Julie?

JULIE (*shy; very feminine*): "Miss!" ——— Call me Julie! There
are no barriers between us any more. Call me Julie!

JEAN (*tormented*): I can't! There'll always be barriers between us
as long as we stay in this house. ——— There's the past and
there's the Count. I've never met anyone I had such respect for.
——— When I see his gloves lying on a chair, I feel small.
——— When I hear that bell up there ring, I jump like a skit-
tish horse. ——— And when I look at his boots standing there
so stiff and proud, I feel like bowing! (*kicking the boots*) Super-
stitions and prejudices we learned as children—but they can
easily be forgotten. If I can just get to another country, a repub-
lic, people will bow and scrape when they see my livery—*they'll*
bow and scrape, you hear, not me! I wasn't born to cringe. I've
got stuff in me, I've got character, and if I can only grab onto
that first branch, you watch me climb! I'm a servant today, but
next year I'll own my own hotel. In ten years I'll have enough to
retire. Then I'll go to Rumania and be decorated. I could—mind
you I said *could*—end up a count!

JULIE: Wonderful, wonderful!

JEAN: Ah, in Rumania you just buy your title, and so you'll be a
countess after all. My countess!

JULIE: But I don't care about that—that's what I'm putting behind
me! Show me you love me, otherwise—otherwise, what am I?

JEAN: I'll show you a thousand times—afterwards! Not here! And
whatever you do, no emotional outbursts, or we'll both be lost!
We must think this through coolly, like sensible people. (*He*

takes out a cigar, snips the end, and lights it.) You sit there, and I'll sit here. We'll talk as if nothing happened.

JULIE (*desperately*): Oh, my God! Have you no feelings?

JEAN: Me? No one has more feelings than I do, but I know how to control them.

JULIE: A little while ago you could kiss my shoe—and now!

JEAN (*harshly*): Yes, but that was before. Now we have other things to think about.

JULIE: Don't speak harshly to me!

JEAN: I'm not—just sensibly! We've already done one foolish thing, let's not have any more. The Count could return any minute, and by then we've got to decide what to do with our lives. What do you think of my plans for the future? Do you approve?

JULIE: They sound reasonable enough. I have only one question: for such a big undertaking you need capital—do you have it?

JEAN (*chewing on the cigar*): Me? Certainly! I have my professional expertise, my wide experience, and my knowledge of languages. That's capital enough, I should think!

JULIE: But all that won't even buy a train ticket.

JEAN: That's true. That's why I'm looking for a partner to advance me the money.

JULIE: Where will you find one quickly enough?

JEAN: That's up to you, if you want to come with me.

JULIE: But I can't; I have no money of my own. (*pause*)

JEAN: Then it's all off . . .

JULIE: And . . .

JEAN: Things stay as they are.

JULIE: Do you think I'm going to stay in this house as your lover? With all the servants pointing their fingers at me? Do you imagine I can face my father after this? No! Take me away from here, away from shame and dishonor ——— Oh, what have I done! My God, my God! (*She cries.*)

JEAN: Now, don't start that old song! ——— What have you done? The same as many others before you.

JULIE (*screaming convulsively*): And now you think I'm contemptible! ——— I'm falling, I'm falling!

JEAN: Fall down to my level and I'll lift you up again.

JULIE: What terrible power drew me to you? The attraction of the weak to the strong? The falling to the rising? Or was it love? Was this love? Do you know what love is?

JEAN: Me? What do you take me for? You don't think this was my first time, do you?

JULIE: The things you say, the thoughts you think!

JEAN: That's the way I was taught, and that's the way I am! Now don't get excited and don't play the grand lady, because we're in the same boat now! ———— Come on, Julie, I'll pour you a glass of something special! (*He opens a drawer in the table, takes out a wine bottle, and fills two glasses already used.*)

JULIE: Where did you get that wine?

JEAN: From the cellar.

JULIE: My father's burgundy!

JEAN: That'll do for his son-in-law, won't it?

JULIE: And I drink beer! Beer!

JEAN: That only shows I have better taste.

JULIE: Thief!

JEAN: Planning to tell?

JULIE: Oh, oh! Accomplice of a common thief! Was I drunk? Have I been walking in a dream the whole evening? Midsummer eve! A time of innocent fun!

JEAN: Innocent, eh?

JULIE (*pacing back and forth*): Is there anyone on earth more miserable than I am at this moment?

JEAN: Why should you be? After such a conquest? Think of Kristine in there. Don't you think she has feelings, too?

JULIE: I thought so awhile ago, but not any more. No, a servant is a servant . . .

JEAN: And a whore is a whore!

JULIE (*on her knees, her hands clasped*): Oh, God in Heaven, end my wretched life! Take me away from the filth I'm sinking into! Save me! Save me!

JEAN: I can't deny I feel sorry for you. When I lay in that onion bed and saw you in the rose garden, well . . . I'll be frank . . . I had the same dirty thoughts all boys have.

JULIE: And you wanted to die for me!

JEAN: In the oat bin? That was just talk.

JULIE: A lie, in other words!

JEAN (*beginning to feel sleepy*): More or less! I got the idea from a newspaper story about a chimney sweep who curled up in a firewood bin full of lilacs because he got a summons for not supporting his illegitimate child . . .

JULIE: So, that's what you're like . . .

JEAN: I had to think of something. And that's the kind of story women always go for.

JULIE: Swine!

JEAN: *Merde!*

JULIE: And now you've seen the hawk's back . . .

JEAN: Not exactly its *back* . . .

JULIE: And I was to be the first branch . . .

JEAN: But the branch was rotten . . .

JULIE: I was to be the sign on the hotel . . .

JEAN: And I the hotel . . .

JULIE: Sit at your desk, entice your customers, pad their bills . . .

JEAN: That I'd do myself . . .

JULIE: How can anyone be so thoroughly filthy?

JEAN: Better clean up then!

JULIE: You lackey, you menial, stand up, when I speak to you!

JEAN: Menial's strumpet, lackey's whore, shut up and get out of here! Who are you to lecture me on coarseness? None of my kind is ever as coarse as you were tonight. Do you think one of your maids would throw herself at a man the way you did? Have you ever seen any girl of my class offer herself like that? I've only seen it among animals and streetwalkers.

JULIE (*crushed*): You're right. Hit me, trample on me. I don't deserve any better. I'm worthless. But help me! If you see any way out of this, help me, Jean, please!

JEAN (*more gently*): I'd be lying if I didn't admit to a sense of triumph in all this, but do you think that a person like me would have dared even to look at someone like you if you hadn't invited it? I'm still amazed . . .

JULIE: And proud . . .

JEAN: Why not? Though I must say it was too easy to be really exciting.

JULIE: Go on, hit me, hit me harder!

JEAN (*rising*): No! Forgive me for what I've said! I don't hit a man when he's down, let alone a woman. I can't deny though, that I'm pleased to find out that what looked so dazzling to us from below was only tinsel, that the hawk's back was only gray, after all, that the lovely complexion was only powder, that those polished fingernails had black edges, and that a dirty handkerchief is still dirty, even if it smells of perfume . . .! On the other hand, it hurts me to find out that what I was striving for wasn't finer, more substantial. It hurts me to see you sunk so low that you're inferior to your own cook. It hurts like watching flowers beaten down by autumn rains and turned into mud.

JULIE: You talk as if you were already above me.

JEAN: I am. You see, I could make you a countess, but you could never make me a count.

JULIE: But I'm the child of a count—something you could never be!

JEAN: That's true. But I could be the father of counts—if . . .

JULIE: But you're a thief. I'm not.

JEAN: There are worse things than being a thief! Besides, when I'm working in a house, I consider myself sort of a member of the family, like one of the children. And you don't call it stealing when a child snatches a berry off a full bush. (*His passion is aroused again.*) Miss Julie, you're a glorious woman, much too good for someone like me! You were drinking and you lost your head. Now you want to cover up your mistake by telling yourself that you love me! You don't. Maybe there was a physical attraction—but then your love is no better than mine. ———— I could never be satisfied to be no more than an animal to you, and I could never arouse real love in you.

JULIE: Are you sure of that?

JEAN: You're suggesting it's possible ———— Oh, I could fall in love with you, no doubt about it. You're beautiful, you're refined ———— (*approaching and taking her hand*) ———— cultured, lovable when you want to be, and once you start a fire in a man, it never goes out. (*putting his arm around her waist*) You're like hot, spicy wine, and one kiss from you . . . (*He tries to lead her out, but she slowly frees herself.*)

JULIE: Let me go!? ———— You'll never win me like that.

JEAN: *How* then? ——— Not like that? Not with caresses and pretty speeches. Not with plans about the future or rescue from disgrace! *How* then?

JULIE: How? How? I don't know! ——— I have no idea!——— I detest you as I detest rats, but I can't escape from you.

JEAN: Escape with me!

JULIE (*pulling herself together*): Escape? Yes, we must escape! ——— But I'm so tired. Give me a glass of wine? (JEAN *pours the wine. She looks at her watch.*) But we must talk first. We still have a little time. (*She drains the glass, then holds it out for more.*)

JEAN: Don't drink so fast. It'll go to your head.

JULIE: What does it matter?

JEAN: What does it matter? It's vulgar to get drunk! What did you want to tell me?

JULIE: We must escape! But first we must talk, I mean I must talk. You've done all the talking up to now. You told about your life, now I want to tell about mine, so we'll know all about each other before we go off together.

JEAN: Just a minute! Forgive me! If you don't want to regret it afterwards, you'd better think twice before revealing any secrets about yourself.

JULIE: Aren't you my friend?

JEAN: Yes, sometimes! But don't rely on me.

JULIE: You're only saying that. ——— Besides, everyone already knows my secrets. ——— You see, my mother was a commoner—very humble background. She was brought up believing in social equality, women's rights, and all that. The idea of marriage repelled her. So, when my father proposed, she replied that she would never become his wife, but he could be her lover. He insisted that he didn't want the woman he loved to be less respected than he. But his passion ruled him, and when she explained that the world's respect meant nothing to her, he accepted her conditions.

But now his friends avoided him and his life was restricted to taking care of the estate, which couldn't satisfy him. I came into the world—against my mother's wishes, as far as I can understand. She wanted to bring me up as a child of nature, and, what's more, to learn everything a boy had to learn, so that I might be an example of how a woman can be as good as a man. I had to wear boy's clothes and learn to take care of horses, but I was never allowed in the cowshed. I had to groom and harness the horses and go hunting—and even had to watch them slaughter animals—that was disgusting! On the estate men were put on women's jobs and women on men's jobs—with the result that the property became run down and we became the laughing stock of the district. Finally, my father must have awakened from his trance because he rebelled and changed everything his way. My parents were then married quietly. Mother became ill—I don't know what illness it was—but she often had convulsions, hid in the attic and in the garden, and sometimes stayed out all night. Then came the great fire, which you've heard about. The house, the stables, and the cowshed all burned down, under very curious circumstances, suggesting arson, because the accident happened the day after the insurance had expired. The quarterly premium my father sent in was delayed because of a messenger's carelessness and didn't arrive in time. (*She fills her glass and drinks.*)

JEAN: Don't drink any more!

JULIE: Oh, what does it matter. ——— We were left penniless and had to sleep in the carriages. My father had no idea where to find money to rebuild the house because he had so slighted his old friends that they had forgotten him. Then my mother suggested that he borrow from a childhood friend of hers, a brick manufacturer who lived nearby. Father got the loan without having to pay interest, which surprised him. And that's how the estate was rebuilt. ——— (*drinks again*) Do you know who started the fire?

JEAN: The Countess, your mother.

JULIE: Do you know who the brick manufacturer was?

JEAN: Your mother's lover?

JULIE: Do you know whose money it was?

JEAN: Wait a moment—no, I don't.

JULIE: It was my mother's.

JEAN: You mean the Count's, unless they didn't sign an agreement when they were married.

JULIE: They didn't. ——— My mother had a small inheritance which she didn't want under my father's control, so she entrusted it to her—friend.

JEAN: Who stole it!

JULIE: Exactly! He kept it. ——— All this my father found out, but he couldn't bring it to court, couldn't repay his wife's lover, couldn't prove it was his wife's money! It was my mother's revenge for being forced into marriage against her will. It nearly drove him to suicide—there was a rumor that he tried with a pistol, but failed. So, he managed to live through it and my mother had to suffer for what she'd done. You can imagine that those were a terrible five years for me. I loved my father, but I sided with my mother because I didn't know the circumstances. I learned from her to hate men—you've heard how she hated the whole male sex—and I swore to her I'd never be a slave to any man.

JEAN: But you got engaged to that lawyer.

JULIE: In order to make him my slave.

JEAN: And he wasn't willing?

JULIE: He was willing, all right, but I wouldn't let him. I got tired of him.

JEAN: I saw it—out near the stable.

JULIE: What did you see?

JEAN: I saw—how he broke off the engagement.

JULIE: That's a lie! I was the one who broke it off. Has he said that he did? That swine . . .

JEAN: He was no swine, I'm sure. So, you hate men, Miss Julie?

JULIE: Yes! ——— Most of the time! But sometimes—when the weakness comes, when passion burns! Oh, God, will the fire never die out?

JEAN: Do you hate me, too?

JULIE: Immeasurably! I'd like to have you put to death, like an animal . . .

JEAN: I see—the penalty for bestiality—the woman get two years at hard labor and the animal is put to death. Right?

JULIE: Exactly!

JEAN: But there's no prosecutor here—and no animal. So, what'll we do?

JULIE: Go away!

JEAN: To torment each other to death?

JULIE: No! To be happy for—two days, a week, as long as we can be happy, and then—die...

JEAN: Die? That's stupid! It's better to open a hotel!

JULIE (*without listening*): ——— on the shore of Lake Como, where the sun always shines, where the laurels are green at Christmas and the oranges glow.

JEAN: Lake Como is a rainy hole, and I never saw any oranges outside the stores. But tourists are attracted there because there are plenty of villas to be rented out to lovers, and that's a profitable business. ——— Do you know why? Because they sign a lease for six months—and then leave after three weeks!

JULIE (*naively*): Why after three weeks?

JEAN: They quarrel, of course! But they still have to pay the rent in full! And so you rent the villas out again. And that's the way it goes, time after time. There's never a shortage of love—even if it doesn't last long!

JULIE: You don't want to die with me?

JEAN: I don't want to die at all! For one thing, I like living, and for another, I think suicide is a crime against the Providence which gave us life.

JULIE: You believe in God? *You?*

JEAN: Of course I do. And I go to church every other Sunday. ——— To be honest, I'm tired of all this, and I'm going to bed.

JULIE: Are you? And do you think I can let it go at that? A man owes something to the woman he's shamed.

JEAN (*taking out his purse and throwing a silver coin on the table*): Here! I don't like owing anything to anybody.

JULIE (*pretending not to notice the insult*): Do you know what the law states...

JEAN: Unfortunately the law doesn't state any punishment for the woman who seduces a man!

JULIE (*as before*): Do you see any way out but to leave, get married, and then separate?

JEAN: Suppose I refuse such a *mésalliance?*

JULIE: *Mésalliance*...

JEAN: Yes, for me! You see, I come from better stock than you. There's no arsonist in my family.

JULIE: How do you know?

JEAN: You can't prove otherwise. We don't keep charts on our ancestors—there's just the police records! But I've read about your family. Do you know who the founder was? He was a miller who let the king sleep with his wife one night during the Danish War. I don't have any noble ancestors like that. I don't have any noble ancestors at all, but I could become one myself.

JULIE: This is what I get for opening my heart to someone unworthy, for giving my family's honor . . .

JEAN: Dishonor!———— Well, I told you so: when people drink, they talk, and talk is dangerous!

JULIE: Oh, how I regret it! ———— How I regret it! ———— If you at least loved me.

JEAN: For the last time—what do you want? Shall I cry; shall I jump over your riding crop? Shall I kiss you and lure you off to Lake Como for three weeks, and then God knows what . . . ? What shall I do? What do you want? This is getting painfully embarrassing! But that's what happens when you stick your nose in women's business. Miss Julie! I see that you're unhappy. I know you're suffering, but I can't understand you. We don't have such romantic ideas; there's not this kind of hate between us. Love is a game we play when we get time off from work, but we don't have all day and night, like you. I think you're sick, really sick. Your mother was crazy, and her ideas have poisoned your life.

JULIE: Be kind to me. At least now you're talking like a human being.

JEAN: Be human yourself, then. You spit on me, and you won't let me wipe myself off ————

JULIE: Help me! Help Me! Just tell me what to do, where to go!

JEAN: In God's name, if I only knew myself!

JULIE: I've been crazy, out of my mind, but isn't there any way out?

JEAN: Stay here and keep calm! No one knows anything!

JULIE: Impossible! The others know and Kristine knows.

JEAN: No they don't, and they'd never believe a thing like that!

JULIE (*hesitantly*): But—it could happen again!

JEAN: That's true!

JULIE: And then?

JEAN (*frightened*): Then? ——— Why didn't I think about that? Yes, there is only one thing to do—get away from here! Right away! I can't come with you, then we'd be finished, so you'll have to go alone—away—anywhere!

JULIE: Alone? ——— Where? ——— I can't do that!

JEAN: You must! And before the Count gets back! If you stay, you know what'll happen. Once you make a mistake like this, you want to continue because the damage has already been done ... Then you get bolder and bolder—until finally you're caught! So leave! Later you can write to the Count and confess everything—except that it was me! He'll never guess who it was, and he's not going to be eager to find out, anyway.

JULIE: I'll go if you come with me.

JEAN: Are you out of your head? Miss Julie runs away with her servant! In two days it would be in the newspapers, and that's something your father would never live through.

JULIE: I can't go and I can't stay! Help me! I'm so tired, so terribly tired. ——— Order me! Set me in motion—I can't think or act on my own ...

JEAN: What miserable creatures you people are! You strut around with your noses in the air as if you were the lords of creation! All right, I'll order you. Go upstairs and get dressed! Get some money for the trip, and then come back down!

JULIE (*in a half-whisper*): Come up with me!

JEAN: To your room? ——— Now you're crazy again! (*hesitates for a moment*) No! Go, at once! (*takes her hand to lead her out*)

JULIE (*as she leaves*): Speak kindly to me, Jean!

JEAN: An order always sounds unkind—now you know how it feels. (JEAN, *alone, sighs with relief. He sits at the table, takes out a notebook and pencil, and begins adding up figures, counting aloud as he works. He continues in dumb show until* KRISTINE *enters, dressed for church. She is carrying a white tie and shirt front.*)

KRISTINE: Lord Jesus, what a mess! What have you been up to?

JEAN: Oh, Miss Julie dragged everybody in here. You mean you didn't hear anything? You must have been sleeping soundly.

KRISTINE: Like a log.

JEAN: And dressed for church already?

KRISTINE: Of course! You remember you promised to come with me to communion today!

JEAN: Oh, yes, that's right. ———— And you brought my things. Come on, then! (*He sits down.* KRISTINE *starts to put on his shirt front and tie. Pause.* JEAN *begins sleepily*) What's the gospel text for today?

KRISTINE: On St. John's Day?—the beheading of John the Baptist, I should think!

JEAN: Ah, that'll be a long one, for sure. ———— Hey, you're choking me! ———— Oh, I'm sleepy, so sleepy!

KRISTINE: Yes, what have you been doing, up all night? Your face is absolutely green.

JEAN: I've been sitting here gabbing with Miss Julie.

KRISTINE: She has no idea what's proper, that one! (*pause*)

JEAN: You know, Kristine...

KRISTINE: What?

JEAN: It's really strange when you think about it. ———— Her!

KRISTINE: What's so strange?

JEAN: Everything! (*pause*)

KRISTINE (*looking at the half-empty glasses standing on the table*): Have you been drinking together, too?

JEAN: Yes.

KRISTINE: Shame on you! ———— Look me in the eye!

JEAN: Well?

KRISTINE: Is it possible? Is it possible?

JEAN (*thinking it over for a moment*): Yes, it is.

KRISTINE: Ugh! I never would have believed it! No, shame on you, shame!

JEAN: You're not jealous of her, are you?

KRISTINE: No, not of her! If it had been Clara or Sofie I'd have scratched your eyes out! ———— I don't know why, but that's the way I feel. ———— Oh, it's disgusting!

JEAN: Are you angry at her, then?

KRISTINE: No, at you! That was an awful thing to do, awful! Poor girl! ———— No, I don't care who knows it—I won't stay in a house where we can't respect the people we work for.

JEAN: Why should we respect them?

KRISTINE: You're so clever, you tell me! Do you want to wait on people who can't behave decently? Do you? You disgrace your-self that way, if you ask me.

JEAN: But it's a comfort to know they aren't any better than us.

KRISTINE: Not for me. If they're no better, what do we have to strive for to better ourselves. ——— And think of the Count! Think of him! As if he hasn't had enough misery in his life! Lord Jesus! No, I won't stay in this house any longer! ——— And it had to be with someone like you! If it had been that lawyer, if it had been a real gentleman . . .

JEAN: What do you mean?

KRISTINE: Oh, you're all right for what you are, but there are men and gentlemen, after all! ——— No, this business with Miss Julie I can never forget. She was so proud, so arrogant with men, you wouldn't have believed she could just go and give herself—and to someone like you! And she was going to have poor Diana shot for running after the gatekeepers' mutt! ——— Yes, I'm giving my notice, I mean it—I won't stay here any longer. On the twenty-fourth of October, I leave!

JEAN: And then?

KRISTINE: Well, since the subject has come up, it's about time you looked around for something since we're going to get married, in any case.

JEAN: Where am I going to look? I couldn't find a job like this if I was married.

KRISTINE: No, that's true. But you can find work as a porter or as a caretaker in some government office. The state doesn't pay much, I know, but it's secure, and there's a pension for the wife and children . . .

JEAN (*grimacing*): That's all very well, but it's a bit early for me to think about dying for a wife and children. My ambitions are a little higher than that.

KRISTINE: Your ambitions, yes! Well, you have obligations, too! Think about them!

JEAN: Don't start nagging me about obligations, I know what I have to do! (*listening for something outside*) Besides, this is something we have plenty of time to think over. Go and get ready for church.

KRISTINE: Who's that walking around up there?

JEAN: I don't know, unless it's Clara.

KRISTINE (*going*): You don't suppose it's the Count, who came home without us hearing him?

JEAN (*frightened*): The Count? No, I don't think so. He'd have rung.

KRISTINE (*going*): Well, God help us! I've never seen anything like this before. (*The sun has risen and shines through the treetops in the park. The light shifts gradually until it slants in through the windows.* JEAN *goes to the door and signals.* MISS JULIE *enters, dressed in travel clothes and carrying a small birdcage, covered with a cloth, which she places on a chair.*)

JULIE: I'm ready now.

JEAN: Shh! Kristine is awake.

JULIE (*very nervous during the following*): Does she suspect something?

JEAN: She doesn't know anything. But my God, you look awful!

JULIE: Why? How do I look?

JEAN: You're pale as a ghost and—excuse me, but your face is dirty.

JULIE: Let me wash up then. ——— (*She goes to the basin and washes her hands and face.*) Give me a towel! ——— Oh—the sun's coming up.

JEAN: Then the goblins will disappear.

JULIE: Yes, there must have been goblins out last night! ——— Jean, listen, come with me! I have some money now.

JEAN (*hesitantly*): Enough?

JULIE: Enough to start with. Come with me! I just can't travel alone on a day like this—midsummer day on a stuffy train— jammed in among crowds of people staring at me. Eternal delays at every station, while I'd wish I had wings. No, I can't, I can't! And then there'll be memories, memories of midsummer days when I was little. The church—decorated with birch leaves and lilacs; dinner at the big table with relatives and friends; the afternoons in the park, dancing, music, flowers, and games. Oh, no matter how far we travel, the memories will follow in the baggage car, with remorse and guilt!

JEAN: I'll go with you—but right away, before it's too late. Right this minute!

JULIE: Get dressed, then! (*picking up the bird cage*)

JEAN: But no baggage! It would give us away!

JULIE: No, nothing! Only what we can have in the compartment with us.

JEAN (*has taken his hat*): What've you got there? What is it?

JULIE: It's only my greenfinch. I couldn't leave her behind.

JEAN: What? Bring a birdcage with us? You're out of your head! Put it down!

JULIE: It's the only thing I'm taking from my home—the only living being that loves me, since Diana was unfaithful. Don't be cruel! Let me take her!

JEAN: Put the cage down, I said! ———— And don't talk so loudly— Kristine will hear us!

JULIE: No, I won't leave her in the hands of strangers! I'd rather you killed her.

JEAN: Bring the thing here, then, I'll cut its head off!

JULIE: Oh! But don't hurt her! Don't . . . no, I can't.

JEAN: Bring it here! I can!

JULIE (*taking the bird out of the cage and kissing it*): Oh, my little Serena, must you die and leave your mistress?

JEAN: Please don't make a scene! Your whole future is at stake! Hurry up! (*He snatches the bird from her, carries it over to the chopping block, and picks up a meat cleaver.* MISS JULIE *turns away.*) You should have learned how to slaughter chickens instead of how to fire pistols. (*He chops off the bird's head.*) Then you wouldn't feel faint at the sight of blood.

JULIE (*screaming*): Kill me, too! Kill me! You, who can slaughter an innocent animal without blinking an eye! Oh, how I hate, how I detest you! There's blood between us now! I curse the moment I set eyes on you! I curse the moment I was conceived in my mother's womb!

JEAN: What good does cursing do? Let's go!

JULIE (*approaching the chopping block, as if drawn against her will*): No, I don't want to go yet. I can't . . . until I see . . . Shh! I hear a carriage ———— (*She listens, but her eyes never leave the cleaver and the chopping block.*) Do you think I can't stand the sight of blood? You think I'm so weak . . . Oh—I'd like to see your blood and your brains on a chopping block! ———— I'd like

to see your whole sex swimming in a sea of blood, like my little
bird . . . I think I could drink from your skull! I'd like to bathe
my feet in your open chest and eat your heart roasted whole!
———— You think I'm weak. You think I love you because my
womb craved your seed. You think I want to carry your spawn
under my heart and nourish it with my blood—bear your child
and take your name! By the way, what is your family name? I've
never heard it. ———— Do you have one? I was to be Mrs. Boot-
black—or Madame Pigsty. ———— You dog, who wears my collar, you lackey, who bears my coat of arms on your buttons—do
I have to share you with my cook, compete with my own servant? Oh! Oh! Oh! ———— You think I'm a coward who wants
to run away! No, now I'm staying—and let the storm break! My
father will come home . . . to find his desk broken open . . . and
his money gone! Then he'll ring—that bell . . . twice for his valet—and then he'll send for the police . . . and then I'll tell everything! Everything! Oh, what a relief it'll be to have it all
end—if only it will end! ———— And then he'll have a stroke
and die . . . That'll be the end of all of us—and there'll be peace
. . . quiet . . . eternal rest! ———— And then our coat of arms will
be broken against his coffin—the family title extinct—but the
valet's line will go on in an orphanage . . . win laurels in the gut-
ter, and end in jail!

JEAN: There's the blue blood talking! Very good, Miss Julie! Just
    don't let that miller out of the closet! (KRISTINE *enters, dressed
    for church, with a psalmbook in her hand.*)

JULIE (*rushing to* KRISTINE *and falling into her arms, as if seeking
    protection*): Help, me Kristine! Help me against this man!

KRISTINE (*unmoved and cold*): What a fine way to behave on a
    Sunday morning! (*sees the chopping block*) And look at this
    mess! ———— What does all this mean? Why all this screaming
    and carrying on?

JULIE: Kristine! You're a woman and my friend! Beware of this
    swine!

JEAN (*uncomfortable*): While you ladies discuss this, I'll go in and
    shave. (*slips off right*)

JULIE: You must listen to me so you'll understand!

KRISTINE: No, I could never understand such disgusting behavior!

Where are you off to in your traveling clothes? —— And he had his hat on. —— Well? —— Well? ——

JULIE: Listen to me, Kristine! Listen, and I'll tell you every-thing ——

KRISTINE: I don't want to hear it . . .

JULIE: But you must listen to me . . .

KRISTINE: What about? If it's about this silliness with Jean, I'm not interested, because it's none of my business. But if you're thinking of tricking him into running out, we'll soon put a stop to that!

JULIE (*extremely nervous*): Try to be calm now, Kristine, and lis-ten to me! I can't stay here, and neither can Jean—so we must go away . . .

KRISTINE: Hm, hm!

JULIE (*brightening*): You see, I just had an idea —— What if all three of us go—abroad—to Switzerland and start a hotel togeth-er? —— I have money, you see—and Jean and I could run it—and I thought you, you could take care of the kitchen . . . Wouldn't that be wonderful? —— Say yes! And come with us, and then everything will be settled! —— Oh, do say yes! (*embracing* KRISTINE *and patting her warmly*)

KRISTINE (*coolly, thoughtfully*): Hm, hm!

JULIE (*presto tempo*): You've never traveled, Kristine. —— You must get out and see the world. You can't imagine how much fun it is to travel by train—always new faces—new countries. —— And when we get to Hamburg, we'll stop off at the zoo—you'll like that. —— and then we'll go to the theatre and the opera—and when we get to Munich, dear, there we have museums, with Rubens and Raphael, the great painters, as you know. —— You've heard of Munich, where King Ludwig lived—the king who went mad. —— And then we'll see his castles—they're still there and they're like castles in fairy tales. —— And from there it isn't far to Switzerland—and the Alps. —— Imagine—the Alps have snow on them even in the middle of summer! —— And oranges grow there and lau-rel trees that are green all year round —— (JEAN *can be seen in the wings right, sharpening his razor on a strop which he holds with his teeth and his left hand. He listens to the conver-*

sation with satisfaction, nodding now and then in approval. MISS
JULIE *continues tempo prestissimo.*) And then we'll start a hotel—and I'll be at the desk, while Jean greets the guests . . . does
the shopping . . . writes letters. ———— You have no idea what a
life it'll be—the train whistles blowing and the carriages arriving and the bells ringing in the rooms and down in the restaurant. ———— And I'll make out the bills—and I know how to salt
them! . . . You'll never believe how timid travelers are when
they have to pay their bills! ———— And you—you'll be in
charge of the kitchen. ———— Naturally, you won't have to
stand over the stove yourself. ———— And since you're going to
be seen by people, you'll have to wear beautiful clothes. ————
And you, with your looks—no, I'm not flattering you—one fine
day you'll grab yourself a husband! ———— You'll see! ———— A
rich Englishman—they're so easy to ———— (*slowing down*) ————
catch—and then we'll get rich—and build ourselves a villa on
Lake Como. ———— It's true it rains there a little now and then,
but ———— (*dully*) ———— the sun has to shine sometimes—
although it looks dark—and then . . . of course we could always
come back home again ———— (*pause*) ———— here—or somewhere else ————

KRISTINE: Listen, Miss Julie, do you believe all this?

JULIE (*crushed*): Do I believe it?

KRISTINE: Yes!

JULIE (*wearily*): I don't know. I don't believe in anything any more.
(*She sinks down on the bench and cradles her head in her arms
on the table.*) Nothing! Nothing at all!

KRISTINE (*turning right to where* JEAN *is standing*): So, you
thought you'd run out!

JEAN (*embarrassed; puts the razor on the table*): Run out? That's
no way to put it. You hear Miss Julie's plan, and even if she is
tired after being up all night, it's still a practical plan.

KRISTINE: Now you listen to me! Did you think I'd work as a cook
for that . . .

JEAN (*sharply*): You watch what you say in front of your mistress!
Do you understand?

KRISTINE: Mistress!

JEAN: Yes!

KRISTINE: Listen to him! Listen to him!

JEAN: Yes, you listen! It'd do you good to listen more and talk less! Miss Julie is your mistress. If you despise her, you have to despise yourself for the same reason!

KRISTINE: I've always had enough self-respect ———

JEAN: ——— to be able to despise other people!

KRISTINE: ——— to stop me from doing anything that's beneath me. You can't say that the Count's cook has been up to something with the groom or the swineherd! Can you?

JEAN: No, you were lucky enough to get hold of a gentleman!

KRISTINE: Yes, a gentleman who sells the Count's oats from the stable.

JEAN: You should talk—taking a commission from the grocer and bribes from the butcher.

KRISTINE: What?

JEAN: And you say you can't respect your employers any longer. You, you, you!

KRISTINE: Are you coming to church with me, now? You could use a good sermon after your fine deed!

JEAN: No, I'm not going to church today. You'll have to go alone and confess what you've been up to.

KRISTINE: Yes, I'll do that, and I'll bring back enough forgiveness for you, too. The Savior suffered and died on the Cross for all our sins, and if we go to Him with faith and a penitent heart, He takes all our sins on Himself.

JEAN: Even grocery sins?

JULIE: And do you believe that, Kristine?

KRISTINE: It's my living faith, as sure as I stand here. It's the faith I learned as a child, Miss Julie, and kept ever since. "Where sin abounded, grace did much more abound!"

JULIE: Oh, if I only had your faith. If only . . .

KRISTINE: Well, you see, we can't have it without God's special grace, and that isn't given to everyone ———

JULIE: Who is it given to then?

KRISTINE: That's the great secret of the workings of grace, Miss Julie, and God is no respecter of persons, for the last shall be the first . . .

JULIE: Then He does respect the last.

KRISTINE (*continuing*): . . . and it is easier for a camel to go through the eye of a needle, than for a rich man to enter the Kingdom of God. That's how it is, Miss Julie! Anyhow, I'm going now—alone, and on the way I'm going to tell the groom not to let any horses out, in case anyone wants to leave before the Count gets back! ——— Goodbye! (*leaves*)

JEAN: What a witch! ——— And all this because of a greenfinch!
———

JULIE (*dully*): Never mind the greenfinch! ——— Can you see any way out of this? Any end to it?

JEAN (*thinking*): No!

JULIE: What would you do in my place?

JEAN: In your place? Let's see—as a person of position, as a woman who had—fallen. I don't know—wait, now I know.

JULIE (*taking the razor and making a gesture*): You mean like this?

JEAN: Yes! But—understand—*I* wouldn't do it! That's the difference between us!

JULIE: Because you're a man and I'm a woman? What sort of difference is that?

JEAN: The usual difference—between a man and a woman.

JULIE (*with the razor in her hand*): I want to, but I can't! ———
My father couldn't either, the time he should have done it.

JEAN: No, he shouldn't have! He had to revenge himself first.

JULIE: And now my mother is revenged again, through me.

JEAN: Didn't you ever love your father, Miss Julie?

JULIE: Oh yes, deeply, but I've hated him, too. I must have done so without realizing it! It was he who brought me up to despise my own sex, making me half woman, half man. Whose fault is what's happened? My father's, my mother's, my own? My own? I don't have anything that's my own. I don't have a single thought that I didn't get from my father, not an emotion that I didn't get from my mother, and this last idea—that all people are equal—I got that from my fiancé. ——— That's why I called him a swine! How can it be my fault? Shall I let Jesus take on the blame, the way Kristine does? ——— No, I'm too proud to do that and too sensible—thanks to my father's teachings.
——— And as for someone rich not going to heaven, that's a lie. But Kristine won't get in—how will she explain the money

she has in the savings bank? Whose fault is it? ———— What does it matter whose fault it is? I'm still the one who has to bear the blame, face the consequences . . .

JEAN: Yes, but . . . (*the bell rings sharply twice.* MISS JULIE *jumps up.* JEAN *changes his coat.*) The Count is back! Do you suppose Kristine — (*He goes to the speaking tube, taps the lid, and listens.*)

JULIE: He's been to his desk!

JEAN: It's Jean, sir! (*listening; the audience cannot hear the Count's voice.*) Yes, sir! (*listening*) Yes, sir! Right away! (*listening*) At once, sir! (*listening*) I see, in half an hour!

JULIE (*desperately frightened*): What did he say? Dear Lord, what did he say?

JEAN: He wants his boots and his coffee in half an hour.

JULIE: So, in half an hour! Oh, I'm so tired. I'm not able to do anything. I can't repent, can't run away, can't stay, can't live— can't die! Help me now! Order me, and I'll obey like a dog! Do me this last service, save my honor, save his name! You know what I *should* do, but don't have the will to . . . You will it, you order me to do it!

JEAN: I don't know why ———— but now I can't either ———— I don't understand. ———— It's as if this coat made it impossible for me to order you to do anything. ———— And now, since the Count spoke to me—I—I can't really explain it—but—ah, it's the damn lackey in me! ———— I think if the Count came down here now—and ordered me to cut my throat, I'd do it on the spot.

JULIE: Then pretend you're he, and I'm you! ———— You gave such a good performance before when you knelt at my feet. ———— —— You were a real nobleman. ———— Or—have you ever seen a hypnotist in the theatre? (JEAN *nods.*) He says to his subject: "Take the broom," and he takes it. He says: "Sweep," and he sweeps ————

JEAN: But the subject has to be asleep.

JULIE (*ecstatically*): I'm already asleep. ———— The whole room is like smoke around me . . . and you look like an iron stove . . . shaped like a man in black, with a tall hat—and your eyes glow like coals when the fire is dying—and your face is a white patch, like ashes ——— (*The sunlight has reached the floor and now shines on* JEAN.) ——— it's so warm and good ——— (*She rubs her hands as if warming them before a fire.*) ——— and bright—and so peaceful!

JEAN (*taking the razor and putting it in her hand*): Here's the broom! Go now while it's bright—out to the barn—and ... (*whispers in her ear*)

JULIE (*awake*): Thank you. I'm going now to rest! But just tell me—that those who are first can also receive the gift of grace. Say it, even if you don't believe it.

JEAN: The first? No, I can't! ——— But wait—Miss Julie—now I know! You're no longer among the first—you're now among—the last!

JULIE: That's true. ——— I'm among the very last. I'm the last one of all! Oh! ——— But now I can't go! ——— Tell me once more to go!

JEAN: No, now I can't either! I can't!

JULIE: And the first shall be the last!

JEAN: Don't think, don't think! You're taking all my strength from me, making me a coward. ——— What was that? I thought the bell moved! ——— No! Shall we stuff paper in it? ——— To be so afraid of a bell! ——— But it isn't just a bell. ——— There's someone behind it—a hand sets it in motion—and something else sets the hand in motion. ——— Maybe if you cover your ears—cover your ears! But then it rings even louder! rings until someone answers. ——— And then it's too late! And then the police come—and—then ——— (*The bell rings twice loudly.* JEAN *flinches, then straightens up.*) It's horrible! But there's no other way! ——— Go! (MISS JULIE *walks firmly out through the door.*)

The Dance of Death

(1900)

PART I

Characters

EDGAR, *Captain in the Coast Artillery*
ALICE, *his wife, a former actress*
KURT, *Quarantine Master*
JENNY, *a maid*
THE OLD WOMAN
THE SENTRY

(The interior of a round tower in a granite fortress. Upstage, a pair of large arches inset with glass doors through which are visible a shoreline with artillery emplacements and the sea. On either side of the arches are windows with flowers and birds in them. To the right of the arches an upright piano; below this a sewing table and two armchairs. To the left center a writing table with a telegraph apparatus on it. Below this a whatnot with family photographs. Nearby a chaise longue. Close to the wall a sideboard. A lamp hangs from the ceiling. On the wall near the piano a portrait of a woman in theatrical costume. On

113

each side of the portrait a laurel wreath with ribbons. Near the door a free-standing coatrack with uniform accessories, sabers, and so forth. Nearby an upright bureau desk. To the left of the door hangs a barometer. In the lower left corner is a round porcelain stove.*)

Act I
Scene 1

(It is a mild autumn evening. The upstage glass doors are open and a SENTRY *is visible out on the shore battery, wearing a plumed helmet. From time to time his saber glitters in the red light of the setting sun. The sea is dark and still. The* CAPTAIN *sits in an armchair to the left of the sewing table, fingering a cigar which has gone out. He is dressed in a worn fatigue uniform with riding boots and spurs. He looks tired and disgusted.* ALICE *sits in the armchair to the right, doing nothing. She looks tired and expectant.)*

CAPTAIN: Won't you play something for me?

ALICE (*indifferently but not snappishly*): What shall I play?

CAPTAIN: Whatever you want.

ALICE: You don't like my repertoire.

CAPTAIN: And you don't like mine.

ALICE (*changing the subject*): Do you want the doors left open?

CAPTAIN: It's up to you.

ALICE: We'll leave them open then . . . (*pause*) Why aren't you smoking?

CAPTAIN: I can't stand strong tobacco any more.

ALICE (*almost friendly*): Smoke a milder kind then. You say it's your only pleasure.

CAPTAIN: Pleasure? What's that?

ALICE: Don't ask me. I have as little knowledge of it as you . . . Isn't it time for your whiskey?

---

*The stove, not mentioned in the opening stage directions, is referred to in the beginning of Act II, Scene 2 (translator).

CAPTAIN: I'll wait awhile . . . What've you got for supper?

ALICE: How should I know? Ask Kristine.

CAPTAIN: Aren't the mackerel running? It's autumn.

ALICE: Yes, it's autumn.

CAPTAIN: Outside and inside. But despite the chill that comes with autumn, outside and inside, the idea of a grilled mackerel with a slice of lemon and a glass of white burgundy doesn't sound half-bad.

ALICE: How eloquent you're getting.

CAPTAIN: Is there any white burgundy left in the wine cellar?

ALICE: I wasn't aware we'd had a wine cellar for the past five years . . .

CAPTAIN: You never could keep track of things. Anyway, we *must* put in a store for our twenty-fifth anniversary . . .

ALICE: You mean you want to celebrate that?

CAPTAIN: Yes, naturally.

ALICE: It would be more natural for us to hide our misery, our twenty-five years of misery . . .

CAPTAIN: Even if it has been miserable, sweetheart, we've had fun, at times. And we have to enjoy the short time that's left, before the end.

ALICE: The end? If only it would be!

CAPTAIN: It'll be the end. With just enough left to put in a wheelbarrow and dump on the garden plot.

ALICE: And all this bother for a garden plot!

CAPTAIN: That's the way it is. I didn't arrange it.

ALICE: All this bother! (*pause*) Did you get the mail?

CAPTAIN: Yes.

ALICE: Did the butcher's bill come?

CAPTAIN: Yes.

ALICE: How big was it?

CAPTAIN (*takes a paper out of his pocket and puts his glasses on, but before long puts them away*): Read it yourself. I can't see any more . . .

ALICE: What's the matter with your eyes?

CAPTAIN: I don't know.

ALICE: Old age.

CAPTAIN: Nonsense! Me?

ALICE: Well not me!

CAPTAIN: Hm!

ALICE (*looking at the bill*): Can you pay it?

CAPTAIN: Yes, but not now.

ALICE: Later, I suppose—a year from now, when they retire you, with a little pension, and then it'll be too late. Later, when the sickness comes again . . .

CAPTAIN: Sickness? I've never been sick in my life, except that once when I felt poorly. I'll live another twenty years.

ALICE: That's not what the Doctor says.

CAPTAIN: The Doctor!

ALICE: Yes, and who knows better what sickness is?

CAPTAIN: I don't have any sickness, and never did. Won't get any either. One day I'll just keel over, like an old soldier.

ALICE: Speaking about doctors—you know that the Doctor is having a party this evening.

CAPTAIN (*upset*): Well, what of it? We're not invited because we don't associate with the Doctor and his wife, and we don't associate with them because we don't want to, because I despise them both. They're rabble!

ALICE: You say that about everybody.

CAPTAIN: Because they're all rabble!

ALICE: All except you.

CAPTAIN: Yes, because I've always known what's respectable and decent. That's why I'm not rabble. (*pause*)

ALICE: Do you want to play cards?

CAPTAIN: Why not?

ALICE (*takes a pack of cards out of the sewing table and begins to shuffle them*): Imagine, the Doctor got the band to play for a private party.

CAPTAIN (*angry*): That's because he's cozy with the Colonel in town. Cozy, you see! . . . Anybody can do that.

ALICE: I used to be friends with Gerda, but she played false with me . . .

CAPTAIN: They're all false, every one of them! . . . What's trump?

ALICE: Put your glasses on!

CAPTAIN: They don't help . . . Oh, well.

ALICE: Spades are trump.

CAPTAIN (*unhappy*): Spades? . . .

ALICE (*playing a card*): That may well be, but as far as the new officers' wives are concerned, we're outcasts.

CAPTAIN (*taking a trick*): So what? Since we never invite anyone here, nobody notices. I don't mind being alone . . . never have!

ALICE: Neither do I. But the children. The children are growing up without any friends.

CAPTAIN: They'll have to find their own in town. . . . That's my trick. Any trumps left?

ALICE: I have one! That one was mine.

CAPTAIN: Six and eight are fifteen . . .

ALICE: Fourteen, fourteen!

CAPTAIN: Six and eight give me fourteen . . . I think I'm forgetting how to count too. And two make sixteen . . . (*yawning*) Your deal.

ALICE: You're tired.

CAPTAIN (*dealing*): Not at all.

ALICE (*listening to something outside*): You can hear the music all the way here. (*pause*) Do you think Kurt's invited?

CAPTAIN: He got here this morning, so he's had plenty of time to unpack his evening clothes—even if he hasn't had time to pay us a visit.

ALICE: Quarantine Master. Will there be a quarantine station here?

CAPTAIN: Yes . . .

ALICE: He is my cousin, after all, and I once had the same name as his . . .

CAPTAIN: No honor in that . . .

ALICE: Now, listen . . . (*sharply*) You leave my relatives alone, and I'll leave yours alone!

CAPTAIN: All right, all right. Want to start again?

ALICE: Is a quarantine master a doctor?

CAPTAIN: No. He's only a kind of civilian administrator or bookkeeper. Kurt never became much of anything.

ALICE: Poor man, he just . . .

CAPTAIN: . . . cost me money . . . And he lost all respect when he left his wife and children.

ALICE: Don't be so hard, Edgar.

CAPTAIN: But it's true—no matter what he did later in America. Yes. I can't say I'm looking forward to seeing him. He was a decent boy, though, and I enjoyed discussing things with him.

ALICE: Because he was so submissive . . .

CAPTAIN (*arrogantly*): Submissive or not, he was someone you could have a conversation with . . . On this island, there isn't a single person who knows what I'm talking about . . . this is a colony of idiots . . .

ALICE: It is strange, though, that Kurt should arrive just in time for our silver anniversary . . . whether we celebrate it or not . . .

CAPTAIN: Why is it strange? . . . Oh, of course, he was the one who brought us together, or married you off, as everybody said.

ALICE: He didn't do that.

CAPTAIN: He certainly did! . . . It was his idea . . . I leave it to you to judge how good it was.

ALICE: Just a light-hearted notion . . .

CAPTAIN: Which we had to suffer for, not him.

ALICE: Yes, think if I'd stayed in the theater. All my friends are stars now.

CAPTAIN (*rising*): Yes, of course . . . I'll have my drink now. (*He crosses to the sideboard and pours a brandy and soda, which he drinks while standing.*) There should be a rail here, to put your foot on. Then you could dream you were in Copenhagen, at the American Bar!

ALICE: We'll have a rail made if only to remind us of Copenhagen. They were the best times we had.

CAPTAIN (*drinking hastily*): Yes! Remember Nimb's wonderful *navarin aux pommes*! Mmmm! Delicious!

ALICE: No, but I remember the concerts in Tivoli Gardens!

CAPTAIN: You have such elegant taste!

ALICE: You should be happy to have a wife with taste!

CAPTAIN: I am . . .

ALICE: The times you need to brag about her . . .

CAPTAIN (*drinking*): They must be dancing at the Doctor's . . . I hear the bass tubas playing three-quarter time . . . *Boom*, boom-boom!

ALICE: They're playing the "Alcazar Waltz." Yes . . . the last time I danced a waltz . . . wasn't yesterday . . .

CAPTAIN: Think you're still up to it?

ALICE: Still?

CAPTAIN: Yes. Aren't your dancing days over, as mine are?

ALICE: I'm ten years younger than you.

CAPTAIN: Then we're the same age, since the wife is supposed to be ten years younger!

ALICE: Shame on you! You're an old man. I'm still in my prime!

CAPTAIN: Oh yes, I know you can be charming when you want to be—to other people.

ALICE: Can we have the lamp lit now?

CAPTAIN: Gladly!

ALICE: Then ring. (*The* CAPTAIN *crosses unhurriedly to the writing table and rings.* JENNY *enters from right.*)

CAPTAIN: Jenny, would you please light the lamp.

ALICE (*sharply*): Light the lamp!

JENNY: Yes, your grace. (*She lights the ceiling lamp as the* CAPTAIN *watches her.*)

ALICE (*curtly*): Did you wipe the glass properly?

JENNY: Sure, a bit.

ALICE: What sort of answer is that?

CAPTAIN: Now, now . . .

ALICE (*to Jenny*): Get out! It's better if I light the lamp myself.

JENNY: I think so too. (*going*)

ALICE (*rising*): Get out!

JENNY (*pausing*): I wonder what you'd say if I really went. (ALICE *is silent.* JENNY *leaves. The* CAPTAIN *crosses and lights the lamp.*)

ALICE (*uneasy*): Do you think she'll leave?

CAPTAIN: It wouldn't surprise me, and then we'd be in a real fix.

ALICE: It's your fault, you know. You spoil them!

CAPTAIN: Oh, no. You see how polite they always are to me.

ALICE: Because you crawl before them! For that matter, you crawl before all your inferiors, because you're a despot with the soul of a slave.

CAPTAIN: Ha!

ALICE: Yes, you crawl before your own orderly and your subordinates. And you can't get along with your peers and superiors.

CAPTAIN: Stuff!

ALICE: That's the way all tyrants are! ... Do you think she'll leave?

CAPTAIN: Yes, if you don't go out and say a friendly word to her.

ALICE: I?

CAPTAIN: If I did it, you'd say I was flirting with the maids.

ALICE: Imagine if she goes. Then I'll have to do everything myself, like the last time, and ruin my hands again.

CAPTAIN: That's not the worst part! If Jenny goes, so will Kristine, and we'll never get another servant to come to this island. The steamboat pilot scares away all the new ones looking for work ... and if he forgets, my own corporals do it!

ALICE: Yes, your corporals! I have to feed them in my kitchen, and you don't dare order them out ...

CAPTAIN: No, because then they'd leave too, when their enlistments were up ... and we'd have to close down the garrison.

ALICE: We'd be ruined!

CAPTAIN: That's why the officer corps has decided to petition the crown for special food allowances ...

ALICE: For whom?

CAPTAIN: For the corporals.

ALICE (*laughing*): You must be crazy!

CAPTAIN: Yes, let's have a little laughter. I can use it.

ALICE: I'll soon have forgotten how to laugh ...

CAPTAIN (*lighting his cigar*): That's something we should never forget ... Life is dreary enough as it is.

ALICE: It's certainly no fun ... Do you want to play some more?

CAPTAIN: No, it tires me. (*pause*)

ALICE: Oh, it makes me angry that the new quarantine master is my own cousin, and he pays his first visit to people who aren't even our friends.

CAPTAIN: There's no use talking about it.

ALICE: Did you see that the newspaper announcement of new arrivals described him as having "independent means"? He must have come into some money.

CAPTAIN: Independent means! So! A wealthy relative. That's the first one in this family!

ALICE: In your family, yes. But we've had many wealthy people in my family.

CAPTAIN: If he's come into money, he's probably gotten arrogant.

Well, I know how to beat him at that game. (*The telegraph apparatus begins to click.*)

ALICE: Who could that be?

CAPTAIN (*standing still*): A little quiet, please.

ALICE: Well, go over to it.

CAPTAIN: I don't have to. I can hear what they're saying ... It's the children. (*He crosses to the telegraph and taps out an answer. The telegraph continues again for a time, and the CAPTAIN answers.*)

ALICE: Well?

CAPTAIN: Wait a minute! ... (*He clicks an end of message signal.*) It was the children. They're at the main guardhouse in town. Judith isn't feeling well again and she's staying home from school.

ALICE: Again? What else did they want?

CAPTAIN: Money, of course!

ALICE: Why is Judith in such a hurry? If she waited till next year to take her exam, that would be soon enough.

CAPTAIN: You tell her that and see if it helps!

ALICE: You're the one to tell her.

CAPTAIN: How many times haven't I already told her? You know yourself that children do as they please.

ALICE: In this house, anyway ... (*The CAPTAIN yawns.*) Do you have to yawn in your wife's face?

CAPTAIN: What else should I do? ... Haven't you noticed that we say the same things every day? Just now, when you said your old familiar "in this house, anyway," I should have answered with my old "I'm not the only one in this house." But since I've already said that five hundred times, I yawned instead. My yawn can be taken to mean either that I don't have the energy to answer, or that "You're right, my angel," or "Let's end it there."

ALICE: You're really charming this evening.

CAPTAIN: Isn't it time to eat soon?

ALICE: Did you know that the Doctor ordered supper from town, from the Grand Hotel?

CAPTAIN: Oh? Then they're having grouse! Mmmm! Delicious! Do you know, grouse is the finest bird there is, but frying it like they do in lard is barbaric!

ALICE: Ugh! Must you talk about food?

CAPTAIN: About wine then? I wonder what those barbarians are drinking with their grouse.

ALICE: Shall I play for you?

CAPTAIN (*sitting at the writing table*): The last resort! All right, as long as you stay away from those funeral marches and dirges you use to stir up sympathy. I can always hear the plaintive: "Listen to how unhappy I am! Meow, meow! Listen to what a terrible husband I have! Grumble, grumble, grumble! Oh, if he would only die soon!" Then a snappy drum roll and some fanfares and we finish with the "Alcazar Waltz" and the "Champagne Gallop"! Speaking of champagne, there should be two bottles left. Shall we bring them up and pretend we have company?

ALICE: No, we won't, because they're mine. I got them as gifts!

CAPTAIN: Always economical!

ALICE: And you're always stingy, toward your wife, anyway!

CAPTAIN: Then I don't know what there is to do . . . Shall I dance for you?

ALICE: No, thanks. Your dancing days are over, remember?

CAPTAIN: You should have a female companion.

ALICE: Thank you! . . . And you should have a male companion.

CAPTAIN: Thank you! We tried that to our mutual dissatisfaction. But it was interesting as an experiment that the moment a stranger came into the house, we were happy . . . to start with . . .

ALICE: But later!

CAPTAIN: Yes, don't talk about that! (*There is a knock at the door left.*)

ALICE: Who can that be this late?

CAPTAIN: Jenny doesn't usually knock.

ALICE: Go and open the door! And don't yell "Come in!" like some worker in a shop!

CAPTAIN (*crossing to the door*): Even the thought of work bothers you, doesn't it? (*There is another knock.*)

ALICE: Well, open it!

CAPTAIN (*opens it and is handed a calling card*): It's Kristine . . . Has Jenny gone? (*The reply is inaudible. He turns to* ALICE.) Jenny's gone.

ALICE: Then I become a maid again.

CAPTAIN: And I a janitor.

ALICE: Can't we get one of the enlisted men to help in the kitchen?

CAPTAIN: Not these days.

ALICE: But surely Jenny didn't leave a calling card?

CAPTAIN (*looks at the card with his glasses on, then hands it to* ALICE.) You read it, I can't.

ALICE (*reading*): Kurt! It's Kurt! Go out and greet him!

CAPTAIN (*exits left*): Kurt! What a pleasure! (ALICE *straightens her hair and seems to come to life. The* CAPTAIN *reenters from left with* KURT.) See, here he is, the traitor! Welcome, my boy! (*embraces him*)

ALICE (*crossing to* KURT): Welcome to my house, Kurt.

KURT: Thank you . . . It's been a long time since we saw each other last.

CAPTAIN: What is it? Fifteen years! And we've gotten old . . .

ALICE: But Kurt hasn't changed a bit.

CAPTAIN: Sit down, sit down! . . . But first of all, what are your plans? Are you invited anywhere this evening?

KURT: I am invited to the Doctor's, but I haven't promised to go.

ALICE: Then you'll stay with your relatives!

KURT: That seems like the natural thing to do, but the Doctor is sort of my superior, and there could be problems later.

CAPTAIN: What nonsense! I've never been afraid of my superiors . . .

KURT: It's not fear, it's just that I don't want any unnecessary problems.

CAPTAIN: On this island, I'm in charge! You stick with me and no one will bother you!

ALICE: That's enough now, Edgar. (*taking* KURT'S *hand*) Never mind about superiors or who's in charge, you stay with us! Everyone will think it right and proper.

KURT: All right . . . Especially since I seem so welcome here.

CAPTAIN: Why shouldn't you be welcome . . . There's no hard feelings . . . (KURT *cannot conceal a certain embarrassment.*) Why should there be? You were a bit thoughtless, but you were young and I've forgotten all about it. I don't hold grudges. (ALICE *is upset. They all sit down at the sewing table.*)

ALICE: So, you've been out in the wide world.

KURT: And now I've landed here with you ...

CAPTAIN: Whom you married off twenty-five years ago.

KURT: That wasn't the way it was, but never mind. It's good to see you're still together after twenty-five years ...

CAPTAIN: Yes, we're dragging along. It's been touch and go sometimes, but as you say, we're still together. And Alice has nothing to complain about. She's never wanted for anything, especially money. Maybe you don't know that I'm a famous writer ... of textbooks ...

KURT: Yes, I remember when we last saw each other that you'd published a rifle instruction manual that sold well. Is it still used in army schools?

CAPTAIN: It's still in print and it's the best seller, although they've tried to replace it with an inferior book ... which is being used, it's true, but is completely worthless. (*a painful silence*)

KURT: You traveled abroad, I heard.

ALICE: Yes, we've been to Copenhagen five times—imagine!

CAPTAIN: Sure! You know that I took Alice away from the theatre ...

ALICE: You took me?

CAPTAIN: Yes, I took you the way a wife should be taken ...

ALICE: How courageous you've become!

CAPTAIN: But afterwards, because I had to swallow the blame for having cut short her brilliant career ... hm ... I had to make amends by promising to take her to Copenhagen ... and I've kept that promise—with honor! Five times we've been there! Five. (*He holds up the fingers on his left hand.*) ... Have you ever been in Copenhagen?

KURT (*smiling*): No, I spent most of my time in America.

CAPTAIN: America? That's a terribly rough place, isn't it?

KURT (*embarrassed*): Well, it's not Copenhagen.

ALICE: Have you ... heard anything ... from your children?

KURT: No.

ALICE: I'm sorry, Kurt dear, but it was rather thoughtless to leave them like that ...

KURT: I didn't leave them. The court granted their mother custody ...

CAPTAIN: We're not going to talk about that now. I think it was good for you to get away from that mess.

KURT (*to* ALICE): How are your children?

ALICE: Oh, fine. They go to school in town. They're almost grown.

CAPTAIN: Yes, they're clever children, and the boy has a brilliant mind. Brilliant! He'll be on the General Staff.

ALICE: If they take him.

CAPTAIN: Him? A future Minister of War?

KURT: To change the subject, . . . There's going to be a quarantine station here . . . examining ships for bubonic plague, cholera, and so forth. And the Doctor will be my superior, as you know . . . What sort of man is he?

CAPTAIN: Man? He's not a man. He's an ignorant scoundrel.

KURT (*to* ALICE): Worse luck for me.

ALICE: He's not as bad as Edgar says, but I have to admit I find him unsympathetic . . .

CAPTAIN: He's a scoundrel! and so are they all—the customs officer, the postmaster, the telephone girls, the druggist, the pilot, the . . . what-do-you-call-him . . . alderman—scoundrels the lot of them, and so I have nothing to do with them.

KURT: You're at odds with all of them?

CAPTAIN: All of them!

ALICE: Yes, it's true. We can't associate with these people.

CAPTAIN: It's as if every tyrant in the country has been interned on this island.

ALICE (*ironically*): Yes, exactly!

CAPTAIN (*good-naturedly*): Hm! Is that a reference to me? I'm no tyrant, at least not in my own house.

ALICE: Just be careful you aren't.

CAPTAIN (*to* KURT): Don't pay any attention to her. I'm a very good husband, and this old lady is the best wife in the world.

ALICE: Do you want something to drink, Kurt?

KURT: Thanks, not now.

CAPTAIN: Have you become a . . . ?

KURT: Just temperate, that's all.

CAPTAIN: Is that American?

KURT: Yes.

CAPTAIN: I say intemperate, or leave it be! A man should be able to hold his liquor.

KURT: To return to your neighbors here on the island. My work will put me in contact with everyone, so it's not going to be smooth sailing. You get mixed up in people's schemes, even if you try to avoid them.

ALICE: You do what you have to do, but you can always come back to us. Here you have real friends.

KURT: Isn't it terrible to sit here alone, surrounded by unfriendly people?

ALICE: It's no fun.

CAPTAIN: It's not terrible at all! I've known nothing but unfriendly people my whole life, and they've helped me rather than hurt me. When the time comes for me to die, I'll be able to say that I don't owe anybody anything, and I never got anything for nothing. Everything I own I had to fight for.

ALICE: Yes, Edgar's path hasn't been strewn with roses...

CAPTAIN: Over thorns and stones, flinty stones... but you have to trust in your own strength. Have you learned that?

KURT (*simply*): Ten years ago I learned how inadequate that was.

CAPTAIN: Then you're a miserable wretch!

ALICE (*to the* CAPTAIN): Edgar!

CAPTAIN: Yes, he's a miserable wretch if he can't trust in his own strength. It's true that when the mechanism is finished, it's into the wheelbarrow and onto a garden plot. But as long as the mechanism keeps running, then it's kick and fight with your hands and feet for all you're worth. That's my philosophy.

KURT (*smiling*): It's amusing to listen to you.

CAPTAIN: But you don't believe it's true.

KURT: No, I don't.

CAPTAIN: Well, it is, anyway. (*The wind has begun to blow, slamming one of the upstage doors. The* CAPTAIN *rises.*) A storm's starting up. I felt it coming. (*He goes to the doors, closes them, and taps the barometer.*)

ALICE (*to* KURT): You'll stay for supper, won't you?

KURT: Yes, thank you.

ALICE: But it'll be very simple. Our maid has left.

KURT: That's fine with me.

ALICE: You're so easy to please, dear Kurt.

CAPTAIN (*at the barometer*): You should see how the barometer is falling! I could feel it changing.

ALICE (*aside to* KURT): It's his nerves.

CAPTAIN: It's time to eat soon!

ALICE (*rising*): I was just going to see to it. You two sit here and philosophize ... (*aside to* KURT) But don't contradict him or he'll lose his temper. And don't ask him why he never became major! (KURT *nods, and* ALICE *starts out right.*)

CAPTAIN (*sitting at the sewing table with* KURT): Fix something good for us now, woman!

ALICE: You give me the money, and I will.

CAPTAIN: Always money! (ALICE *leaves.*) Money, money, money. I went around so long with my wallet open that I started to imagine that I was a wallet. Do you know what I mean?

KURT: Oh yes. The difference was that I thought I was a check book.

CAPTAIN: Ha ha! Yes, you've been down that road! Women! Ha ha! But you really picked one!

KURT (*patiently*): Let's not dig up that old story.

CAPTAIN: She was a real jewel ... Anyway, what I found—when all is said and done—was a good woman.

KURT (*smiling good-naturedly*): When all is said and done!

CAPTAIN: Don't you laugh!

KURT (*as before*): When all is said and done.

CAPTAIN: Yes, she's been a faithful wife ... a splendid mother, excellent ... it's just that ——— (*looking at the door right*) ——— she has the devil's own temper. Do you know, there were times when I cursed you for saddling me with her?

KURT (*good-naturedly*): But I didn't do that! Listen, my friend ...

CAPTAIN: Never mind, never mind! You talk nonsense and you forget the things that are unpleasant to remember. Don't take it badly! You know how I am—used to shouting and giving orders. You're not offended, are you?

KURT: Not at all. But I didn't bring you two together, on the contrary.

CAPTAIN (*not listening to* KURT's *argument*): But life is strange, after all, isn't it?

KURT: That it is.

CAPTAIN: And getting old. It's no fun, but it is interesting. Not that I'm old, but I'm *starting* to feel it. Everyone you know dies off and you're left so alone.

KURT: Fortunate the man who has a wife to grow old with.

CAPTAIN: Fortunate? Yes, it is fortunate, because your children leave you too. You shouldn't have left yours.

KURT: But I didn't. They were taken from me . . .

CAPTAIN: Now you mustn't be offended when I say that . . .

KURT: But that's not the way it was . . .

CAPTAIN: However it was, it's forgotten. But you are alone.

KURT: You get used to everything, my friend.

CAPTAIN: Can you . . . can you even get used to . . . to being entirely alone, as well?

KURT: Look at me!

CAPTAIN: What have you been doing these past fifteen years?

KURT: What a question! Fifteen years!

CAPTAIN: They say you've come into money and are rich.

KURT: I'm not rich . . .

CAPTAIN: I wasn't thinking of borrowing . . .

KURT: If you were, I'd be ready to . . .

CAPTAIN: Thanks anyway, I have enough debts as it is. You see ——— (*looking at the door right*) ——— we can't be out of anything in this house. And the day I didn't have any money . . . she'd go her way!

KURT: Oh no!

CAPTAIN: No? I'm sure of that! . . . Do you know, whenever I'm short of money, *that's* when she wants to buy things, just for the pleasure of showing me that I can't provide for my family.

KURT: But you said before that you had a big income.

CAPTAIN: Oh, I do . . . but it's not enough.

KURT: Then it's not big in the usual sense . . .

CAPTAIN: Life is strange, and so are we! (*The telegraph starts clicking.*)

KURT: What's that?

CAPTAIN: Only a time signal.

KURT: Don't you have a telephone?

CAPTAIN: Yes, in the kitchen, but we use the telegraph because the telephone girls repeat everything they hear.

KURT: You must have a difficult social life out here by the sea.

CAPTAIN: Yes, it's dreadful, simply dreadful. All of life is dreadful! You believe in a hereafter, don't you? ——— Do you think there'll be any peace there?

KURT: There'll surely be battles and storms there too.

CAPTAIN: There too—if there is anything there. Then annihilation would be better!

KURT: Don't you think annihilation will be painful?

CAPTAIN: I'll just keel over painlessly.

KURT: Oh? And you know that for certain?

CAPTAIN: Yes, I do.

KURT: You don't seem very satisfied with your life.

CAPTAIN (*sighing*): Satisfied? I'll be satisfied the day I die.

KURT (*rises*): That you can't know for certain . . . Tell me: what's going on in this house? What's the matter? The moment I entered, I felt sick. I would have left if I hadn't promised Alice I'd stay. There's a poisonous stench in here. Is it the wallpaper, or is something rotting under the floorboards? The hate is so thick, I find it hard to breathe. (*The* CAPTAIN *slumps in his chair and stares blankly into space.*) What's the matter? Edgar! (*The* CAPTAIN *does not move.* KURT *slaps him on the shoulder.*) Edgar!

CAPTAIN (*coming to*): Did you say something? (*looking around*) I thought it was Alice . . . Oh, it's you . . . Listen, I . . . (*falls into a stupor again*)

KURT: This is dreadful! (*He crosses to the door right and opens it.*) Alice!

ALICE (*enters wearing an apron*): What is it?

KURT: I don't know! Look at him!

ALICE (*calmly*): He goes off like that sometimes . . . If I play something, he'll wake up.

KURT: No, don't do that! Don't . . . Let me try! . . . Can he hear? Can he see?

ALICE: He neither hears nor sees when he's like this.

KURT: And you say that so calmly! . . . Alice, what's going on in this house?

ALICE: Ask him, that one!

KURT: That one? . . . He's your husband!

ALICE: To me, he's a stranger, as much a stranger as he was twenty-five years ago. I know nothing about this man . . . except that . . .

KURT: Stop! He'll hear you!

ALICE: He can't hear anything now. (*A trumpet call sounds outside.*)

CAPTAIN (*jumping up and getting his saber and uniform cap*): Excuse me! I just have to inspect the posts. (*leaves through the upstage doors*)

KURT: Is he sick?

ALICE: I don't know.

KURT: Has he lost his reason?

ALICE: I don't know.

KURT: Does he drink?

ALICE: Not as much as he boasts he does.

KURT: Sit down and tell me everything, but calmly and factually.

ALICE (*sits*): What shall I say? That I've been locked up in this tower for a generation, guarded by a man I've always hated and now hate so immeasurably that the day he died I'd laugh out loud?

KURT: Why didn't you separate?

ALICE: Good question! We separated twice when we were engaged. Since then we've tried to separate every day that's passed . . . but we're welded together and can't get free. Once we lived apart . . . in the same house . . . for five years. Now only death can separate us. We know that, and so we wait for it as a liberator!

KURT: Why are you both so alone?

ALICE: Because he's isolated me! First, he rooted out all my relatives from the house—those are the words he used himself, "rooted out"—then my closest friends and others . . .

KURT: But *his* relatives. Did you root them out?

ALICE: Yes, because after depriving me of honor and respect, they were killing me . . . Finally, my last contact with the world became that telegraph—because the telephone girls were listening in on our calls . . . I taught myself to telegraph without him knowing it. You mustn't tell him—he'd kill me!

KURT: This is terrible, terrible! . . . But why does he blame me for your marriage? Let me tell you how it was. . . . Edgar was a childhood friend. The first time he saw you, he fell in love. He asked me to act as go-between. I said no immediately, my dear Alice, because I knew how tyrannical and cruel you could be. That's why I warned him. . . . And when he kept hounding me, I sent him to ask your brother to plead for him.

ALICE: I believe you, but he's been fooling himself for so long, you'll never get him to change his opinion.

KURT: Let him blame me then, if it makes him feel better.

ALICE: But that's not right . . .

KURT: I'm used to it . . . The thing that really hurts is his unjust accusation that I abandoned my children . . .

ALICE: That's the way he is. He says what he thinks, then afterward believes it. But he seems to like you, mostly because you don't contradict him . . . Please try not to tire of us . . . I think you arrived at a fortunate time for us. In fact, I take it as a sign that you were sent! . . . Kurt! You mustn't tire of us, because we're the most unfortunate people on the face of the earth! *(weeps)*

KURT: I've seen *one* marriage up close . . . and that was horrible! But this is almost worse!

ALICE: Do you think so?

KURT: Yes!

ALICE: Whose fault is it?

KURT: Alice, the moment you stop asking whose fault it is, you'll find peace. Try to accept things as they are, as a trial you have to bear . . .

ALICE: I can't! It's too much! *(rises)* It's past help!

KURT: Poor people! . . . Do you know why you hate each other so?

ALICE: No! It's a groundless hate, without cause, without purpose, but also without end. Can you guess why he fears death most? He's afraid I'll remarry.

KURT: Then he does love you!

ALICE: Probably, but that doesn't stop him from hating me.

KURT *(as if to himself)*: This is what they call love-hate, and it's from the abyss! . . . Does he like you to play for him?

ALICE: Yes, but only ugly melodies . . . for example, that awful "Entry of the Boyars." When he hears it, he feels possessed and wants to dance.

KURT: He dances?

ALICE: Yes, he's so funny sometimes.

KURT: Forgive my asking . . . but where are the children?

ALICE: Did you know that two of them died?

KURT: Have you also suffered that?

ALICE: What haven't I suffered?

KURT: But the other two?

ALICE: In town. They couldn't stay here. He turned them against me . . .

KURT: And you turned them against him?

ALICE: Naturally. And so everyone had to take sides, and there were intrigues and bribes. . . . To avoid destroying the children, we sent them away. What should have drawn us together, pulled us apart. What should have been a blessing, became a curse. . . . Yes, sometimes I think our whole family is cursed!

KURT: After the Fall, that's what it is.

ALICE (*with a venomous glance, her voice cutting*): What fall?

KURT: Adam and Eve's.

ALICE: Oh, I thought you meant something else. (*embarrassed silence;* ALICE *wrings her hands.*) Kurt! My cousin, my oldest friend. I haven't always treated you as I should. But now I've been punished, and you've gotten revenge.

KURT: Not revenge! There'll be no revenge here! Hush!

ALICE: Do you remember that time when you were engaged? I had invited you to Sunday dinner.

KURT: Hush!

ALICE: Be patient with me, I must speak! . . . When you arrived, we were gone, and you had to return home.

KURT: But you had been invited away yourself. That's nothing to talk about now.

ALICE: Kurt, a moment ago when I invited you to supper, I thought there was something in the pantry. (*hiding her face in her hands*) But there's nothing, not even a crust of bread! . . . (*weeps*)

KURT: My poor Alice.

ALICE: But when *he* comes back and wants to eat and discovers that there isn't anything, he'll be furious. You've never seen him angry! . . . Oh God, it's so humiliating!

KURT: Let me go out and find something!

ALICE: There's nothing to find on this island.

KURT: We must do something . . . not for my sake, but for his and yours. . . . We'll make light of the subject when he returns. . . . I'll suggest we have a drink, and meanwhile I'll think of something. . . . To put him in a good mood, you can play something for him, anything at all. . . . Sit down at the piano and be ready!

ALICE: Look at my hands—do you think I can play with them? After polishing brass, wiping out lamps, keeping the fire going, cleaning the house. . . .

KURT: But you have two servants.

ALICE: We say that because he's an officer. . . . Servants come and go, and sometimes—most of the time—we have none at all. . . . How am I going to manage this business about supper? Oh, if only the house would catch fire. . . .

KURT: Alice! Shhh!

ALICE: If only the sea would rise and carry us off!

KURT: No, no, no, I can't listen to you!

ALICE: What will he say, what will he say? . . . Don't go, Kurt, don't leave me!

KURT: No, dear . . . I *won't* leave!

ALICE: Yes, but when you do go . . .

KURT: Does he beat you?

ALICE: Me? Oh no, he knows I'd leave if he did that! I've some pride left! (*Offstage shouts: "Halt! Who goes there? . . . Pass, friend."*)

KURT (*rising*): Is that him?

ALICE (*frightened*): Yes, it's him! (*pause*)

KURT: What in God's name shall we do?

ALICE: I don't know, I don't know!

CAPTAIN (*entering upstage, cheerfully*): There, now I'm free! . . . Well, now she's had time to complain. She's so unfortunate . . . isn't she? . . .

KURT: What's the weather like out there?

CAPTAIN: Stormy! . . . (*opening one of the doors slightly; jokingly*) Sir Bluebeard and the maiden in the tower. And outside, the sentry marches, saber drawn, guarding the lovely maiden. . . . And then her brothers come, but the sentry's at his post. Look at him! One, two, one two! What a good sentry! Look at him! Meli-tam-tam-ta meli-ta-lia-lay! Shall we have the sword dance? Kurt has to see that!

KURT: No, let's have "The Entry of the Boyars" instead!

CAPTAIN: Do you know that? . . . Alice, in her apron, come on and play! Come on, I said! (ALICE *goes reluctantly to the piano. The*

CAPTAIN *pinches her arm.*) You've been slandering me!

ALICE: I? (KURT *turns away.* ALICE *plays "The Entry of the Boyars." The* CAPTAIN *performs a kind of Hungarian dance behind the writing table, his spurs clanging. Then he sinks to the floor, unnoticed by the others.* ALICE *continues playing until the piece is finished. She begins speaking without looking around.*) Shall we take it again? (*When there is silence,* ALICE *turns and sees the* CAPTAIN *lying senseless and concealed from view behind the writing table.*) Lord Jesus! (*She stands, her arms crossed on her chest, and sighs, as if grateful or relieved.*)

KURT (*turning and rushing to the* CAPTAIN): What is it? What's the matter?

ALICE (*very tensely*): Is he dead?

KURT: I don't know! Help me!

ALICE (*remaining standing*): I can't touch him . . . is he dead?

KURT: No! He's alive! (ALICE *sighs.* KURT *helps the* CAPTAIN *into a chair.*)

CAPTAIN: What is it? (*silence*) What is it?

KURT: You fell.

CAPTAIN: Did something happen?

KURT: You fell to the floor. Is something wrong?

CAPTAIN: With me? Of course not! I don't know what you're talking about. What are you standing there yelling about?

KURT: You're sick!

CAPTAIN: Nonsense! Keep on playing, Alice . . . Oh, it's coming on again! (*clutching his head*)

ALICE: Don't you see that you're sick?!

CAPTAIN: Stop screaming! It's only a fainting spell!

KURT: You must have a doctor! . . . I'll use the telephone! . . .

CAPTAIN: I don't want any doctor!

KURT: You must! We'll call him for our sake—otherwise we'll be responsible.

CAPTAIN: If he comes, I'll throw him out! . . . I'll shoot him down! . . . Oh, it's coming on again! (*clutching his head*)

KURT (*crossing to door right*): I'm going to telephone! (*He exits.* ALICE *takes off her apron.*)

CAPTAIN: Will you get me a glass of water?

ALICE: I guess I'll have to. (*She gives him a glass of water.*)

CAPTAIN: How loving!

ALICE: Are you sick?

CAPTAIN: Forgive me for not being perfectly well.

ALICE: Can you take care of yourself?

CAPTAIN: You don't seem to want to!

ALICE: You can be sure of that.

CAPTAIN: The moment you've been waiting for has finally come.

ALICE: Yes, the moment you believed never would come.

CAPTAIN: Don't be angry with me!

KURT (*entering right*): It's a disgrace!

ALICE: What did he say?

KURT: He hung up—just like that!

ALICE (*to the* CAPTAIN): There we have the consequences of your boundless arrogance!

CAPTAIN: I think I'm getting worse! ... Try to get a doctor from town!

ALICE (*crossing to the telegraph*): It'll have to be by telegraph then!

CAPTAIN (*half-rising, amazed*): Can—you—telegraph?

ALICE (*telegraphing*): Yes, I can.

CAPTAIN: Is that so? ... Go on then! ... How deceitful she is! (*to* KURT) Come sit beside me! (KURT *sits beside the* CAPTAIN.) Hold my hand! I feel like I'm sitting and falling at the same time. Can you imagine? Like falling down something. It's strange.

KURT: Have you ever had such an attack before?

CAPTAIN: Never! ...

KURT: While we're waiting for an answer from town, I'm going to talk to the Doctor here. Has he ever treated you?

CAPTAIN: He certainly has!

KURT: Then he's familiar with your history ... (*crossing left*)

ALICE: It'll be awhile before there's an answer. This is kind of you, Kurt. But hurry back!

KURT: As fast as I can! (*exits*)

CAPTAIN: Kurt is kind. And so changed.

ALICE: Yes, and for the better. It's bad luck for him, though, getting mixed up in our misery just now.

CAPTAIN: But good luck for us. I wonder how things really are for him. Did you notice that he didn't want to talk about himself?

ALICE: Yes, but I also noticed no one asked him to.

CAPTAIN: Think of his life .... and ours! Do you suppose every-one has it like this?

ALICE: Perhaps, but they don't talk about it as much as we do.

CAPTAIN: Sometimes I think that misery is attracted to misery, and that if people are happy it's because they avoid unhappi-ness. That's why you and I will never know anything but mis-ery.

ALICE: Do you know of any happy people?

CAPTAIN: Let me think ... No ... Yes ... the Ekmarks!

ALICE: What are you talking about? She was operated on last year ...

CAPTAIN: That's true. Then I don't know of ... wait: the von Kraffts.

ALICE: Yes, for fifty years that family lived idyllically: prosperous and respected, with good children who married well. Then that cousin went and murdered someone, and the scandal put an end to their peace. The family name was disgraced in all the news-papers ... The murder made it impossible for any of the Kraffts to show their faces. Their children had to be taken out of school ... Oh, God!

CAPTAIN: I wonder what's wrong with me.

ALICE: What do you think it is?

CAPTAIN: My heart, or my head. It's as if my soul wanted to fly out and dissolve in a cloud of smoke.

ALICE: Are you hungry?

CAPTAIN: Yes. How's supper coming?

ALICE (*pacing uneasily*): I'll ask Jenny.

CAPTAIN: But she's gone.

ALICE: Yes, of course.

CAPTAIN: Ring for Kristine so I can get some fresh water.

ALICE (*rings*): Imagine ... (*rings again*) She doesn't hear!

CAPTAIN: Go out and look for her ... What if she's gone too?

ALICE (*crosses and opens the door left*): What's this? Her trunk is standing in the hallway.

CAPTAIN: Then she's gone!

ALICE: This is hell! (*She bursts into tears, falls to her knees, and lays her head on a chair, sobbing.*)

CAPTAIN: Everything happens at once! And Kurt arrives to witness our troubles! If there's a humiliation left, let it come now, right now!

ALICE: Do you know what I suspect? That Kurt is never coming back!

CAPTAIN: I can believe it of him.

ALICE: Yes, we are cursed . . .

CAPTAIN: What do you mean?

ALICE: Don't you see how everyone shuns us?

CAPTAIN: I don't give a damn! (*The telegraph begins to click.*) There's the answer! Quiet, I'm listening! . . . No one has the time. Excuses, excuses . . . The rabble!

ALICE: That's what you get for despising your doctors . . . and neglecting to pay their bills!

CAPTAIN: That's not true . . .

ALICE: Even when you could pay, you didn't want to, because you look down on their work, just as you look down on my work, or anyone else's . . . They don't want to come! And the telephone has been cut off because you thought that was worthless too! Nothing is worth anything any more except your rifles and cannons.

CAPTAIN: Don't stand there chattering . . .

ALICE: All the birds have come home to roost!

CAPTAIN: Superstition . . . old wives' tales!

ALICE: You'll see! . . . Do you know that we owe Kristine six months' wages?

CAPTAIN: She's stolen that much!

ALICE: What's more, I had to borrow money from her.

CAPTAIN: I'm not surprised.

ALICE: You ingrate! I borrowed it so the children could get to town.

CAPTAIN: Well, Kurt certainly came back to roost. The scoundrel! And coward! Didn't dare say he's had enough and that it would be more fun at the Doctor's. Probably expected a bad meal here! . . . He's still the wretch he always was!

KURT (*rushes in from left*): Well, my dear Edgar! This is how it is! . . . The Doctor knows all about your heart . . .

CAPTAIN: Heart?

KURT: Yes, for a long time you've had a calcified heart . . .

CAPTAIN: Heart of stone?

KURT: And . . .

CAPTAIN: Is that serious?

KURT: Yes . . . that is to say . . .

CAPTAIN: It is serious!

KURT: Yes!

CAPTAIN: Fatal?

KURT: You must be very careful! The first thing is to get rid of those cigars! (*The* CAPTAIN *throws away his cigar.*) Next is the whiskey! . . . After that, into bed!

CAPTAIN (*afraid*): Never! Not into bed! That would be the end. I'd never get up again! I'll lie on the sofa tonight. What else did he say?

KURT: He was very friendly. He'll come at once if you call him.

CAPTAIN: He was friendly, eh, that hypocrite! I don't want to see him! . . . Is it all right for me to eat?

KURT: Not tonight. And for the next few days only milk.

CAPTAIN: Milk! I can't stand the taste!

KURT: Then you'll have to learn.

CAPTAIN: No, I'm too old to learn! (*clutching his head*) Oh! It's coming on again! (*He sits still, staring into space.*)

ALICE (*to* KURT): What did the Doctor say?

KURT: That he *could* die!

ALICE: God be praised!

KURT: Alice, be careful! Be careful! Go get a pillow and a blanket, and I'll put him to bed here on the sofa! Afterward, I'll spend the night in this chair.

ALICE: And I?

KURT: You go to bed. Your presence only makes him worse.

ALICE: You command! I'll obey, for you mean well by us both. (*exiting left*)

KURT: By you *both*, remember that! I won't take sides. (*He takes the water pitcher and exits right. The storm outside grows louder. An upstage door blows open and a shabby and disagreeable* OLD WOMAN *looks in. The* CAPTAIN *comes to, sits up, and looks around.*)

CAPTAIN: So, they've left me alone, the scoundrels! (*When he catches sight of the* OLD WOMAN, *he becomes frightened.*) Who are you? What do you want?

OLD WOMAN: I only wanted to close the door, sir.

CAPTAIN: Why? What for?

OLD WOMAN: Because it blew open just as I was passing.

CAPTAIN: You meant to steal something!

OLD WOMAN: Not much worth taking, according to Kristine.

CAPTAIN: Kristine!

OLD WOMAN: Good night, sir. Sleep well! (*She closes the door and exits.* ALICE *enters left with pillows and a blanket.*)

CAPTAIN: Who was that at the door? Was there anyone?

ALICE: Yes, old Maia from the poorhouse went by.

CAPTAIN: Are you sure?

ALICE: Are you frightened?

CAPTAIN: I, frightened? Of course not!

ALICE: Since you won't go to bed, you can lie here.

CAPTAIN (*crosses to the sofa*): I'll lie down here. (*He tries to grasp* ALICE'S *hand, but she pulls it away.* KURT *enters with a water pitcher.*) Kurt, don't leave me!

KURT: I'll stay with you through the night. Alice is going to bed.

CAPTAIN: Good night, Alice.

ALICE (*to* KURT): Good night, Kurt!

KURT: Good night. (*takes a chair and sits by the* CAPTAIN) Don't you want to take off your boots?

CAPTAIN: No! A soldier always wants to be ready!

KURT: Are you expecting a battle?

CAPTAIN: Perhaps! . . . (*raises himself*) Kurt! You're the only person I've ever confided in. Promise me one thing! . . . If I die during the night . . . look after my children!

KURT: I will.

CAPTAIN: Thank you. I trust you.

KURT: Can you explain why you trust me?

CAPTAIN: It's true we've never been friends. I don't believe in friendship. And our families were born enemies, always fighting . . .

KURT: And yet you trust me?

CAPTAIN: Yes! And I don't know why. (*silence*) Do you think I'm going to die?

KURT: You, too, just like everyone else. There'll be no exception made in your case.

CAPTAIN: Are you bitter?

KURT: Yes! . . . Are you afraid of death? The wheelbarrow and the garden plot!

CAPTAIN: What if it isn't the end?

KURT: Many people think it isn't.

CAPTAIN: And what then?

KURT: Endless surprises, I should imagine!

CAPTAIN: But we can't know for certain.

KURT: No, that's just it. That's why we have to be prepared for anything.

CAPTAIN: You're not so childish as to believe there's a hell, are you?

KURT: Don't you believe in it? You, who are in the midst of it?

CAPTAIN: Only metaphorically.

KURT: Your description of it was so real, a metaphor is out of the question. (*silence*)

CAPTAIN: If you only knew the torment I'm suffering.

KURT: Physical?

CAPTAIN: No, not physical.

KURT: Then it must be spiritual. There's no third possibility. (*pause*)

CAPTAIN (*raising himself*): I don't want to die!

KURT: A while ago you talked of annihilation.

CAPTAIN: Yes, if it's painless.

KURT: But it isn't!

CAPTAIN: Is this annihilation, then?

KURT: The beginning of it.

CAPTAIN: Good night!

KURT: Good night!

Scene 2

(*The setting is the same except that the lamp is about to go out. Through the windows and the panes of the upstage doors a cloudy sky is visible over the sea. The* SENTRY *is at his post as before. The* CAPTAIN *lies asleep on the chaise longue.* KURT *is sitting in a chair close by, pale and spent from his all-night vigil.*)

ALICE (*entering from left*): Is he asleep?

KURT: Yes, since about sunup.

ALICE: What sort of night was it?

KURT: He dozed off at times, but mostly he's been talking.

ALICE: About what?

KURT: He's been arguing about religion like a schoolboy who's solved all the riddles of the universe. Toward morning, he discovered the immortality of the soul.

ALICE: *He* discovered it!

KURT: Exactly! . . . He's really the most arrogant person I've ever met. "*I* exist, therefore there is a God."

ALICE: Now you know . . . Look at those boots. They would have trampled the earth flat if he'd had his way! They've trampled other people's fields and gardens, trampled on other people's toes and on my head! . . . The killer bear has finally been brought down!

KURT: He'd be comic if he weren't tragic. But even his pettiness has a touch of grandeur. Can't you find a single good thing to say about him?

ALICE (*sits*): Of course, as long as he doesn't hear it. One word of encouragement makes him impossibly conceited.

KURT: He can't hear anything. He's had morphine.

ALICE: Edgar came from a poor home with many brothers and sisters. Quite early he had to help support them by tutoring. His father was a good-for-nothing or worse. It's hard for a boy to have to give up youthful pleasures and slave for a pack of ungrateful children that he didn't bring into the world. The first time I saw him I was a little girl and he was a young man with no overcoat in the middle of winter . . . while his little sisters had thick wool coats . . . I thought it was wonderful and I admired him, but his ugliness repelled me. Don't you think he's uncommonly ugly?

KURT: Yes, sometimes even hideous. I noticed it most when we'd separate after a quarrel. His image in my mind would take on horrible shapes and dimensions. He'd literally haunt me.

ALICE: Imagine, then, how it was for me! . . . In any case, his early career as an officer was a martyrdom. He was helped from time to time by wealthy people, although he'll never admit it. Whatever he received he took as a tribute he was due, without a word of thanks.

KURT: We were going to speak well of him.

ALICE: After he's dead! Anyway . . . I don't remember anything else.

KURT: Only the meanness.

ALICE: Yes, but he can be kind and sensitive too . . . As an enemy he's a monster!

KURT: Why did he never make major?

ALICE: Can't you see why? Who would want him as a superior when he was already a tyrant as a subordinate? But you must never mention this! He says he never wanted to be a major . . . Did he talk about the children?

KURT: Yes, he misses Judith.

ALICE: I can believe that. Oh! Do you know what Judith is? The very image of her father, and he's trained her to spite me. Think of it, my own daughter . . . raised her hand against me!

KURT: That's terrible!

ALICE: Shhh! He's moving! . . . What if he's been listening? . . . He can be cunning that way!

KURT: He's just waking up.

ALICE: Doesn't he look like the devil himself? I'm afraid of him! (*silence*)

CAPTAIN (*Awakening, he raises up and looks around.*): It's morning! At last . . .

KURT: How do you feel now?

CAPTAIN: Bad.

KURT: Do you want the doctor?

CAPTAIN: No! . . . I want to see Judith! My child!

KURT: Wouldn't it be better to put your house in order, before, or in case something should happen?

CAPTAIN: What do you mean? What could happen?

KURT: That which happens to us all.

CAPTAIN: Oh, nonsense! You don't think I'm going to die that easily, do you? It's not time to celebrate yet, Alice.

KURT: Think of your children! Make out a will so at least your wife won't lose all the furniture.

CAPTAIN: And you want her to inherit it while I'm still alive?

KURT: No! But if something happens, she musn't be thrown out on the street! Someone who's cleaned, dusted, and polished these possessions for twenty-five years should have some right to hold onto them! Can I send for the judge advocate?

CAPTAIN: No!

KURT: You're a cruel man, crueler than I thought.

CAPTAIN: It's coming on again! (*falling back unconscious on the chaise*)

ALICE (*crosses to right*): There's someone in the kitchen. I must go.

KURT: Yes, go! There's nothing to be done here. (ALICE *exits.*)

CAPTAIN (*awakening*): Kurt, how do you intend to set up the quarantine station?

KURT: I'll manage all right.

CAPTAIN: Listen, I'm the commandant on this island. You have to deal with me, and don't you forget it!

KURT: Have you ever seen a quarantine station?

CAPTAIN: Have I? Before you were born! And I'll give you some advice: don't put the disinfecting ovens too near the shore.

KURT: I thought the point was to place them near water . . .

CAPTAIN: That shows how much you know your business. Bacilli thrive in water—it's their life-giving element.

KURT: But salt water is necessary to wash away impurities.

CAPTAIN: Idiot! . . . Anyway, when you find a place to live, send for your children.

KURT: Do you think they'll come?

CAPTAIN: Naturally, if you're any sort of man at all! It'll make a good impression on the people here to see you meet your responsibilities in this area . . .

KURT: I have always met my responsibilities in this area!

CAPTAIN (*raising his voice*): . . . in this area in which you've failed so miserably!

KURT: But I've already told you . . .

CAPTAIN (*continuing*): . . . Because people don't desert their children that way . . .

KURT: How you do go on!

CAPTAIN: As your relation, an older relation, I feel I have the right to tell you the truth, even it if is bitter . . . So, you mustn't resent it . . .

KURT: Are you hungry?

CAPTAIN: Yes, I am! . . .

KURT: Would you like something light?

CAPTAIN: No, something substantial.

KURT: That would finish you!

CAPTAIN: Isn't it enough that I'm sick? Do I have to starve too?

KURT: That's the way it is!

CAPTAIN: And no drinking or smoking. Then life isn't worth much.

KURT: Death doesn't bargain. He demands sacrifices or he comes at once.

ALICE (*enters carrying bouquets of flowers, telegrams, and letters*): These are for you! (*throws the flowers on the writing table*)

CAPTAIN (*flattered*): For me? . . . Let me see! . . .

ALICE: They're only from the noncommissioned officers, the band, and your corporals!

CAPTAIN: You're jealous!

ALICE: Oh no! If they were laurel wreaths . . . that would be something else. But you could never get them.

CAPTAIN: Hm! . . . Here's a telegram from the Colonel . . . You read it, Kurt. The Colonel is a gentleman, after all . . . even if he is a little idiot! . . . This one's from . . . what does it say? It's from Judith! . . . Please wire her to come on the next boat! . . . This one . . . yes! . . . I'm not without friends, anyway, and it's wonderful of them to think of a sick man, a man deserving beyond his rank, fearless and blameless!

ALICE: I don't understand. Are they congratulating you for being sick?

CAPTAIN: Hyena!

ALICE (*to* KURT): Do you know, we had a doctor on this island who was so hated that they held a banquet for him—after he left!

CAPTAIN: Put the flowers in vases . . . I'm not a gullible man, and people are rabble, but this simple tribute is sincere, by God . . . It can't be anything but sincere!

ALICE: Idiot!

KURT (*reading the telegram*): Judith says she can't come because the steamboat's been held up by the storm.

CAPTAIN: Is that all?

KURT: Er, no—there is a postscript.

CAPTAIN: Out with it!

KURT: Well, she begs her poppa not to drink so much.

CAPTAIN: What impudence! . . . That's children for you! My own beloved daughter . . . my Judith! My idol!

ALICE: And mirror image!

CAPTAIN: That's life for you, and its greatest blessing! Damn it to hell!

ALICE: Now you're reaping what you've sown! You turned her against her mother, now she's going against her father! Tell me there is no God!

CAPTAIN (*to* KURT): What does the Colonel say?

KURT: He's granted you a leave of absence—with no explanation.

CAPTAIN: A leave of absence? I didn't ask for that.

ALICE: But I did.

CAPTAIN: I won't accept it!

ALICE: The orders have already been cut.

CAPTAIN: I don't care!

ALICE: You see, Kurt, for this man, no laws exist, no statutes apply, no human ordinances are valid ... He's above everything and everyone! The universe was created for his personal use! The sun and moon move in order to carry his praises to the stars! That's my husband! This insignificant Captain, who couldn't even make major, whose pompousness makes him a laughingstock while he thinks he's feared. This wretch who's afraid of the dark and believes only in barometers. And what will all this add up to at the final curtain? a wheelbarrow full of manure, and not even of prime quality!

CAPTAIN (*fanning himself complacently with a bunch of flowers, not listening to* ALICE): Did you ask Kurt to breakfast?

ALICE: No.

CAPTAIN: Then prepare two really fine chateaubriand right away.

ALICE: Two?

CAPTAIN: I'm having one as well!

ALICE: But there are three of us!

CAPTAIN: You too? Well, three then.

ALICE: Where am I going to get them? Last night you invited Kurt to supper and there wasn't a crust of bread in the house. Kurt has had to keep watch all night on an empty stomach, without so much as a cup of coffee, because there isn't any, because our credit's been cut off!

CAPTAIN: She's angry at me for not dying yesterday.

ALICE: No, for not dying twenty-five years ago, for not dying before I was born!

CAPTAIN (*to* KURT): Listen to her! . . . Do you see the kind of marriage you arranged, my dear Kurt! It wasn't arranged in heaven, that's for certain! (ALICE *and* KURT *look at each other meaningfully. The* CAPTAIN *rises and crosses toward the door.*) However! I don't care what anyone says, I'm going on duty! (*He puts on an old-fashioned artillery helmet, his saber, and his cape.* ALICE *and* KURT *try to stop him, but in vain.*) Out of the way! (*leaves*)

ALICE: Yes, go! You always turn tail and run when the battle goes against you! And then you let your wife cover your retreat! The great soldier! The only thing great about you is your drinking, boasting, and lying! (*spits*)

KURT: This is the bottomless pit!

ALICE: You don't know the half of it!

KURT: What more could there be?

ALICE: I'm too ashamed to . . .

KURT: Where is he going now? And how does he find the strength?

ALICE: Yes, you may well ask! Oh, now he'll go to the noncommissioned officers to thank them for the flowers . . . And then he'll eat and drink with them and slander the other officers . . . If you knew how many times he's been threatened with dismissal! Only pity for his family has prevented it. And he thinks it's because they're afraid of him, because he's superior to them. And then he hates and slanders the poor officers' wives when they put in a good word for us!

KURT: I must confess that I applied for this job to find a little peace out by the sea . . . I knew nothing about your circumstances . . .

ALICE: Poor Kurt! . . . How will you get something to eat?

KURT: Oh, I'll go to the Doctor's, but what about you? Let me see to it for you.

ALICE: As long as he doesn't find out! He'd kill me!

KURT (*looking out through the window*): Look, he's standing out on the rampart in the storm.

ALICE: It's a pity that . . . he has to be this way.

KURT: It's a pity that both of you have to suffer like this . . . Isn't there anything that can be done?

ALICE: I don't know! . . . And there's a new pack of bills too, that he hasn't noticed yet! . . .

KURT: Sometimes not seeing things can be a blessing.

ALICE (*at the window*): Now he's opened his coat and is letting the storm blow against him. He wants to die!

KURT: I don't think so. A little while ago, when he felt his own life slipping away, he clutched onto mine, and began prying into my affairs, as if he wanted to crawl into my skin and live my life.

ALICE: That's his vampire nature . . . Because he finds his own life so totally without interest, he bleeds excitement from other people, interfering in their lives, manipulating their destinies. Whatever you do, Kurt, never let him feel part of your family, never let him get to know your friends, for he'll take them away from you and make them his own . . . He's absolutely a magician at that . . . If he gets to your children, he'll soon make them his. He'll determine how they'll be raised, and *always* against your wishes.

KURT: Alice! He was the one who took my children away from me when I separated, wasn't he?

ALICE: Since it's all in the past, yes, it was he!

KURT: I suspected it, but wasn't certain! He was the one!

ALICE: When you trusted Edgar so, that you sent him as a peacemaker to your wife, he proceeded to flirt with her and teach her how to get custody of the children!

KURT: Oh, God! . . . God in heaven!

ALICE: There you have another side of him! (*silence*)

KURT: Do you know, last night . . . when he thought he was going to die . . . he made me promise to look after his children.

ALICE: You surely don't want to find revenge through my children, do you?

KURT: By keeping my promise? Of course! I'll look after your children.

ALICE: That would be the cruelest revenge you could take, for there's nothing he despises more than generosity.

KURT: Then I could be revenged—without taking revenge.

ALICE: I love when vengeance and justice are one and the same! And I hunger to see evil punished!

KURT: You're still harping on that?

ALICE: I always will. The day I could forgive or love an enemy, I'd be a hypocrite!

KURT: Alice! Sometimes we have a duty not to say everything or see everything! It's called charity, and we all need it.

ALICE: Not me. My life is open and clear, and all my cards are always on the table.

KURT: That's saying a lot.

ALICE: No, it's not saying enough. What I've suffered blamelessly for a man I never loved ...

KURT: Then why did you marry him?

ALICE: Yes, why? ... Because he took me! Seduced me! I don't know. And then I wanted to advance myself socially ...

KURT: So you abandoned your career.

ALICE: Because people looked down on it! ... But, you know, he cheated me! He promised me a good life ... a beautiful home, and there's been nothing but debts ... The only gold was on his uniform, and even that wasn't real. He cheated me!

KURT: Wait a moment! When a young man falls in love, he's always hopeful about the future. Maybe it's his fault if the hopes aren't always realized, but we must forgive him. I have the same fault on my conscience, but I don't think I cheated anyone ... What are you looking at?

ALICE: I'm looking to see if he's fallen.

KURT: Has he fallen?

ALICE: No, unfortunately. He's still cheating me.

KURT: Well, I'm going to see the Doctor and the Governor.

ALICE (*sits by the window*): You go, Kurt dear. I'll sit here and wait. I've learned to wait.

Act II

Scene I

(*The same setting by daylight. The* SENTRY *paces, as before.* ALICE *is sitting in the armchair right. Her hair is gray.* KURT *enters from left after knocking.*)

KURT: Good morning, Alice!

ALICE: Good morning, dear! Sit down!

KURT (*sits in the armchair left*): The steamboat's arriving.

ALICE: Then I know what to expect if he's on it.

KURT: He is on it. I could see his helmet gleaming. . . . What's he been doing in town?

ALICE: I can guess. He was in full-dress uniform, so he must have gone to the Colonel's, and he had his white gloves on, so he must have paid some calls.

KURT: Did you notice how quiet he was yesterday? Since he stopped drinking, he's been a different person: calm, reserved, considerate . . .

ALICE: Yes, I felt that. The world would have been in danger long ago if that man had always stayed sober. Maybe it's a blessing that whiskey made him harmless and ridiculous.

KURT: The genie in the bottle restrained him. Have you noticed that ever since death set its mark on him he's acquired a kind of dignity or elegance. Maybe these new thoughts about immortality have given him another perspective on life.

ALICE: You're deceiving yourself. He's up to no good. And you can't believe a word he says. He's a congenital liar and master schemer . . .

KURT (*looking at* ALICE): Alice! What's this? Your hair has turned gray in two nights!

ALICE: No, my dear, it's been like that for a long time. It's just that I stopped bothering to darken it since my husband is practically dead. Twenty-five years in a fortress . . . Did you know that this was a prison at one time?

KURT: A prison! So, that's why the walls look that way!

ALICE: And my complexion! Even the children had a prison pallor in here.

KURT: It's hard for me to imagine little children prattling within these walls.

ALICE: There was seldom any prattling. And the two who died perished from the lack of light.

KURT: What is it you're expecting?

ALICE: The decisive attack against *us*! I saw a familiar flash of hate in his eye when you read him the telegram from Judith. It was meant for her, of course, but as you know, she always gets off scot free, so the hate struck you instead.

KURT: What does he want with me, do you think?

ALICE: Hard to say, but he has incredible talent or luck when it comes to ferreting out other people's secrets ... Didn't you notice all day yesterday how he seemed to be *living* in your quarantine station, how he was bleeding you for information, devouring your children ... A cannibal, you see—I know him. His own life is running out, or has run out ...

KURT: I got the same impression: that he's already on the other side. His face seems to glow in the dark, as if it were decomposing ... And his eyes blaze like marsh gas flaming over graves or swamps ... He's coming! Has it occurred to you that he might be jealous?

ALICE: No, he's too conceited for that! ... "Show me the man I need to be jealous of!" That's what he says.

KURT: So much the better. His faults have some merits, after all ... Shouldn't I at least be polite and greet him?

ALICE: Don't! He'll think you're up to something. And when he begins to lie, pretend to believe him. I have my own dictionary for translating his lies and getting at the truth ... I'm afraid something terrible is going to happen ... but, Kurt, don't lose control of yourself! ... In my long war with him, my sole advantage was that I was always sober and so kept my wits about me! ... Whiskey always did him in! ... Now we'll have to see!

(*The* CAPTAIN *enters left in full-dress uniform, with helmet, cape, and white gloves. Calm, dignified, but pale and hollow-eyed. He stumbles forward and sits right, away from* KURT *and* ALICE, *still wearing his helmet and cape. During the following, he holds the saber between his knees.*)

CAPTAIN: Good morning! ... Forgive me for sitting down like this, but I'm a little tired.

ALICE and KURT: Good morning!

ALICE: How do you feel?

CAPTAIN: Fine. Just a little tired. ...

ALICE: Any news from town?

CAPTAIN: Oh, this and that. Among other things, I went to the Doctor. He said it was nothing and that I could live another twenty years if I took care of myself.

ALICE (*to* KURT): Now he's lying! (*to the* CAPTAIN) That's good news, dear.

CAPTAIN: Yes it is. (*A silence during which the* CAPTAIN *stares at*

ALICE *and* KURT, *as if imploring them to speak*)

ALICE (*to* KURT): Don't say anything. Let him speak first, then he'll show his hand.

CAPTAIN (*to* ALICE): Did you say something?

ALICE: No, I didn't say anything.

CAPTAIN (*slowly*): Listen, Kurt . . .

ALICE (*to* KURT): You see, now it's coming!

CAPTAIN: I, I was in town, as you know. (KURT *nods assent.*) Well, uh, I made the acquaintance . . . among others . . . with a young cadet —— (*hesitating*) —— in the artillery! (*pause, during which* KURT *looks uneasy*) Since . . . we're short of cadets on the island, I arranged with the Colonel for him to come here . . . It should please you, you especially, when I tell you that it . . . was . . . your own son!

ALICE (*to* KURT): There's the vampire!

KURT: Most fathers would be pleased by such news, but, under the circumstances, for me it's only painful.

CAPTAIN: I don't understand.

KURT: You don't need to, it's enough that I don't want it.

CAPTAIN: So, that's how you feel! . . . Then you should know that the young man has been ordered to report here, under my command!

KURT: Then I'll force him to ask for a transfer to another regiment.

CAPTAIN: You can't do that because you have no rights over your son.

KURT: I don't?

CAPTAIN: No, the court granted them to his mother.

KURT: Then I'll get in touch with his mother.

CAPTAIN: It's not necessary.

KURT: Not necessary?

CAPTAIN: No, I've already done it! Yep! (KURT *starts to rise, but slumps back.*)

ALICE (*to* KURT): Now he must die!

KURT: He *is* a cannibal!

CAPTAIN: So much for *that*! (*quickly*) Did either of you say something?

ALICE: No, are you having trouble hearing?

CAPTAIN: Yes, a bit!...But if you'll come closer, I'll tell you something privately.

ALICE: It's not necessary. Besides, a witness can be an advantage to both sides.

CAPTAIN: You're right there. It's always good to have witnesses... But first, have you got the will ready?

ALICE *(handing him a document)*: The judge advocate himself drew it up!

CAPTAIN: In your favor!...Good!...(*he reads the document and then carefully tears it into strips, which he throws on the floor.*) So much for that! Yep!

ALICE *(to* KURT): Have you ever seen such a man?

KURT: He's not a man!

CAPTAIN: I've something to tell you, Alice!...

ALICE *(uneasy)*: Go right ahead!

CAPTAIN *(calmly, as before)*: Because of your long expressed desire to put an end to the misery suffered in this unhappy marriage, and because of the lack of love shown to your husband and children, and because of the negligence with which you've handled the family finances, I filed in court, during my trip to town, a petition of divorce!

ALICE: Ohh? And the grounds?

CAPTAIN *(calmly, as before)*: In addition to the grounds already named, I have purely personal ones. Since it's been established that I may live another twenty years, I have been considering replacing this unfortunate union with a more suitable one. I intend to unite my destiny with that of a woman who, with devotion for her husband, can bring to this home youth and...maybe even...a little beauty!

ALICE *(taking off her ring and throwing it at the* CAPTAIN): There you are!

CAPTAIN *(picking up the ring and putting it in his vest pocket)*: She throws away her wedding ring. Will the witness kindly note that?

ALICE *(rising indignantly)*: And you intend to throw me out and bring another woman into my house?

CAPTAIN: Yep!

ALICE: Then it's time for the whole truth to be out...Kurt, my cousin, this man is guilty of attempting to murder his wife!

KURT: Murder?

ALICE: Yes, he pushed me into the sea!

CAPTAIN: Where are the witnesses?

ALICE: Judith was there!

CAPTAIN: So what?

ALICE: She can testify!

CAPTAIN: No, she can't. She said she didn't see anything.

ALICE: You've taught her to lie!

CAPTAIN: I didn't have to. You'd already taught her.

ALICE: Did you see Judith?

CAPTAIN: Yep!

ALICE: Oh, God! Oh, God!

CAPTAIN: The fortress has been taken! The enemy is granted ten minutes to evacuate under safe-conduct. (*puts his watch on the table*) Ten minutes, by my watch! (*suddenly clutches his heart*)

ALICE (*crosses and grasps the* CAPTAIN's *arm*): What is it?

CAPTAIN: I don't know!

ALICE: Do you want something, something to drink?

CAPTAIN: Whiskey? No thanks, Alice, I don't want to die! . . . (*straightens up*) Don't touch me! . . . Ten minutes, or the garrison will be cut down! (*draws his saber*) Ten minutes! (*exits upstage*)

KURT: Who is this man?

ALICE: He's a demon, not a man!

KURT: What does he want with my son?

ALICE: He wants him as hostage so he can get you in his power. He wants to isolate you from the island's authorities . . . Do you know that the natives here call the island "Little Hell"?

KURT: I didn't know that . . . Alice, you're the first woman who's aroused my pity. All the others I thought deserved their fate.

ALICE: Don't desert me now! Don't leave me! He beats me . . . He's beaten me for twenty-five years . . . and in the presence of the children . . . he pushed me into the sea . . .

KURT: Hearing that was the last straw for me. I came here without any bitterness, forgetting how he used to slander and humiliate me. I forgave him even when you told me it was he who separated me from my children . . . because he was sick and dying . . . But wanting to take my son, for that he must die, he—or I!

ALICE: Good! We won't surrender the fortress! Rather blow it up and him with it, even if it means us too! I'll see to the gunpowder!

KURT: I wasn't angry when I came here, and I thought of fleeing when I felt your hate infecting me. Now I feel an irresistible calling to hate this man as I've hated evil itself . . . What can we do?

ALICE: He taught me the strategy. Round up his enemies and look for allies.

KURT: Imagine—he's managed to track down my wife. Why couldn't those two have met a generation ago? That collision would have made the earth tremble!

ALICE: But now that they've met . . . they must be parted! I know where he's vulnerable, I've long suspected it . . .

KURT: Who's his worst enemy on the island?

ALICE: The Ordnance Officer.

KURT: Can he be trusted?

ALICE: Yes, he can! . . . And he knows what I . . . yes, I know it too! . . . He knows what the Sergeant Major and the Captain have been up to!

KURT: Been up to? What do you mean?

ALICE: Embezzlement!

KURT: That's disgusting! No, I won't have anything to do with that!

ALICE: Ha! Can't you strike back at an enemy?

KURT: I could once, but not any more.

ALICE: Why not?

KURT: Because I discovered that . . . sooner or later justice is done.

ALICE: But why wait for it? Your son is being taken away from you. And my hair is getting grayer . . . feel how thick it is . . . If he remarries, I'll be free—to do the same! . . . I'll be free! And ten minutes later he'll be sitting down below here, under arrest, down below ———— (*stamps on the floor*) ———— down below . . . and I'll dance over his head, I'll dance the "Entry of the Boyars" . . . (*takes several dance steps, her hands on her hips*) . . . Ha ha ha ha! And I'll play the piano loud enough for him to hear it! (*hammers on the piano*) Oh! The tower will open its portals and the sentry with his saber drawn will no longer guard me, but *him* . . . Meli-tam-tam-ta meli-ta-lia-lay! Guard him, him him!

KURT (*watching her, fascinated*): Alice! Are you a devil too?

ALICE (*jumps up on a chair and takes down the laurel wreaths*): These I'll take with me when we march off ... laurels for the moment of triumph! And fluttering ribbons! A bit dusty, but eternally green—like my youth! ... I'm not old, Kurt!

KURT (*his eyes shining*): You are a devil!

ALICE: In Little Hell! ... Look, I'm getting ready ... (*lets down her hair*) ... in two minutes I'll be dressed ... in another two minutes we'll be at the Ordnance Officer's ... and then the fortress will go sky high!

KURT (*as before*): You are a devil!

ALICE: You said that all the time when we were children too! Do you remember when we were children and pretended we were engaged? Ha ha! You were shy, of course ...

KURT (*in earnest*): Alice!

ALICE: Yes, you were! And it was becoming. You see, there are coarse women who like shy men. And they say ... there are shy men who like coarse women! ... You did like me then, a little, didn't you?

KURT: I don't know where I am!

ALICE: With an actress who doesn't feel bound by any rules, though she's still a fine woman! Yes! I'm free, free, free! ... Turn away while I change my blouse! (*She unbuttons her blouse.* KURT *rushes to her, takes her in his arms, lifts her high in the air, and bites her on the neck until she screams. Then he throws her aside on to the chaise longue and dashes out left.*)

Scene 2

(*The same setting in the evening. The* SENTRY *is still visible through the upstage doors. The laurel wreaths are hanging on the arm of a chair. The ceiling lamp is lit. Soft music.*

The CAPTAIN, *pale and hollow-eyed, grizzled, dressed in a worn fatigue uniform with riding boots, is sitting at the writing table, playing solitaire. He has his glasses on.*

The intermission music continues after the curtain goes up, until the next character enters.

The CAPTAIN *lays out his cards, but now and then gives a start and looks up anxiously, listening.*

He seems unable to get all the cards out, becomes impatient, and sweeps them together. Then he goes to the window left, opens it, and throws the cards out. The window remains open, shaking on its hinges.

He crosses to the sideboard. The noise made by the window so alarms him that he turns to see what it is. He takes out three dark, square whiskey bottles, examines them carefully—and throws them out the window. He takes out cigar boxes, smells inside one of them, and throws them out the window.

He takes off his glasses, wipes them, and tests to see how he can see through them. Then he throws them out the window, stumbles among the furniture, as if having difficulty seeing properly, and lights a six-candled candelabra on the bureau desk. Catching sight of the laurel wreaths, he picks them up and starts toward the window, then stops. He takes a cloth from the piano and carefully wraps the wreaths in it, fastening the corners with pins from the writing table. He then places the bundle on a chair. He crosses to the piano, bangs on the keys with his fists, closes and locks the lid, and throws the key through the window. Then he lights the candles on the piano. He crosses to the whatnot, picks up his wife's picture, looks at it, and tears it up, throwing the pieces on the floor. The window shakes on its hinges, and he becomes alarmed again. After calming down, he takes the pictures of his son and daughter, gives them a fleeting kiss, and puts them in his breast pocket. He sweeps the remaining pictures away with his elbow and kicks them into a pile with his boot.

Tired, he sits at the writing table and clutches at his heart. He lights the candle on the table and sighs. He stares into space as though he saw terrible visions . . . He rises, crosses to the bureau desk, folds the lid down, takes out a bundle of letters tied with blue silk ribbon, and throws it into the stove. He closes the bureau desk. The telegraph clicks once and is silent. Scared to death, the CAPTAIN *shrinks back, standing still, listening, his hand on his heart. When he hears nothing more from the telegraph, he listens toward the door left. He crosses to it, opens it, takes a step inside, and emerges with a cat on his arm; he strokes its back. Then he exits right. The music stops.*

ALICE *enters upstage, dressed for walking. Her hair is black and she is wearing a hat and gloves. She is surprised when she sees all the candles lit.* KURT *enters left, nervously.*)

ALICE: It looks like Christmas Eve in here.

KURT: Well?

ALICE (*holds out her hand for him to kiss*): Thank me! (*He kisses her hand reluctantly.*) Six witnesses, four of them as good as gold. The charges have been filed, and the reply will come here by telegraph—here in the heart of the fortress!

KURT: I see.

ALICE: Say "thank you" instead of "I see"!

KURT: Why has he lit so many candles?

ALICE: Because he's afraid of the dark, of course! Look at the telegraph. Doesn't the key look like the handle of a coffee mill? . . . I grind and grind and the beans crunch like the sound of teeth being pulled . . .

KURT: What has he done to the room?

ALICE: It looks as though he planned to move. Down below—that's where he'll move!

KURT: Don't talk like that, Alice! It's awful . . . He was my friend when we were young, and he was often kind to me when I needed help . . . I feel sorry for him.

ALICE: More than for me—who did nothing wrong and had to sacrifice a career for that monster?

KURT: What about that career—was it really so brilliant?

ALICE (*furious*): What are you saying? Do you know who I am, what I was?

KURT: All right, all right!

ALICE: Are you starting too, already?

KURT: Already? (ALICE *flings her arms around his neck and kisses him.* KURT *grabs her by the arms and bites her neck until she screams.*)

ALICE: You're biting me!

KURT (*beside himself*): Yes, I want to bite your throat and suck your blood like a lynx! You've aroused animal feelings in me that I've tried for years to suppress and deny. I came here think-

ing I was a bit better than you two, and now I am the vilest of
us all! With lust distorting my vision, I saw you in all your terrible nakedness! Now I know the full power of evil. It makes ugliness seem beautiful and goodness seem ugly and weak ...
Come, let me choke you ... with a kiss! (*He embraces her.*)

ALICE (*showing her left hand*): Do you see the mark of the shackle
you severed? I was a slave, and now I'm freed! ...

KURT: But I shall bind you!

ALICE: You?

KURT: I!

ALICE: I thought for awhile that you might be ...

KURT: Religious?

ALICE: Yes, with all that talk about the Fall ...

KURT: Is that so?

ALICE: I thought you'd come to preach ...

KURT: You did, eh? ... In an hour we'll be in town. Then you'll
see who I am ...

ALICE: Then we'll go to the theatre tonight, and be sure to be
seen. You understand, don't you, that if I run away, the shame
will be his?

KURT: I'm beginning to understand. It's not enough, putting him
in prison ...

ALICE: No, it's not enough! He has to know shame too!

KURT: A strange world! You act shamefully and he's the one who's
shamed.

ALICE: Since the world is so stupid!

KURT: It's as if these prison walls had soaked up all the evil, and
we have only to breathe to take it in! You're thinking about the
theatre and dinner, I suppose. I'm thinking about my son!

ALICE (*strikes him on the mouth with her glove*): What a prude!
(KURT *raises his hand to slap her face.* ALICE *shrinks back.*) *Tout
beau!*

KURT: Forgive me!

ALICE: On your knees, then! (*He drops to his knees.*) On your face!
(*His forehead touches the floor.*) Kiss my foot! (*He kisses her
foot.*) And never try that again! ... Get up!

KURT (*rising*): Where have I come to? Where am I?

ALICE: You know where!

KURT (*looking around in terror*): I almost think I'm ...

CAPTAIN (*enters right, leaning on a walking stick and looking miserable*): Can I speak with Kurt? Alone!

ALICE: Is it about the safe-conduct?

CAPTAIN (*sits at the sewing table*): Kurt, will you please sit with me a while? And Alice, will you give us a few minutes' . . . peace?

ALICE: What's all this now? . . . New signals! (*to* KURT) You can sit down. (KURT *sits reluctantly.*) And listen to the words of age and wisdom . . . If a telegram comes . . . call me! (*exits left*)

CAPTAIN (*with dignity, after a pause*): Have you understood a fate like mine, like ours?

KURT: No more than I've understood my own.

CAPTAIN: Do you see any purpose in this chaos?

KURT: In my better moments I believed that the purpose was that we should bend and submit without understanding why . . .

CAPTAIN: Bend and submit! Without a fixed point outside myself, I can't bend.

KURT: That's absolutely correct! But as a mathematician you know that having certain given points you can find the unknown point . . .

CAPTAIN: I've looked for it, but—I haven't found it.

KURT: Your calculations were wrong. Begin again.

CAPTAIN: I will begin again! . . . Tell me, where have you learned your resignation?

KURT: I have none left. Don't overestimate me.

CAPTAIN: Maybe you noticed that my approach to life has been to forget what's past: cross it out and go on! Early in life I made myself a sack in which to stuff all humiliations, and when it was full, I threw it in the sea! ———— I don't think any human being has suffered as many humiliations as I have. But when I crossed them out and went on, they ceased to exist!

KURT: I have noticed how you transform the world into a figment of your imagination.

CAPTAIN: How could I survive otherwise? How would I have been able to stand it? (*clutches at his heart*)

KURT: How are you feeling?

CAPTAIN: Bad! (*pause*) There comes a moment when the ability to create figments, as you call them, is gone. Then reality stands revealed in all its nakedness! . . . It's terrible! (*Now he speaks like an old man, with a tearfulness in his voice, and his jaw drooping.*) You see, my dear friend . . . (*controls himself and speaks in a normal voice*) I'm sorry! . . . When I was in town just now and saw the Doctor ——— (*tearful again*) ——— he said that I was finished . . . ——— (*in a normal voice*) ——— and that I couldn't live much longer!

KURT: He said *that?*

CAPTAIN: Yes, that's what he said.

KURT: Then it wasn't true?

CAPTAIN: Which? Oh, . . . no, it wasn't true. (*pause*)

KURT: And the other thing wasn't true either, was it?

CAPTAIN: What do you mean?

KURT: That my son was to report here as a cadet.

CAPTAIN: There's been no talk of that.

KURT: Your ability to cross out your own evildoing is incredible.

CAPTAIN: Kurt, my friend, I don't understand what you're saying.

KURT: Then you are finished.

CAPTAIN: Yes, there's not much left.

KURT: Maybe you haven't filed for divorce either?

CAPTAIN: Divorce! No, I never did that.

KURT (*rising*): Will you admit you lied then?

CAPTAIN: Those are strong words from a friend. We all need to be charitable.

KURT: So you've realized that?

CAPTAIN (*in a clear, determined voice*): Yes, I've realized that! . . . That's why I want you to forgive me, Kurt! Forgive everything!

KURT: Now you're talking like a man! ——— But I have nothing to forgive you for. And I'm not the man you think I am, not any more. Least of all someone worthy to accept your confessions!

CAPTAIN (*in a clear voice*): Life was always so strange! So contrary, so mean, right from childhood . . . and people so mean that I became mean too . . . (KURT *paces uneasily and stares at the telegraph.*) What are you looking at?

KURT: Can the telegraph be turned off?

CAPTAIN: No, not easily.

KURT (*increasingly uneasy*): What sort of man is Sergeant Major Oestberg?

CAPTAIN: He's honest enough. Of course, he does a little business on the side.

KURT: And the Ordnance Officer?

CAPTAIN: He's my enemy, definitely, but I can't say anything bad about him.

KURT (*stares through the window at a lantern moving in the distance*): What are they doing with a lantern out on the battery?

CAPTAIN: Is there a lantern?

KURT: Yes, and a group of people.

CAPTAIN: It's probably a special detail.

KURT: What for?

CAPTAIN: It's a corporal and some enlisted men. Some poor devil is going to be arrested.

KURT: Oh! (*pause*)

CAPTAIN: Now that you know Alice, what do you think of her?

KURT: I can't say . . . I don't understand people at all! She's as inexplicable to me as you are or I myself. I'm starting to reach that age, you see, when wisdom forces me to admit that I know nothing and understand nothing! ———— When I see something happen, though, I'm curious to know the reason . . . Why did you push her in the sea?

CAPTAIN: I don't know. She was standing on a pier, and it seemed like the natural thing to do.

KURT: Have you never regretted it?

CAPTAIN: Never.

KURT: That's strange.

CAPTAIN: Yes, of course it is. So strange, that I can't believe I did such an awful thing.

KURT: Hasn't it occurred to you that she might seek revenge?

CAPTAIN: Oh, she's had plenty, and I find that just as natural.

KURT: How have you managed so quickly to become so cynically resigned?

CAPTAIN: Ever since I stared death in the eye, I've seen life in a different light . . . Kurt, if you had to judge between Alice and myself, which would you say was in the right?

KURT: Neither! But I pity you both profoundly, perhaps you a little more than her.

CAPTAIN: Give me your hand, Kurt!

KURT (*holds out one hand and puts the other on the* CAPTAIN's *shoulder*): Old friend!

ALICE (*entering from left, carrying a parasol*): My, how intimate!

That's friendship! ... Hasn't the telegram come yet?

KURT (*coolly*): No.

ALICE: This waiting makes me impatient, and when I get impatient, I like to hurry things along! ... Watch, Kurt, while I deliver the coup de grace! This will bring him down! First, I load— I'm familiar with the rifle manual, you see, the famous rifle manual that didn't sell five thousand copies—and now I aim, and fire! (*She aims the parasol.*) How is your new wife? The young, beautiful, secret one. You don't know! But I know how my lover is! (*She puts her arms around* KURT's *neck and kisses him. He pushes her away.*) He's fine, but still shy! ... You poor wretch, whom I never loved! You were too conceited to be jealous, and you never noticed how I led you by the nose! (*The* CAPTAIN *draws his saber and stumbles toward her, slashing away, but succeeds only in hitting the furniture.*) Help! Help! (KURT *stands motionless.*)

CAPTAIN (*falling, his saber in his hand*): Judith! Avenge me!

ALICE: Hurrah! He's dead! (KURT *moves toward the upstage door.*)

CAPTAIN (*rising*): Not yet! (*He sheathes his saber and crosses to sit in the armchair by the sewing table.*) Judith! Judith!

ALICE (*crosses to* KURT): Now I'm going—with you!

KURT (*shoves her from him so she falls to her knees*): Back to the abyss, where you came from! ——— Good-bye forever! (*starts out*)

CAPTAIN: Don't leave me, Kurt, she'll kill me!

ALICE: Kurt! Don't desert me, don't desert me!

KURT: Good-bye! (*exits*)

ALICE (*in a completely altered tone*): What a wretch! That's a friend for you!

CAPTAIN (*gently*): Forgive me, Alice! Come here! Come quickly!

ALICE (*crossing to him*): He's the worst wretch and hypocrite I ever met! ——— You're a man, whatever else you are!

CAPTAIN: Alice, listen! ... I haven't long to live!

ALICE: What?

CAPTAIN: That's what the Doctor said!

ALICE: Then you were lying about everything!

CAPTAIN: Yes!

ALICE (*beside herself*): Oh God! What have I done? ...

CAPTAIN: There's no damage done.

ALICE: Oh yes, there is!

CAPTAIN: No damage is done as long as you cross it out and go on!

ALICE: But the telegram! The telegram!

CAPTAIN: What telegram?

ALICE (*on her knees beside him*): Are we damned? Must this be? I've destroyed myself, destroyed us both? Oh, why did you lie? And why did this man have to come and tempt me? . . . We're lost! Everything would have been all right! You, with your generous nature, would have forgiven everything.

CAPTAIN: What is it that can't be forgiven? What have I not forgiven you?

ALICE: You're right . . . but there's no remedy for this!

CAPTAIN: I can't imagine what it could be, though I know how inventive you are when it comes to meanness . . .

ALICE: Oh, if I could undo it! If I could just undo it, I would take care of you . . . Edgar, I would love you!

CAPTAIN: Listen to her! I can't believe my ears!

ALICE: Is there no one who can help us? No! No human being can!

CAPTAIN: Who else then?

ALICE (*looking him in the eye*): I don't know . . . Oh! What will the children do with their name disgraced? . . .

CAPTAIN: Have you disgraced our name?

ALICE: Not I! Not I! . . . They'll have to leave school! And when they come out in the world, they'll be alone, as we are, and as mean! —————— Am I right in assuming that you didn't see Judith either?

CAPTAIN: Yes. But cross it out! (*The telegraph begins to click.* ALICE *jumps up.*)

ALICE (*shrieking*): Now we're done for! (*to the* CAPTAIN) Don't listen to it!

CAPTAIN (*calmly*): I won't listen to it, my dear child! Calm down! . . .

ALICE (*stands near the telegraph and rises on her toes to look out the window*): Don't listen! Don't listen!

CAPTAIN (*covering his ears*): I'm covering my ears, Lissa, my child!

ALICE (*on her knees, her arms outstretched*): God, help us! —————— They're coming, the special detail is coming . . . (*weeps*) God in heaven! (*She moves her lips as if praying silently. The telegraph continues clicking a while longer, and then is silent. A long strip of paper has appeared.* ALICE *rises, tears off the strip, and reads it silently. Then she raises her eyes to heaven, crosses to the* CAPTAIN, *and kisses him on the forehead.*) It's over, we're safe! —— It was nothing! (*She sits in the other chair and weeps violently into her handkerchief.*)

CAPTAIN: What secrets have you got there?

ALICE: Don't ask me! It's over now!

CAPTAIN: As you wish, my child.

ALICE: You wouldn't have spoken like that three days ago. Why now?

CAPTAIN: Well, dear, when I fell the first time, I had a glimpse of the other side of the grave. I've forgotten what I saw, but an impression remains.

ALICE: Of what?

CAPTAIN: Hope—of something better.

ALICE: Something better?

CAPTAIN: Yes, I've never really believed that this was life itself . . . This is death! Or something even worse . . .

ALICE: But what of us? . . .

CAPTAIN: Our purpose was to torment each other . . . so it seems.

ALICE: And have we tormented each other enough?

CAPTAIN: Yes, I think so! And look at the mess we made! (*looks around*) Shall we clean it up? And put things right?

ALICE (*rising*): Yes, if it's possible.

CAPTAIN (*looking around the room*): It'll take more than a day! That's for sure.

ALICE: Two days then! A week!

CAPTAIN: Let's hope we can! . . . (*pause; he sits down again.*) Well, you didn't get away this time, did you? And you didn't get me locked up either. (ALICE *is dumbfounded.*) Yes, I know you wanted to have me put in prison, but I'm crossing it out! . . . You've done worse things than that before . . . (ALICE *has no answer.*) And I was innocent of embezzlement!

ALICE: And now, I suppose, I have to be your nurse?

CAPTAIN: If you wish.

ALICE: What else can I do?

CAPTAIN: I don't know.

ALICE (*sits, listless and forlorn*): These must be the everlasting fires! Is there no end?

CAPTAIN: Yes, if we have patience. Perhaps when death comes, life begins.

ALICE: If only that were true! (*pause*)

CAPTAIN: You think Kurt was a hypocrite, don't you?

ALICE: Of course I do!

CAPTAIN: I don't. But everyone who comes close to us becomes evil, and goes his way ... Kurt was weak, and evil is strong! (*pause*) Think how banal life is nowadays! In the old days, we fought. Now we just shake our fists! ——— I'm ready to bet that in three months we'll be celebrating our silver wedding anniversary ... with Kurt as best man ... and the Doctor and Gerda will come ... The Quartermaster will propose the toast, and the Sergeant Major will lead the cheering! If I know the Colonel, he'll invite himself! ——— Yes, you laugh! Do you remember Adolf's silver anniversary ... the fellow in the infantry? His wife had to wear her wedding ring on her right hand because in a tender moment he'd hacked off her left ring finger with a machete. (ALICE *holds a handkerchief in front of her mouth to keep from laughing.*) Are you crying? ——— No, I believe you're laughing! ——— Yes, child, that's what it's been for us, part tears and part laughter! Don't ask me which is more appropriate! ... The other day I read in the paper that a man who'd been divorced seven times—and so of course married seven times—finally, at the age of ninety-eight, ran off with his first wife and remarried her! That's love! ... I've never been clever enough to know whether to take life seriously. It can be its most painful when it's a joke, and its most pleasant and tranquil when it's serious ... And then, when you finally do take it seriously, someone comes along and makes a fool of you! Kurt, for example! ... Well, shall we have an anniversary party? (ALICE *is silent.*) Say yes, come on! ——— They'll laugh at us, but so what? We'll laugh too, or be serious, whatever we feel like!

ALICE: Sure, why not!

CAPTAIN (*seriously*): A silver anniversary it'll be! ... (*rises*) Cross it out and go on! ——— That's it! We'll go on!

The Dance of Death

PART II

Characters

EDGAR
ALICE
KURT
ALLAN, *Kurt's son*
JUDITH, *Edgar's daughter*
THE LIEUTENANT

(*An oval drawing room in white and gold. The upstage wall is broken by glass doors, which stand open and reveal a garden terrace outside with a balustrade of stone pillars and bluish-white faïence pots of petunias and scarlet geraniums. The terrace is a public promenade. In the background the shore battery is visible with an artilleryman on guard. In the distance the open sea. To the left in the drawing room a gilded sofa with table and chairs. To the right a grand piano, a writing table, and a fireplace. Downstage an American easy chair. Beside the writing table is a small table with a copper lamp attached on a standard. On the walls several old oil paintings.*)

Act I
Scene I

(ALLAN *is sitting at the writing table working on mathematical problems.* JUDITH *enters upstage, wearing a short summer dress; her hair is in a braid down her back. She has a hat in one hand, a tennis racket in the other. She stops in the doorway.* ALLAN *rises, serious and respectful.*)

JUDITH (*serious but friendly*): Why didn't you come to play tennis?

ALLAN (*shy, struggling with his emotions*): I'm too busy . . .

JUDITH: Didn't you see that I put my bicycle facing *toward* the oak and not *away* from it?

ALLAN: Yes, I saw that.

JUDITH: And what does that mean?

ALLAN: It means . . . that you want me to come and play tennis with you . . . but my duties . . . I have problems to solve . . . and your father is a very strict teacher . . .

JUDITH: Do you like him?

ALLAN: Yes, I do. He takes an interest in all his students . . .

JUDITH: He takes an interest in everyone and everything. —— Do you want to come?

ALLAN: You know I want to—but I'd better not.

JUDITH: I'll ask Poppa to give you permission.

ALLAN: Don't do that! It'll just start talk.

JUDITH: Don't you think I can manage him? He wants what I want.

ALLAN: That's because you're so hard—yes!

JUDITH: You should be too.

ALLAN: I don't belong to the wolf family.

JUDITH: Then you'd rather be a sheep?

ALLAN: Yes!

JUDITH: Tell me why you won't come and play tennis.

ALLAN: Oh, you know . . .

JUDITH: Tell me anyway . . . It's the Lieutenant . . .

ALLAN: You don't care a bit about me. You just want me there when you're with the Lieutenant because it's no fun for you unless you can watch me being tortured!

JUDITH: Am I so cruel? I didn't know that.

ALLAN: Now you know.

JUDITH: Then I'll improve, because I don't want to be cruel, I don't want to be a bad person ... in your eyes.

ALLAN: You're only saying that so you'll get me to do what you want. I'm already your slave, but you're not satisfied with that. The slave has to be tortured and thrown to the wild beasts! ... You already have *him* in your claws; what do you want with me? Let me go my way, and you go yours!

JUDITH: Are you sending me away? (ALLAN *does not answer.*) Then I'll go. ——— As cousins we do have to see each other now and then, but I won't bother you. (Allan *sits at the table and returns to his mathematics. Instead of leaving,* JUDITH *comes further into the room, slowly approaching the table where* ALLAN *is sitting.*) Don't be afraid, I'm going soon ... I just want to see how the Quarantine Master lives ... (*looks around*) White and gold! ——— A grand piano, a Bechstein! ——— Well! ——— And since Poppa retired, we're still in the fortress tower ... the tower where Momma has been for twenty-five years ... and even that means accepting charity. You, you're rich ...

ALLAN (*calmly*): We're not rich.

JUDITH: You say that, but you're always so well-dressed—for that matter, whatever you wear becomes you ... Do you hear what I'm saying? (*comes closer*)

ALLAN (*submissively*): I hear.

JUDITH: How can you hear, when you're busy staring at your mathematics, or whatever it is you're doing?

ALLAN: I don't hear with my eyes!

JUDITH: Your eyes, yes! ... Have you ever looked at them in a mirror? ...

ALLAN: Will you go?

JUDITH: You despise me, I know ...

ALLAN: Listen, I'm not even thinking about you.

JUDITH (*coming closer*): Archimedes, sits and calculates, while the soldier comes up and runs him through! (*stirs his papers with her racquet*)

ALLAN: Don't touch my papers!

JUDITH: That's what Archimedes said too ... Now you're imagining things, of course. You think I can't live without you ...

ALLAN: Why can't you leave me in peace!

JUDITH: If you're polite, I'll help you with your exam.

ALLAN: You?

JUDITH: Yes, I know the examiners ...

ALLAN (*sternly*): So?

JUDITH: Don't you know that it pays to be friendly with your teachers?

ALLAN: You mean your father and the Lieutenant?

JUDITH: And the Colonel!

ALLAN: And you mean that with your protection I wouldn't have to work so hard?

JUDITH: You're a bad translator!

ALLAN: Of a bad original!

JUDITH: Aren't you ashamed?

ALLAN: Yes I am—of you and me! ——— I'm ashamed that I listened to you ... Why don't you leave?

JUDITH: Because I know you appreciate my company. ———- Why else do you always manage to pass by under my window? And whenever you go to town on errands, it's always on the same boat I'm on. And you can't go out sailing unless I crew for you.

ALLAN (*shyly*): A young girl shouldn't talk like that!

JUDITH: Do you mean I'm a child?

ALLAN: Sometimes you're a good child, sometimes an evil woman. And I've been chosen to be your sheep, it seems.

JUDITH: You are a sheep, but I'll protect you.

ALLAN (*rising*): Wolves always make bad shepherds! ... The truth is you want to devour me ... You want to pawn your beautiful eyes in order to redeem my head.

JUDITH: Oh, so you've noticed my eyes. I didn't think you were that bold! (ALLAN *gathers his papers and starts out right.* JUDITH *blocks the doorway.*)

ALLAN: Get out of my way, or ...

JUDITH: Or what?

ALLAN: If you were a boy, I'd ... But you're a girl!

JUDITH: And so?

ALLAN: If you had a spark of pride, you'd have left! Consider your-self thrown out!

JUDITH: I'll get even with you for that!

ALLAN: I'm sure you will!

JUDITH (*furious, crosses upstage*): I'll—get—even—with—you—for—that! (*exits*)

KURT (*enters from left*): Where are you going, Allan?

ALLAN: Oh, it's you.

KURT: Who was that leaving so stormily . . . that the bushes shook?

ALLAN: It was Judith.

KURT: Yes, she is a bit stormy, but she's a fine girl.

ALLAN: Whenever a girl is coarse and mean, people say she's a fine girl!

KURT: You mustn't be so hard on her, Allan! . . . Don't you like your new relatives?

ALLAN: I like Uncle Edgar . . .

KURT: Yes, he has many good qualities . . . but more than your other teachers? The Lieutenant, for example?

ALLAN: He's so unpredictable! Sometimes I think he has a grudge against me.

KURT: Oh, no! . . . You "think" too much about other people. Don't brood. You do your work the best you can and let others do theirs.

ALLAN: I do, but . . . they won't leave me in peace! They drag a person into things . . . just like those squid down by the pier . . . They don't bite, but they stir up a whirlpool that sucks you under . . .

KURT (*kindly*): What I think is that you tend to look on the gloomy side. Don't you like it here with me? Is there something you miss?

ALLAN: I've never had it so good, but . . . but there's something here that's suffocating me.

KURT: Here, by the sea? Don't you like the sea?

ALLAN: Yes, the open sea! But along the shore you get tangled in seaweed and squid or stung by jellyfish!

KURT: You stay indoors too much. Go out and play tennis!

ALLAN: It doesn't interest me.

KURT: You're angry at Judith, that's what it is.

ALLAN: Judith?

KURT: You're too critical about other people. You mustn't be that way, or you'll end up all alone.

ALLAN: I'm not critical . . . it's just . . . I feel as if I'm at the bottom of a woodpile . . . and have to wait my turn to join in the fire . . . and everything above me presses and presses down . . .

KURT: Wait, your turn will come! The woodpile gets smaller . . .

ALLAN: Yes, but slowly, so slowly! . . . Oh! And meanwhile I lie there getting moldy.

KURT: It's no fun to be young. And yet people envy you.

ALLAN: They do? Would you change places with me?

KURT: No, thanks!

ALLAN: Do you know what the worst thing is? To have to sit and keep quiet when older people talk nonsense . . . I'm certain I know more about some things than they do . . . and yet I must keep quiet. Oh, excuse me, I don't include you among the older people.

KURT: Why not?

ALLAN: Maybe because we really didn't get to know each other until now . . .

KURT: And because . . . you had a different impression of me before?

ALLAN: Yes.

KURT: I suppose that during the years we were apart you didn't always think kindly of me?

ALLAN: No.

KURT: Did you ever see a picture of me?

ALLAN: Only one, and it was very unflattering.

KURT: And old?

ALLAN: Yes.

KURT: Ten years ago I turned gray overnight . . . Later, it changed back by itself . . . Let's talk about something else. Oh, here's your aunt. What do you think of her?

ALLAN: I'd rather not say.

KURT: Then I won't ask. (ALICE *enters wearing a light-colored summer walking dress and carrying a parasol.*)

ALICE: Good morning, Kurt. (*She glances to indicate that* ALLAN *should leave.*)

KURT (*to* ALLAN): Would you mind leaving, Allan? (ALLAN *exits right.* ALICE *sits to the left on the sofa.* KURT *sits in a nearby chair.*)

ALICE (*ill at ease*): He's coming right behind me, so you needn't be embarrassed.

KURT: Why should I be?

ALICE: With your strict principles . . .

KURT: When it concerns me, yes.

ALICE: Yes . . . well . . . I forgot myself once, when I saw you as my liberator, but you kept your presence of mind . . . and so we have a right to forget—what never was.

KURT: Then forget it.

ALICE: However . . . I don't think *he's* forgotten . . .

KURT: You mean the night he had a heart attack . . . and you re-joiced too soon, thinking he was dead?

ALICE: Yes ! . . . But after he recovered and stopped drinking, he learned to keep his mouth shut, and now he's impossible. He's up to something that I don't understand . . .

KURT: Alice, your husband is an indulgent old fool who shows me nothing but kindness . . .

ALICE: Watch out for his kindnesses! I know them!

KURT: Oh, come now.

ALICE: He's obviously blinded you too . . . Don't you see the dan-ger? Don't you notice the traps?

KURT: No.

ALICE: Then you're doomed to go under.

KURT: Oh, God save us!

ALICE: Think of it—I sit here watching disaster creep up on you like a cat . . . I point it out to you, and you can't see it.

KURT: Even Allan, with those unblinking eyes of his, can't see it. In fact, he has eyes only for Judith. Surely that's a guarantee of good relations.

ALICE: Do you know Judith?

KURT: A little flirt in a pigtail, with skirts a bit too short . . .

ALICE: Exactly! But the other day I saw her in a long skirt . . . and that was a young lady ... and not so young, either, with her hair up.

KURT: She's precocious, I'll admit that.

ALICE: And she's playing with Allan.

KURT: That's all right, as long as it's just play.

ALICE: Really? It's all right? ... Edgar will be here soon, and he'll sit in the easy chair—he loves that chair enough to steal it.

KURT: He can have it.

ALICE: Let him sit there and we'll sit here. And when he talks—he loves to rattle on in the mornings—when he talks about seemingly insignificant things, I'll translate them for you ...

KURT: Oh, you're too clever, *too* clever, dear Alice! What do I have to fear as long as I run the quarantine station properly and otherwise behave myself?

ALICE: You believe in justice and honor and all that.

KURT: Yes, I learned that from experience. There was a time I didn't believe in them ... That cost me dearly.

ALICE: Here he comes ...

KURT: I've never seen you so frightened.

ALICE: My courage was only ignorance of the danger.

KURT: Danger? ... You're beginning to alarm me.

ALICE: Oh, if only I could! ... There he is! (*The* CAPTAIN *enters upstage in civilian clothes: a black, buttoned-up morning coat, his uniform cap, a silver-handled cane. He nods a greeting and crosses to sit in the easy chair.*)

ALICE (*to* KURT): Let him speak first.

CAPTAIN: This is a superb chair you have, my dear Kurt! Absolutely superb!

KURT: It's yours if you'd like it.

CAPTAIN: That wasn't my intention ...

KURT: But it is mine, really! Haven't I gotten a lot from you?

CAPTAIN (*expansively*): Oh, nonsense! ... And when I sit here, I can look out over the whole island. I see all the promenades, all the people on their verandahs, all the ships coming and going ... You've managed to get the best piece of land on the island, which is certainly no Isle of Bliss. Right, Alice? ... Yes, they call it "Little Hell," and here Kurt has built himself a paradise, without an Eve, of course. When she arrives, that's the end of paradise. By the way, did you know that this used to be a royal hunting lodge?

KURT: I've heard that.

CAPTAIN: Yes, you live royally, and I'm ashamed to say it, but you have me to thank for it.

ALICE (*to* KURT): Watch out! He's trying to steal you!

KURT: I have much to thank you for.

CAPTAIN: Stuff! ——— Say, did you get those cases of wine?

KURT: Yes.

CAPTAIN: And you're satisfied?

KURT: Very satisfied, and you can tell your wine merchant that.

CAPTAIN: He carries the best ...

ALICE (*to* KURT): At prices lower than you had to pay for them ...

CAPTAIN: What did you say, Alice?

ALICE: I? Nothing!

CAPTAIN: Yes. When they established this position of Quarantine Master, I thought of applying for it myself ... and so I studied the subject.

ALICE (*to* KURT): He's lying!

CAPTAIN (*boastfully*): I didn't share the outmoded ideas the authorities had about disinfecting procedures. I took the side of the Neptunists—that's what we called them because they advocate the water method ...

KURT: Excuse me! I remember clearly that it was I who preached water and you fire, that time.

CAPTAIN: I? Nonsense!

ALICE (*aloud*): Yes, I remember that too!

CAPTAIN: You? ...

KURT: I remember it clearly because ...

CAPTAIN (*cutting him off*): It's possible, but it's not important! (*raising his voice*) However ... we now stand on the brink ... (*to* KURT *who tries to cut him off*) ... don't interrupt! ... of a new era ... The entire quarantine system is about to take a giant step forward.

KURT: Speaking of that, do you know who's been writing those stupid articles in the journal?

CAPTAIN (*reddens*): No I don't, but why do you call them stupid?

ALICE (*to* KURT): Be careful! He's the one who wrote them!

KURT (*to* ALICE): He? ... (*to the* CAPTAIN) Well, not very sensible, anyway.

CAPTAIN: You're no judge of that!

ALICE: Is it necessary to quarrel?

KURT: No!

CAPTAIN: It's hard enough maintaining peace on this island. We should set a good example ...

KURT: Can you explain something to me? When I first arrived here, I quickly made friends with all the authorities. The Judge Advocate became an especially close friend, as close as one can be at our age. Anyway, after a while—right after you recovered from your attack—people began acting cool toward me, first one and then another. Yesterday, on the promenade, the Judge Advocate avoided me. I can't tell you how hurt I was. (*The* CAPTAIN *is silent.*) Have you noticed people being unfriendly to you?

CAPTAIN: No, on the contrary.

ALICE (*to* KURT): Don't you understand that he's stolen your friends?

KURT (*to the* CAPTAIN): I wonder if it's because I refused to invest in that new issue of stock.

CAPTAIN: Oh, no. But can you tell me why you didn't want to subscribe?

KURT: Because I'd already put my small savings into a soda factory. And also because a new issue means that the old stock is shaky.

CAPTAIN (*preoccupied*): That's a superb lamp you have. Where did you get it?

KURT: In town, of course.

ALICE (*to* KURT): Watch out for your lamp!

KURT (*to the* CAPTAIN): You mustn't think I'm ungrateful or mistrust you, Edgar.

CAPTAIN: No, but it shows lack of confidence that you want to pull out of something that you helped to start.

KURT: Edgar, my friend, ordinary caution dictates that people try to save themselves and what they have, while there's still time.

CAPTAIN: Save themselves? Is there any real danger? Do you think someone's trying to rob you?

KURT: Why such harsh words?

CAPTAIN: Weren't you satisfied when I helped you place your capital at six percent interest?

KURT: Yes, and I was also grateful.

CAPTAIN: You're not grateful—it's not your nature, but that's not your fault.

ALICE (*to* KURT): *Listen* to him!

KURT: My nature is full of flaws and my struggle against them is pretty unsuccessful, but I do recognize my obligations . . .

CAPTAIN: See that you do, then! (*reaches out and picks up a newspaper*) Why, what's this? . . . An announcement! (*reads aloud*) The Director of Public Health is dead!

ALICE (*to* KURT): Now he's speculating in corpses.

CAPTAIN (*as if to himself*): This will mean certain . . . changes . . .

KURT: In what respect?

CAPTAIN (*rising*): We'll have to wait and see!

ALICE (*to the* CAPTAIN): Where are you going?

CAPTAIN: I think I must go into town . . . (*catches sight of a letter on the writing table, picks it up without thinking, reads the address, and puts it down*) Forgive me. I'm so absent-minded.

KURT: No harm done.

CAPTAIN: Why that's Allan's mathematical instrument case. Where's the boy?

KURT: He's out playing with the girls.

CAPTAIN: A big boy like him? I don't like it! And Judith mustn't be allowed to run around like that . . . You keep an eye on your young man, and I'll look after my young lady! (*crossing past the piano, he strikes several chords.*) Superb tone in this instrument! A Steinbech? Right?

KURT: Bechstein!

CAPTAIN: Yes, you have it good! Thanks to me for bringing you here!

ALICE (*to* KURT): He's lying, he tried to prevent it!

CAPTAIN: Good-bye now. I'm taking the next boat. (*As he leaves, he scrutinizes the paintings on the walls.*)

ALICE: Well?

KURT: Well what?

ALICE: I don't know what he's planning yet. But—tell me something! The envelope he looked at . . . who is the letter from?

KURT: I'm sorry to say—that was my only secret.

ALICE: And he smelled it out! Don't you see he's a wizard, as I said before? . . . Is there something printed on the envelope?

KURT: Yes. It says "The Board of Elections."

ALICE: Then he's guessed your secret. I know you want to be a member of Parliament. And now you'll see *him* become one instead.

KURT: Has he ever thought about it?

ALICE: No, but he'll think about it now. I saw it in his face when he looked at the envelope.

KURT: Is that why he's going to town?

ALICE: No, that he decided when he saw the death announcement.

KURT: What can he hope to gain by the death of the Director of Public Health?

ALICE: Yes, you tell me! . . . Maybe he was an enemy who obstructed Edgar's plans.

KURT: If he's as terrible as you say, then there's good reason to fear him.

ALICE: Didn't you hear how he was trying to steal you, to tie your hands by making you feel obliged for debts you never incurred. Saying he got you this position, for example, when he really tried to prevent you getting it. He steals people. He's an insect, a woodworm, who'll devour you from within so that one day you'll be hollow, like a rotted pine tree . . . He hates you, though he's bound to you through the memory of your early friendship.

KURT: Hate seems to sharpen your wits, Alice.

ALICE: And love makes us stupid. Blind and stupid.

KURT: No, don't say that!

ALICE: Do you know what a vampire is? . . . They say it's the soul of a dead person looking for a body to live in as a parasite. Edgar's been dead ever since he fell that time. He has no interests of his own, no personality, no initiative. But the moment he gets hold of someone, he clings to them, sinks down a taproot, and begins to grow and blossom. Now he's sitting on you.

KURT: If he gets too close, I'll shake him off.

ALICE: Try shaking off a burr, and you'll see!...By the way, do you know why he doesn't want Judith and Allan to play together?

KURT: I'm sure he's concerned they're too young to handle their feelings.

ALICE: Oh, no!...He wants to marry Judith off...to the Colonel!

KURT (*upset*): That old widower?

ALICE: Yes!

KURT: That's terrible!...And Judith?

ALICE: If she could get the General, who's eighty years old, she'd do it to humiliate the Colonel, who's sixty. Humiliating people, that's what she lives for, you see. Trample and humiliate is the watchword of that family!

KURT: Judith? That lovely, proud young girl?

ALICE: That's right!...May I sit here and write a letter?

KURT (*clears the writing table*): Of course!

ALICE (*takes off her gloves and sits at the writing table*): Now I'll try my hand at the art of war! I failed the first time I tried to slay my dragon. But I've learned a bit since then.

KURT: Do you know you have to load before you fire?

ALICE: Yes, and with live ammunition! (KURT *exits right.* ALICE *thinks for a moment and then writes.* ALLAN *rushes in without noticing her and throws himself headlong onto the sofa, sobbing into a lace handkerchief.* ALICE *watches him, then rises and crosses to the sofa; gently*) Allan! (ALLAN *sits up, embarrassed, and hides the handkerchief behind his back.* ALICE *continues, gently, womanly, with genuine emotion.*) You mustn't be afraid of me, Allan. You're in no danger with me...What's the matter ——— Are you sick?

ALLAN: Yes!

ALICE: What's wrong?

ALLAN: I don't know.

ALICE: Where's the pain? In your head?

ALLAN: Nooo!

ALICE: In your chest then? An awful pain?

ALLAN: Yes!

ALICE: A pain as if your heart is melting away? And it aches and aches...

ALLAN: How did you know?

ALICE: And then you want to die. If only you were dead. And
everything is so difficult. And you can only think of one thing
... one person ... but if two people think about the same person, one of the two is bound to be terribly unhappy ... (ALLAN
forgets himself and picks at the handkerchief.) This is the sickness no one can cure ... You can't eat or drink. You just want to
cry, and the crying is so bitter ... preferably out in the woods,
so no one can see you, because people laugh at this kind of
sorrow ... those mean people! Ugh! ... What do you want of
her? Nothing! You don't want to kiss her on the mouth, because
you believe that then you'd die. You feel as if death is drawing
closer whenever your thoughts fly to her! And it is death, my
child, the death that brings life. But you don't understand that
yet. I smell violets. It is she. (*approaches* ALLAN *and slowly takes
the handkerchief*) It is she, it is she everywhere, and only she!
Oh my, oh my! (ALLAN *sees no alternative but to bury his face
in* ALICE's *bosom.*) Poor boy! Poor boy! Oh, it hurts so, it hurts
so! (*She wipes his tears away with the handkerchief.*) That's it,
that's it! Cry, go on and cry! You'll feel better! ... All right, get
up now, Allan, and be a man, otherwise she won't want to look
at you. She who's so cruel but not cruel at all. Has she tormented you? ———— With the Lieutenant? Listen! You must become
friends with the Lieutenant, then the two of you can talk about
her. That usually helps.

ALLAN: I don't want to see the Lieutenant.

ALICE: Listen, my boy! It won't be long before the Lieutenant
comes looking for you to talk about her. Because ... (ALLAN
looks up, brightening with hope.) Shall I be nice and tell you?
(ALLAN *bows his head.*) He's just as unhappy as you are.

ALLAN (*happily*): Really?

ALICE: Absolutely. And he needs someone to open his heart to
when Judith hurts him ... It didn't take much to cheer you up.

ALLAN: Doesn't she want the Lieutenant?

ALICE: Allan dear, she doesn't want you either. She wants the Colonel. (ALLAN *is sad again.*) Here comes the rain again. ————
Well, you can't have the handkerchief. Judith is very fussy
about her belongings and keeps track of every one. (ALLAN *looks*

disappointed.) Yes, that's the way Judith is! . . . You sit there while I write another letter, then you can run an errand for me. (*She crosses to the table and writes. The* LIEUTENANT *enters upstage, looking melancholy, but not comically so. He does not notice* ALICE *and crosses directly to* ALLAN.)

LIEUTENANT: Cadet! (ALLAN *rises and snaps to attention.*) At ease! (ALLAN *sits again.* ALICE *watches them. The* LIEUTENANT *crosses to* ALLAN *and sits beside him. He sighs and takes out a handkerchief resembling the one* ALLAN *had and wipes his forehead.* ALLAN *stares enviously at the handkerchief. The* LIEUTENANT *looks at* ALLAN *gloomily.* ALICE *coughs. The* LIEUTENANT *rises and stands at attention.*)

ALICE: At ease, Lieutenant.

LIEUTENANT: I apologize, ma'am.

ALICE: No need to . . . Please sit down and keep the Cadet company. He feels rather deserted on this island. (*writes*)

LIEUTENANT (*disconcerted; talks to* ALLAN *in low tones*): It's tremendously hot out.

ALLAN: Oh, yes.

LIEUTENANT: Have you finished the sixth book yet?

ALLAN: I'm just working on the last proposition.

LIEUTENANT: That's a nasty one! (*silence*) Have you . . . ———— (*looking for the words*) ———— played any tennis today?

ALLAN: No, it's too hot in the sun.

LIEUTENANT (*anguished without becoming comic*): Yes, it is tremendously hot today.

ALLAN (*whispering*): Very hot! (*silence*)

LIEUTENANT: Have you . . . been out sailing today?

ALLAN: Uh, no, I couldn't find anyone to crew for me.

LIEUTENANT: Would you . . . trust me to crew?

ALLAN (*respectful, as before*): That would be too great an honor for me, sir.

LIEUTENANT: Oh no, not at all . . . Do you think . . . there'd be a good wind . . . around noon? That's the only time I'm free.

ALLAN (*slyly*): The wind usually dies around noon, and . . . Miss Judith has her lesson then . . .

LIEUTENANT (*crestfallen*): I see, I see! Hm! ———— Do you think that . . .

ALICE: Could either of you young gentlemen take this letter for me ... (ALLAN *and the* LIEUTENANT *eye each other suspiciously.*) ... to Miss Judith? (*Both men get up and go to* ALICE, *though with a certain dignity, to avoid betraying their feelings.*) Both of you? Well, all the more certain it'll be delivered. (*gives the letter to the* LIEUTENANT) Lieutenant, may I have that handkerchief? My daughter is careful of her things. She's a little finicky by nature ... Give me the handkerchief! ... I don't want to laugh at you, so don't make fools of yourselves—needlessly. Besides, the Colonel wouldn't want to be an Othello! (*takes the handkerchief*) Off with you now, young men, and try to conceal your feelings as best you can! (*The* LIEUTENANT *bows and leaves, followed closely by* ALLAN. ALICE *shouts.*) Allan!

ALLAN (*stopping very reluctantly in the doorway*): Yes, Aunt Alice.

ALICE: Stay!—if you don't want more hurt than you can stand!

ALLAN: But he's going!

ALICE: Let him get burned! You take care!

ALLAN: I don't want to take care!

ALICE: Then there'll be more crying. And I'll have the trouble of comforting you.

ALLAN: I want to go!

ALICE: Then go! But be sure to come back, you young idiot, so I can have a chance to laugh at you! (ALLAN *runs off after the* LIEUTENANT. ALICE *returns to her writing.*)

KURT (*entering*): Alice, I've received an anonymous letter that upsets me.

ALICE: Have you noticed that Edgar has become another person since he stopped wearing his uniform? I never thought clothes could make such a difference.

KURT: You didn't answer my question.

ALICE: It wasn't a question. It was a statement of fact. What are you afraid of?

KURT: Everything.

ALICE: He's gone to town. His trips to town always lead to something terrible.

KURT: But I can't do anything, because I don't know where the attack will come from.

ALICE (*folding the letter*): We'll see if I guessed it . . .

KURT: Then you'll help me?

ALICE: Yes . . . But no further than my interests permit—*my* interests, or rather, my children's.

KURT: I can understand that . . . Listen to how still it is: Nature, the sea, everything!

ALICE: But behind the stillness I hear voices . . . murmurs, cries.

KURT: Shhh! I hear something too . . . No, it was only the seagulls.

ALICE: But I hear something else . . . I'm going to the post office—with this letter.

Scene 2

(*The same setting.* ALLAN *is sitting at the writing table, studying.* JUDITH *stands in the doorway, wearing a tennis hat and holding the handlebars of a bicycle.*)

JUDITH: Can I borrow your wrench?

ALLAN (*without looking up*): No, you can't.

JUDITH: You're being rude just because I asked you for something.

ALLAN (*not harshly*): I'm not anything at all. I just want to be left in peace.

JUDITH (*coming forward*): Allan.

ALLAN: Yes, what is it?

JUDITH: You mustn't be angry with me.

ALLAN: I'm not.

JUDITH: Give me your hand on it!

ALLAN (*gently*): No, I don't want to give you my hand, but I'm not angry . . . What is it you want from me, anyway?

JUDITH: You're so silly!

ALLAN: I guess I am.

JUDITH: You think I'm only mean.

ALLAN: No, I know you're nice too. When you want to be.

JUDITH: Well, it's not my fault . . . that . . . you and the Lieutenant go and cry in the woods. Why do you cry? Tell me. (ALLAN *is embarrassed.*) Tell me . . . I never cry. And why are you such good friends now? . . . What do you talk about, when you walk arm in arm? (ALLAN *has no answer.*) Allan! You'll soon see what I really am, and that I can fight for the people I care about! . . . But I'll give you a piece of advice . . . though I don't want to tell tales . . . Be prepared!

ALLAN: For what?

JUDITH: For something unpleasant.

ALLAN: From which direction?

JUDITH: The direction you least expect.

ALLAN: I'm used to unpleasant things. Life hasn't been much fun for me. . . . What's brewing now?

JUDITH (*wistfully*): You poor boy! . . . Give me your hand! (ALLAN *gives her his hand.*) Look at me! . . . Are you afraid to look at me? (ALLAN *rushes out left to hide his emotion.*)

LIEUTENANT (*enters upstage*): Excuse me! I thought the Cadet . . .

JUDITH: Lieutenant, will you be my friend and confidant?

LIEUTENANT: It would be an honor . . .

JUDITH: Just one thing! . . . Don't desert Allan when trouble comes!

LIEUTENANT: What kind of trouble?

JUDITH: You'll soon see, perhaps today . . . Do you like Allan?

LIEUTENANT: He's my best student, and I admire him personally for his strength of character . . . Yes, there are moments in life when one must have ———— (*with emphasis*) ———— in a word the strength to stand it, to endure, to suffer.

JUDITH: That was more than a word . . . Anyway, you really like Allan?

LIEUTENANT: Yes.

JUDITH: Go find him and keep him company.

LIEUTENANT: That's the reason I came, *that* and *nothing more!* I had no intention of . . .

JUDITH: I didn't suppose you had. Of the kind you mean. Allan went out that way. (*points left*)

LIEUTENANT (*hesitantly, as he exits left*): Well . . . I guess I'll go.

JUDITH: Yes, do. That's good of you.

ALICE (*entering upstage*): What are you doing here?

JUDITH: I came to borrow a wrench.

ALICE: Will you listen to me a moment?

JUDITH: Of course I will. (ALICE *sits on the sofa.* JUDITH *remains standing.*) But whatever you have to say, do it quickly. I don't like long lectures.

ALICE: Lectures? . . . Very well. Put up your hair and wear a long skirt.

JUDITH: Why should I?

ALICE: Because you're not a child any more. And you're too young to pretend you're younger than you are.

JUDITH: What does that mean?

ALICE: That you're old enough to be married. And that your way of dressing is scandalous.

JUDITH: All right, I'll do it.

ALICE: Then you've understood?

JUDITH: Yes, yes.

ALICE: And you agree with me?

JUDITH: Completely.

ALICE: On all points?

JUDITH: Even the most sensitive.

ALICE: Will you also stop playing games—with Allan?

JUDITH: So I have to be serious about everything?

ALICE: Yes.

JUDITH: Then we might as well begin. (*Having put down the handlebars, she lets down her bicycling dress and twists her braid into a knot. She takes a hairpin from her mother's hair and fastens the knot.*)

ALICE: One doesn't make one's toilet in other people's houses!

JUDITH: Is this all right? . . . Then I'm ready. Let the world beware!

ALICE: At least now you look respectable . . . And leave Allan in peace!

JUDITH: I don't understand what you mean by that.

ALICE: Can't you see that he's suffering? . . .

JUDITH: Yes, I think I noticed that, but I can't understand why. I'm not suffering.

ALICE: That's your strength. But you wait . . . oh yes, one day . . . you'll know what it's like . . . Go home now, and don't forget— you're wearing a long skirt.

JUDITH: Does that mean that I have to walk differently?

ALICE: Try and you'll see!

JUDITH (*tries to walk like a lady*): Oh, my feet feel shackled! I'm a prisoner, I can't run any more!

ALICE: Yes, child, you have to learn to walk again, this time on a slow path toward an unknown you already know about, but must pretend to be ignorant of . . . Shorter steps, and slower, much slower. Children's shoes must be exchanged for high button shoes, Judith. ———— You don't remember your first shoes, but I do.

JUDITH: I'll never be able to stand this!

ALICE: And yet you must! You must! (JUDITH *crosses to her mother, kisses her lightly on the cheek, then exits like a lady, with dignity, forgetting the handlebars.*)

JUDITH: Good-bye!

KURT (*enters from left*): So, you're here already?

ALICE: Yes.

KURT: Then he's come back?

ALICE: Yes.

KURT: What was he wearing?

ALICE: His full-dress uniform! ———— So he was at the Colonel's. Two orders on his chest.

KURT: Two? ———— I know he was supposed to get the Order of the Sword when he retired. What's the other one?

ALICE: I don't know, but it was a white cross inside a red one.

KURT: Portuguese then . . . Let me think ———— Wait! ———— Weren't those articles he wrote for the journal about quarantine stations in Portuguese harbors?

ALICE: Yes, as far as I remember.

KURT: And he's never been in Portugal, has he?

ALICE: Never!

KURT: But I have.

ALICE: And you're always so informative. You know he hears well and has a good memory.

KURT: Maybe it was Judith's influence that got him the decoration.

ALICE: Kurt! . . . There are limits, you know . . . (*rising*) And you're overstepping them!

KURT: Are we going to quarrel now?

ALICE: That depends on you! Don't interfere in my interests!

KURT: When they cross mine, I must interfere in them, however gently I can . . . Here he comes!

ALICE: And now it'll happen!

KURT: What'll happen?

ALICE: We'll see.

KURT: Let it be an attack then. This state of siege has got on my nerves. I don't have a friend left on the whole island.

ALICE: Wait! . . . You sit here on this side . . . He'll surely take the easy chair, and I can prompt you. (*The* CAPTAIN *enters upstage, wearing his full-dress uniform with the Order of the Sword and the Portuguese Order of Christ.*)

CAPTAIN: Good morning! ———— So this is where we meet!

ALICE: You're tired. Sit down! (*The* CAPTAIN, *contrary to expectation, sits left on the sofa.*) Why don't you make yourself comfortable?

CAPTAIN: I'm fine here. ———— You're too kind.

ALICE (*to* Kurt): Be careful, he suspects us!

CAPTAIN (*sullenly*): What did you say?

ALICE (*to* KURT): He must have been drinking.

CAPTAIN (*rudely*): No, he hasn't. (*silence*) Well? . . . How have you two been amusing yourselves?

ALICE: What about you?

CAPTAIN: You're looking at my decorations.

ALICE: Not at all.

CAPTAIN: I think you are, and you're jealous. ———— Otherwise, it's customary to congratulate people who receive honors.

ALICE: Congratulations.

CAPTAIN: We get these just as actresses get laurel wreaths.

ALICE: He means my wreaths on the wall back in the tower . . .

CAPTAIN: Which you got from your brother . . .

ALICE: Oh, shut up!

CAPTAIN: And which I had to bow down to for twenty-five years! . . . and it's taken all this time to discover the truth!

ALICE: You saw my brother?

CAPTAIN: Several times! (ALICE *is crushed; silence*) What about you, Kurt? Nothing to say?

KURT: I'm waiting.

CAPTAIN: Listen, you've heard the big news, haven't you?

KURT: No.

CAPTAIN: Well, I hate to be the one to tell you . . .

KURT: Just tell me!

CAPTAIN: The soda factory has gone bust.

KURT: That is bad news! ———— How did you come out?

CAPTAIN: All right. I sold out in time.

KURT: That was wise of you.

CAPTAIN: How will you come out?

KURT: Badly.

CAPTAIN: It's your own fault. You should have sold out in time or subscribed to the new shares.

KURT: Then I'd have lost them too.

CAPTAIN: Not at all. For then the company would have stayed solvent.

KURT: Not the company, the board of directors. In my opinion the new subscription would only have benefited them.

CAPTAIN: But will your opinion save you? That's the question.

KURT: No, I'll have to give up everything.

CAPTAIN: Everything?

KURT: Even the house and furniture.

CAPTAIN: That's horrible!

KURT: I've been through worse. (*silence*)

CAPTAIN: That's what happens when amateurs go in for speculation.

KURT: How can you say that? You know that if I hadn't invested in the first place, I would have been ostracized . . . Didn't you write in the journal about the extra source of income there would be for local people? With unlimited capital, unlimited as the sea . . . a philanthropic project for the good of the nation! . . . And now you call it speculation!

CAPTAIN (*unmoved*): What will you do now?

KURT: I guess I'll have to have an auction.

CAPTAIN: That's a good idea.

KURT: What do you mean?

CAPTAIN: What I said. (*slowly*) There'll be certain changes made here . . .

KURT: Here on the island?

CAPTAIN: Yes!...For instance...you'll have to move into simpler living quarters.

KURT: I see.

CAPTAIN: Yes, the plan is to relocate the quarantine station on the far side of the island, near the water.

KURT: My original idea!

CAPTAIN (*drily*): I know nothing about that...I'm not familiar with your ideas on the subject...However, the advantage in getting rid of the furniture now is that later the...scandal will attract less attention.

KURT: What?

CAPTAIN: The scandal! (*his temper rising*) For it's a scandal to come to a new place and immediately get involved in a financial mess that makes things unpleasant for your relatives...especially for your relatives!

KURT: Surely it'll be most unpleasant for me.

CAPTAIN: I'm going to tell you something, my dear Kurt: if you didn't have me on your side in this matter, you'd be gone from here.

KURT: That too!

CAPTAIN: You have difficulty managing things properly...There have been complaints about your work.

KURT: Justified complaints?

CAPTAIN: Well, the fact is that despite your many admirable qualities, you are negligent! ——— Don't interrupt! ——— You're grossly negligent!

KURT: This is incredible!

CAPTAIN: However! The change I mentioned will take place very soon. So I would advise you to hold an auction immediately, or else try to sell things privately.

KURT: Privately? Where can I find a buyer here?

CAPTAIN: You don't think that I'd go and buy up your furniture, do you? That would make a lovely story ——— (*sporadically*) ——— hum! especially if you...consider what happened...in the past...

KURT: And what was that? ——— Don't you mean what *didn't* happen?

CAPTAIN (*tacking*): Alice is so quiet. What's the matter, old girl?

You're not getting sluggish, are you?

ALICE: I'm just thinking . . .

CAPTAIN: Oh my! Are you thinking? But you have to think quick-
ly, correctly and clearly, if it's going to do any good. ———
Come on, now: One, two, three—think! ——— Aha! You can't!
. . . Well, I'll be off, then! . . . Where's Judith?

ALICE: She's around somewhere.

CAPTAIN: Where's Allan? (ALICE *is silent.*) Where's the Lieutenant? (ALICE *is silent.*) Kurt! ——— What do you intend to do
with Allan now?

KURT: Do with him?

CAPTAIN: Yes, you can't afford to keep him in the artillery.

KURT: Perhaps not.

CAPTAIN: You'll have to try to get him placed as a cadet in some
cheap infantry regiment in Norrland or something.

KURT: Norrland?

CAPTAIN: Yes! Or maybe you should simply let him go into something practical ——— If I were you, I'd put him in an office . . .
Why not? (KURT *is silent.*) In these enlightened times! Well! . . .
Alice is *unusually* quiet! . . . Yes, my children, that's the swing-
ing seasaw of life: one minute you're sitting high up and cock-
sure of yourself, and the next you're down below! But then you
come up again! Et cetera! So much for that, yes . . . (*to* ALICE)
Did you say something? (ALICE *shakes her head.*) We're expecting a visitor here in several days.

ALICE: Are you talking to me?

CAPTAIN: We're expecting a visitor in several days. An important
visitor!

ALICE: Who?

CAPTAIN: You see! You *are* interested! . . . You can just sit there
and guess who's coming, and between guesses you can read this
letter—*again!* (*hands her an opened letter*)

ALICE: That's my letter! Opened! You got it from the post office!

CAPTAIN (*rising*): Yes, as head of the family and your guardian I
watch over the family's most sacred interests, and I'll smash
with an iron hand any attempt to loosen family ties by criminal
correspondence! Understand? (ALICE *is crushed.*) I'm not dead,
you see! But don't be angry, not now when I intend to lift us all

out of this undeserved degradation, undeserved on my part at least.

ALICE: Judith! Judith!

CAPTAIN: And Holofernes? ——— Is that supposed to be me? Bah! (*exits upstage*)

KURT: Who is this man?

ALICE: Don't ask me!

KURT: We're destroyed!

ALICE: Yes! . . . No doubt about it.

KURT: He's ground me to bits, but so cunningly I can't accuse him of anything.

ALICE: On the contrary. You owe him a debt of thanks.

KURT: Does he know what he's doing?

ALICE: No, I don't think so. He follows his nature and his instincts, and for the moment he seems to be in favor with whoever deals out good and bad luck.

KURT: It must be the Colonel who's coming here.

ALICE: Probably. That's why Allan must be sent away.

KURT: And you think that's right?

ALICE: Yes, I do.

KURT: Then this is where we part.

ALICE: (*ready to leave*): For a little while . . . But we'll meet again!

KURT: Presumably.

ALICE: And do you know where?

KURT: Here!

ALICE: Do you sense that?

KURT: It's simple. He'll take the house and buy the furniture.

ALICE: That's what I think too. But don't abandon me!

KURT: Not for so slight a reason.

ALICE (*leaving*): Good-bye.

KURT: Good-bye.

Act II

(*The same setting, but it is cloudy and raining outside.* ALICE *and* KURT *enter upstage, in raincoats, carrying umbrellas.*)

ALICE: So, I got you here ... Kurt, I can't be so cruel as to welcome you to your own home ...

KURT: Oh! Why not? I've gone through three court seizures ... and worse ... It means nothing to me.

ALICE: Did he send for you?

KURT: It was a formal summons, but I don't know the reason.

ALICE: He's not your superior, is he?

KURT: No, but he's made himself king on the island. If anyone offers any opposition, he mentions the Colonel's name, and everyone bows. ——— By the way, isn't the Colonel supposed to arrive today?

ALICE: He's expected—but I'm not sure when ——— Sit down!

KURT (*sitting*): Everything looks the same.

ALICE: Don't think about it! ——— Don't tear open old wounds!

KURT: Wounds? I just think it's a little strange, as strange as that man. ——— Do you know, when I first got to know him as a young man, I ran away from him ... But he pursued me. Flattered me, offered me favors, and bound me ... I tried repeatedly to escape, but in vain ... Now I'm his slave.

ALICE: Yes, and why? He's the one who owes you, but you're the debtor.

KURT: After I was ruined, he offered to help Allan with his exam ...

ALICE: That'll cost you dearly! ... Are you still a candidate for Parliament?

KURT: Yes. There are no obstacles there, as far as I can see. (*silence*)

ALICE: Is Allan really leaving today?

KURT: Yes. Unless I can prevent it.

ALICE: That was a short-lived joy.

KURT: Short, like everything else except life itself, which is horribly long.

ALICE: Yes, that it is ... Won't you come and wait in the drawing room? The surroundings here bother me even if they don't bother you.

KURT: If you wish.

ALICE: I'm ashamed. I'm so ashamed I want to die ... but I can't change anything.

KURT: Let's go then, if you like.

ALICE: Besides, someone's coming. (*They exit left. The* CAPTAIN *and* ALLAN *enter upstage, both in uniforms and cloaks.*)

CAPTAIN: Sit down here, my boy, I want to have a talk with you. (*He sits in the easy chair.* ALLAN *sits in the chair left.*) It's raining today, otherwise I like to sit here and look at the sea. (*silence*) Well? —— You don't want to leave, do you?

ALLAN: I don't want to leave my father.

CAPTAIN: Yes, your father. He's a very unfortunate man. (*silence*) And parents seldom understand what's best for their children. Of course—there are exceptions. Hm. Tell me, Allan, do you have any contact with your mother?

ALLAN: Yes, she writes now and then.

CAPTAIN: You know that she's your guardian?

ALLAN: Yes.

CAPTAIN: And do you know that your mother has given me full power to act in her behalf?

ALLAN: I didn't know that.

CAPTAIN: Well, now you know. Consequently, there'll be no more discussion about your career . . . So, you'll go to Norrland?

ALLAN: But I don't have the money.

CAPTAIN: I've taken care of that.

ALLAN: In that case, all I can do is thank you, Uncle Edgar.

CAPTAIN: I like to see gratitude—it's in short supply around here . . . (*raising his voice*) The Colonel . . . do you know the Colonel?

ALLAN (*startled*): No, I don't.

CAPTAIN: The *Colonel* —— (*with emphasis*) —— is my very special friend —— (*speeding up*) —— as you perhaps know! Hm! The Colonel has taken a personal interest in my family, including my wife's relatives. Using his influence, the Colonel has succeeded in obtaining the money necessary for you to complete your training. —— Now you know how you and your father are indebted—to the Colonel . . . Have I made myself clear? (ALLAN *bows.*) Go now and pack your things! The money will be waiting for you at the gangway. And so, good-bye, my boy! (*waving his little finger*) Good-bye! (*He rises and exits right.* ALLAN, *alone and distressed, looks around the room.* JUDITH *enters upstage, carrying an umbrella. Beneath her hood-*

ed cape she is beautifully dressed, with a long skirt and her hair up.)

JUDITH: Is that you, Allan?

ALLAN (*Turning, he looks at her carefully.*): Is that *you,* Judith?

JUDITH: Don't you recognize me? Where have you been so long? ... What are you looking at? ——— My long skirt ... and my hair ... You've never seen me like this before ...

ALLAN: Oh, no!

JUDITH: Do I look like a woman? (ALLAN *turns away from her.* JUDITH *is suddenly serious.*) What are you doing here?

ALLAN: I came to say good-bye.

JUDITH: What? Are you—going away?

ALLAN: I'm being sent to Norrland.

JUDITH (*crushed*): To Norrland? ——— When?

ALLAN: Today.

JUDITH: Whose idea was this?

ALLAN: Your father's.

JUDITH: I might have known. (*pacing and stamping her foot*) I wish you could have stayed another day!

ALLAN: In order to meet the Colonel?

JUDITH: What do you know about the Colonel? ... Do you really have to go?

ALLAN: I don't have any choice. Besides, now I want to. (*silence*)

JUDITH: Why now?

ALLAN: I want to get away from here! Out into the world!

JUDITH: Yes, it's suffocating here. I understand you, Allan. It's un-bearable! ——— People speculate—in soda factories and hu-man beings. (*silence; sincerely*) Allan, as you know, I'm not the sort who suffers emotionally. But now I'm beginning to feel what it's like.

ALLAN: You?

JUDITH: Yes! ——— I think I am! (*She presses her hands against her breast.*) Oh, it's terrible!

ALLAN: What is it?

JUDITH: I don't know! ——— I'm suffocating! I think I'm dying!

ALLAN: Judith!

JUDITH (*screaming*): Oh! ... Is *this* the way it feels? Is this ... you poor boys!

ALLAN: I should smile, but I'm not as cruel as you!

JUDITH: I'm not cruel. I didn't know any better!...You can't leave!

ALLAN: I must!

JUDITH: Go then!...But give me something to remember you by!

ALLAN: What have I to give you?

JUDITH (*in deep pain*): Allan!...No, I can't live through this! (*screams and clutches her breast*) The pain, the pain...What have you done to me?...I don't want to live any more! ———— Allan, don't go, not alone! We'll go together! We'll take out the little sloop, the little white one, but with the sheets belayed— there's a good wind...and we'll sail until we founder—out there, far out, where there's no seaweed or jellyfish. ———— Well? Say something! ———— But we should have washed the sail yesterday—it has to be absolutely white—I want everything to be white in that moment—and you'll swim with me in your arms until you tire—and then we'll go under...(*changing her tone*) That has style! Much more style than staying here to grieve and smuggle letters to each other which my father will tear open and laugh at! Allan! (*She takes his arms and shakes him.*) Did you hear me?

ALLAN (*who has watched her with shining eyes*): Judith! Judith! Why didn't you say all this before?

JUDITH: I didn't know! How could I say what I didn't know?

ALLAN: And now I have to leave you!...But it's probably best. It's the only way...I can't compete with a man...who...

JUDITH: Don't talk about the Colonel.

ALLAN: Isn't it true?

JUDITH: It's true—and untrue.

ALLAN: Completely untrue?

JUDITH: Or will be. Within an hour.

ALLAN: Will you promise me? I can wait, I can be patient, I can work!...Oh, Judith!

JUDITH: Don't go yet! ———— How long must I wait?

ALLAN: A year!

JUDITH (*jubilantly*): A year? I can wait a thousand years, and if you don't come then, I'll twist the heavens around so the sun comes up in the west...Shhh, someone's coming! ———— Allan, we must part...Shhh! ———— Take me in your arms! (*They em-*

brace.) But you mustn't kiss me! (*turns away her head*) Go now! ——— Go! (ALLAN *crosses upstage and puts on his cloak. Then they fly into each other's arms and* JUDITH *disappears in the cloak. For an instant they kiss.* ALLAN *runs out.* JUDITH *throws herself headlong onto the sofa, weeping.* ALLAN *enters again and kneels by the sofa.*)

ALLAN: No, I can't go! I can't leave you now, not now!

JUDITH (*rising*): If you knew how beautiful you are! If you could only see yourself!

ALLAN: Don't say that! A man can't be beautiful. But you, Judith, you—I see now that when you were kind, another Judith appeared ... *my* Judith! ... But if you deceive me, I'll die!

JUDITH: I think I must die after all! ... Oh, if I could only die now, this moment, when I'm happy!

ALLAN: Someone's coming.

JUDITH: Let them come! I'm not afraid of anything in the world any more. But I wish you'd take me with you under your cloak. (*She pretends to hide herself under his cloak.*) And we could fly away together to Norrland. What'll we do in Norrland? Maybe you'll be one of those infantrymen with a plume in his hat ... That's elegant—you'd look good in that. (*She fondles his hair. He kisses her fingertips, one after the other—then kisses her shoe.*) What are you doing, you lunatic? You'll make your mouth black. (*rising suddenly*) And then I won't be able to kiss you when you go! ... Come, I'm going with you!

ALLAN: No, I'll be arrested!

JUDITH: I'll be arrested with you!

ALLAN: They wouldn't let you be! ... Now we must part.

JUDITH: I'll swim after the steamboat ... And then you'll jump in and save me, and it'll be in the newspapers, and they'll let us get engaged! Shall we do that?

ALLAN: And you can still make jokes?

JUDITH: There'll be time for crying later! ... Say good-bye now! (*They fly into each other's arms.* ALLAN *withdraws through the upstage door, which remains open. They embrace outside, in the rain.*)

ALLAN: You're getting rained on! Judith!

JUDITH: What do I care about that? (*They tear apart from each other.* ALLAN *exits.* JUDITH *stands in the rain and wind, which blows her hair and clothes as she waves good-bye with her handkerchief. Then she rushes back inside, throws herself on the sofa, her face in her hands.* ALICE *enters and crosses to* JUDITH.)

ALICE: What is this? . . . Are you sick? ———— Stand up and let me look at you. (JUDITH *rises.* ALICE *looks her over carefully.*) No, you're not sick . . . And I refuse to comfort you. (*She exits right. The* LIEUTENANT *enters upstage.*)

JUDITH (*rises and puts on her hooded cape*): Lieutenant, would you please come with me to the telegraph office?

LIEUTENANT: Of course, if I can be of service . . . but I don't think it would look right.

JUDITH: So much the better! That's the idea: for you to compromise me—but without any illusions! . . . You go first. (*They exit upstage. The* CAPTAIN *and* ALICE *enter right, the* CAPTAIN *in fatigue uniform. He sits in the easy chair.*)

CAPTAIN: Let him in. (ALICE *crosses left and opens the door, then sits on the sofa.*)

KURT (*enters left*): You wanted to speak to me?

CAPTAIN (*friendly but somewhat condescending*): Yes, I have a number of important things to say to you. ———— Sit down.

KURT (*sits in the chair left*): I'm all ears.

CAPTAIN: Very well . . . (*orating*) You know that the quarantine system in our country has been badly neglected for almost a century . . . hm!

ALICE (*to* KURT): That's the candidate for Parliament talking.

CAPTAIN: . . . but with the extraordinary advances being made today in . . .

ALICE (*to* KURT): Communications, of course.

CAPTAIN: . . . every field imaginable, the government is considering an expansion program. Toward this end, the Ministry of Public Health has appointed inspectors—and . . .

ALICE (*to* KURT): He's dictating.

CAPTAIN: . . . you might as well know it sooner as later. ————
I've been appointed Quarantine Inspector. (*silence*)

KURT: I congratulate you—and at the same time pay my formal respects.

CAPTAIN: Our personal relationship—because of family ties—will remain unchanged. But now, to turn to other matters. ———— At my request your son Allan has been transferred to an infantry regiment in Norrland.

KURT: But that's against my wishes.

CAPTAIN: In this case the wishes of the boy's mother take precedence over yours . . . and since she has authorized me to act for her, I decided on the boy's transfer.

KURT: I admire you.

CAPTAIN: Is that your only reaction to being parted from your son? Have you no human feelings?

KURT: You mean I should be suffering?

CAPTAIN: Yes!

KURT: That would make you happy. You want to see me suffering?

CAPTAIN: Are you capable of suffering? . . . The time I fell sick and you were there . . . the only thing I remember is an expression of undisguised pleasure on your face.

ALICE: That's not true! Kurt sat at your side the whole night and calmed you when your guilty conscience tormented you . . . But when you recovered, you were ungrateful . . .

CAPTAIN (*pretending not to hear* ALICE): So, Allan will leave us.

KURT: Who will provide the money?

CAPTAIN: I've already done that, or rather we have—a consortium interested in the young man's future.

KURT: Consortium!

CAPTAIN: Yes! ———— So that you understand it's been handled correctly, you can look at the list of the people involved. (*hands* KURT *some papers*)

KURT: The list? (*looks at the papers*) But this is charity!

CAPTAIN: You can call it that.

KURT: Have you been begging for my son?

CAPTAIN: Here comes the ingratitude again! An ungrateful person is the heaviest burden the earth has to bear!

KURT: I'll be disgraced! . . . And my candidacy will come to nothing! . . .

CAPTAIN: What candidacy?

KURT: For Parliament, of course!

CAPTAIN: You haven't been dreaming about that, have you? Especially since you should have guessed that I, with the most seniority here, intended to run myself. Apparently, you underestimate my qualifications.

KURT: Well, so that's finished too.

CAPTAIN: It doesn't seem to bother you.

KURT: Now you've taken everything. What more do you want?

CAPTAIN: Do you have anything more? And do you have any reason to reproach me? Think about it: Have I done anything you can reproach me for? (*silence*)

KURT: Strictly speaking, no. Everything has been handled as correctly and legally as any ordinary transaction between honorable men . . .

CAPTAIN: You say that with a resignation I'd call cynical. But that's typical of your cynical nature, my dear Kurt. You know, there are moments when I'm tempted to share Alice's opinion that you're a hypocrite, a first-class hypocrite.

KURT (*calmly*): Is that really Alice's opinion?

ALICE (*to* KURT): It was, once, but no more. For you to bear what you've borne demands truly heroic courage, or—something more.

CAPTAIN: I think we can regard this discussion as closed. Go say good-bye to Allan, Kurt. He's leaving on the next boat.

KURT (*rises*): So soon? . . . Well! I've gone through worse than this.

CAPTAIN: You know, you say that so often, I'm beginning to wonder what sort of life you had in America.

KURT: What sort of life? Oh, yes, I had my share of misery. Every human being has an inalienable right to be miserable.

CAPTAIN (*sharply*): There are self-inflicted miseries. Is that what yours were?

KURT: Isn't that a question of conscience?

CAPTAIN (*bluntly*): Do you have a conscience?

KURT: There are wolves and there are sheep. There's no honor in it, but I'd rather be a sheep than a wolf.

CAPTAIN: Don't you know the truth in the old saying that every man forges his own good luck?

KURT: Is *that* a truth?

CAPTAIN: And you don't know that a man's own strength . . .

KURT: Oh, yes, I know about that, ever since the night your strength deserted you and left you prostrate on the floor.

CAPTAIN (*raising his voice*): A deserving man like myself—yes, look at me—for fifty years I've fought against the whole world, and I finally won, through perseverance, devotion to duty, energy and—honesty!

ALICE: That's for other people to say.

CAPTAIN: But they won't say it, because they're jealous! However! ———— A visitor is expected here! Today my daughter Judith will meet her intended . . . Where is Judith?

ALICE: She's out.

CAPTAIN: In the rain? . . . Send for her.

KURT: Perhaps I may go now.

CAPTAIN: No, wait a while . . . Was Judith dressed . . . properly?

ALICE: Properly enough . . . Did the Colonel say that he was definitely coming?

CAPTAIN (*rising*): Yes, but he'd like his arrival to be a surprise . . . I'm expecting a telegram—at any moment. (*exiting right*) I'll be right back.

ALICE: There you have him! Is he human?

KURT: When you asked me that once before, I answered no. Now I think he's one of the most typical human beings on the face of the earth . . . Maybe we are too—all opportunists, waiting to exploit each other.

ALICE: He's devoured you and yours alive . . . and you defend him?

KURT: I've known worse . . . At least this cannibal has left my soul untouched—that he couldn't swallow up!

ALICE: What "worse" have you known?

KURT: And you ask that? . . .

ALICE: Are you being rude?

KURT: No, and I don't want to be, so . . . don't ask me again!

CAPTAIN (*enters right*): The telegram was here all the time! ———— Read it to me, will you, Alice? I don't see so well . . . (*sits pompously in the easy chair*) Read it! ———— You don't have to leave, Kurt. (ALICE *reads it quickly and quietly to herself first and looks amazed.*) Well? Aren't you pleased? (ALICE *stares at the* CAPTAIN *in silence. He responds ironically.*) Who is it from?

ALICE: It's from the Colonel.

CAPTAIN (*delighted*): I thought so! . . . So what does he say?

ALICE: He says: "Because of Miss Judith's impertinent telephone message, I consider relations broken off—permanently." (*stares at the* CAPTAIN)

CAPTAIN: Once more, if you please.

ALICE (*reading fast*): "Because of Miss Judith's impertinent telephone message, I consider relations broken off—permanently."

CAPTAIN (*turning pale*): That's Judith!

ALICE: And this is Holofernes!

CAPTAIN: What are you then?

ALICE: You'll soon see!

CAPTAIN: You did this!

ALICE: No!

CAPTAIN (*furiously*): You did this!

ALICE: No! (*The* CAPTAIN *tries to rise and draw his sword but has a stroke and falls back in his chair.*) Finally, you got what you deserve!

CAPTAIN (*whimpering like an old man*): Don't be angry at me! I'm so sick!

ALICE: Are you? I'm glad to hear it! . . .

KURT: Alice! Let's get him into bed!

ALICE: No, I don't want to touch him! (*rings*)

CAPTAIN (*as before*): You mustn't be angry with me! (*to* KURT) Look after my children!

KURT: This is sublime! I should look after his children after he has stolen mine!

ALICE: It's the same old self-deception!

CAPTAIN: Look after my children! (*His speech turns into incoherent stuttering.*)

ALICE: At last that tongue has finally stopped! ———— There'll be no more boasts, no more lies, no more insults! ———— Kurt, you who believe in God—thank Him for me! Thank Him for freeing me from the tower, from the wolf, from the vampire!

KURT: Alice, don't!

ALICE (*leaning close to the* CAPTAIN): Where is your "own strength" now? Eh? And your "energy?" (*The* CAPTAIN, *speechless, spits in her face.*) So, the viper can still spit venom!

Then I'll have to tear out your tongue! (*She slaps his face.*) The head is off, but the cheek still reddens! . . . Oh, Judith, magnificent girl, whom I bore like vengeance beneath my heart. You, you've set us all free! —————— If you have any more heads, Hydra, we'll have them too! (*yanks the* CAPTAIN's *beard*) There is justice on earth after all! Sometimes I dreamed there was, but never believed it! Kurt, ask God to forgive me for misjudging Him! Oh, justice does exist! Then I want to be a sheep too! Tell Him that, Kurt! A little happiness makes us better people. It's the endless unhappiness that turns us into wolves! (*The* LIEU-TENANT *enters upstage.*) The Captain has had a stroke. Please help us wheel the chair out.

LIEUTENANT: Ma'am . . .

ALICE: What is it?

LIEUTENANT: Well, Miss Judith . . .

ALICE: Help us with this first. You can tell me about Judith later. (*The* LIEUTENANT *wheels the chair out right.*) Out with the corpse! Out with it, and open up the doors! The place needs airing out! (*She throws open the upstage doors. Outside, it has cleared.*) Ugh! . . .

KURT: Are you abandoning him?

ALICE: You abandon a ship when it founders. The crew has a right to save themselves! . . . There's no need to mourn a rotting dog. Let the scavengers or the garbage collectors have him. A garden plot is too fine a place to dump that barrowload of filth! . . . I'll go and bathe and try to wash off all this dirt, if it's possible ever to be clean again! (JUDITH *appears outside by the balustrade, bareheaded, waving her handkerchief toward the sea.*)

KURT (*crossing upstage*): Who's there? Judith! (*shouting*) Judith!

JUDITH (*enters, crying out*): He's gone!

KURT: Who?

JUDITH: Allan is gone!

KURT: Without saying good-bye?

JUDITH: He and I said good-bye, and he sent you his love, Uncle Kurt!

ALICE: Oh, so that's what happened!

JUDITH (*throwing herself in* KURT's *arms*): He's gone!

KURT: He'll come back, my child.

ALICE: Or we'll follow after him.

KURT (*gesturing toward the door right*): And leave him? ——— People would . . .

ALICE: People! Bah! . . . Judith, come and let me hold you. (JUDITH *goes to* ALICE, *who kisses her on the forehead.*) Do you want to follow him?

JUDITH: Need you ask that?

ALICE: But your father is sick!

JUDITH: What do I care about that?

ALICE: That's my Judith! ——— Oh, I love you, Judith!

JUDITH: Besides, Poppa isn't petty . . . and he doesn't like to be coddled. Say what you like about Poppa, he's got style!

ALICE: Yes, a bit.

JUDITH: And I don't think he's longing to see me, after that telephone call . . . Why did he try to force an old man on me? Oh, Allan, Allan! (*throwing herself in* KURT's *arms*) I want to go to Allan! (*She tears herself loose and runs out to wave.* KURT *follows her and also waves.*)

ALICE: To think that flowers can grow out of filth! (*The* LIEUTENANT *enters right.*) Yes?

LIEUTENANT: Uh . . . is Miss Judith . . . ?

ALICE: Are you so eager to speak her name that you leave a dying man?

LIEUTENANT: But she said that . . .

ALICE: She? You might as well say Judith then. ——— What's happening in there?

LIEUTENANT: It's all over.

ALICE: Over? ——— Oh, God, I thank Thee . . . for myself and all humanity . . . that Thou hast delivered us from this evil! . . . (*to the* LIEUTENANT) Give me your arm. I want to go out where I can breathe. ——— Breathe! (*The* LIEUTENANT *offers his arm.* ALICE *pauses.*) Did he say anything at the last?

LIEUTENANT: A few words.

ALICE: What did he say?

LIEUTENANT: He said: "Forgive them, for they know not what they do."

ALICE: Incredible!

LIEUTENANT: Yes, the Captain was a good and noble man.

ALICE: Kurt! (KURT *enters.*) It's over!

KURT: Oh! . . .

ALICE: Do you know what he said at the last? No, you couldn't. "Forgive them, for they know not what they do". . .

KURT: Can you translate that?

ALICE: I suppose he meant that *he* had always done what was right and that life had wronged him.

KURT: There'll probably be many fine words spoken over his grave.

ALICE: And so many wreaths. From the noncommissioned officers.

KURT: Yes.

ALICE: About a year ago, he said something to the effect that it seemed as if life were playing a colossal joke on us.

KURT: Do you mean he was joking with us even as he was dying?

ALICE: No! . . . But now that he's dead, I feel a strange urge to speak well of him.

KURT: Let's do that then.

LIEUTENANT: Miss Judith's father was a good and noble man.

ALICE (*to* KURT): There—do you hear?

KURT: "They know not what they do." How many times didn't I ask you if he knew what he was doing. And you thought he didn't know. It's time to forgive him.

ALICE: Riddles! Riddles! . . . But finally there's peace in this house! The wonderful peace of death! As wonderful as that solemn, anxious moment when a child is coming into the world. I hear the silence . . . and I see the tracks on the floor from the chair that carried him away. ——— And I feel my life is ended, and I'm beginning to decay . . . You know, it's curious, those simple words of the Lieutenant—and he is a simple soul—they haunt me. They've become true. My husband, the love of my youth— yes, you may laugh—he *was* a good and a noble man . . . in spite of everything!

KURT: In spite of everything? And a valiant one too—the way he fought for what was his.

ALICE: The troubles he suffered! The humiliations! The way he crossed things out—so he could on!

KURT: A man passed over by life. That explains much. Alice, go in to him.

ALICE: No, I can't. While we've been talking, I remembered the way he looked as a young man. ———— I saw him, I see him—now, as he was when he was twenty!...I must have loved that man!

KURT: And hated!

ALICE: And hated!...Peace be with him! (*She goes toward the door right, then stops, her hands clasped.*)

A Dream Play

(1901)

Author's Note

In this dream play, as in his earlier dream play *To Damascus,*
the author has attempted to imitate the disconnected but seemingly logical form of a dream. Anything can happen, everything is
possible and plausible. Time and space do not exist. Upon an insignificant background of real life events the imagination spins
and weaves new patterns: a blend of memories, experiences, pure
inventions, absurdities, and improvisations. [Those who follow the
author during the brief hours of his sleepwalker route will perhaps
find a certain similarity between the apparent jumble of a dream
and life's motley, unmanageable canvas, woven by the "World
Weaveress," who sets up the "warp" of human destinies and then
constructs the "woof" from our intersecting interests and variable
passions.]*

The characters split, double, redouble, evaporate, condense,
fragment, cohere. But one consciousness is superior to them all:
that of the dreamer. For him there are no secrets, no inconsisten-
cies, no scruples, no laws. He neither condemns nor acquits, only

*This sentence, taken from Strindberg's notes, is published here with the play
for the first time (translator).

205

relates. And since dreams are more often painful than happy, a tone of melancholy, and of compassion for all living things, runs through the swaying narrative. Sleep, supposedly a liberator, is often a torturer, but when the torment is at its worst, an awakening reconciles the sufferer with reality. No matter how agonizing reality can be, at this moment, compared with a tormenting dream, it is a pleasure.

Characters*

THE VOICE OF INDRA	SHE, *Victoria*
INDRA'S DAUGHTER, *Agnes*	THE RETIRED MAN
THE GLAZIER	THREE MAIDS
THE OFFICER, *Alfred*	UGLY EDITH
HIS FATHER	EDITH'S MOTHER
HIS MOTHER, *Kristina*	THE NAVAL OFFICER
LINA	ALICE
THE STAGE DOORKEEPER	THE SCHOOLMASTER
THE BILLPOSTER	A BOY, *Nils*
THE VOICE OF VICTORIA	A NEWLYWED HUSBAND
A BALLET DANCER	A NEWLYWED WIFE
A SINGER	THE BLIND MAN
THE PROMPTER	THE FIRST COAL HEAVER
THE POLICEMAN	THE SECOND COAL HEAVER
THE LAWYER, *Axel*	THE GENTLEMAN
THE ONE-ARMED CLERK	HIS WIFE
THE ONE-EYED CLERK	THE CHANCELLOR OF THE
THREE DOCTORAL CANDI-	UNIVERSITY
DATES	THE DEAN OF THEOLOGY
KRISTINE	THE DEAN OF PHILOSOPHY
THE QUARANTINE MASTER	THE DEAN OF MEDICINE
THE DANDY, *Don Juan*	THE DEAN OF LAW
HIS ATTENDANT	DANCERS AND CHORUS
THE COQUETTE	MEMBERS OF THE OPERA
HER "FRIEND"	COMPANY, CHILDREN,
THE POET	SCHOOLBOYS, AND SAILORS
HE	

*There is no list of characters in the original (translator).

Prologue

*(The backdrop represents banks of clouds that resemble crum-
bling slate mountains with ruins of castles and fortresses. The
constellations of Leo, Virgo, and Libra can be seen. Between
them is the planet Jupiter, shining brightly.* INDRA'S DAUGHTER
is standing on the highest cloud.)

INDRA'S VOICE *(from above)*: Where are you daughter, where?

INDRA'S DAUGHTER: Here, Father, here!

INDRA'S VOICE: You have strayed, child,
> Beware, you're falling ...
> How did you get here?

INDRA'S DAUGHTER: Racing on a cloud, I followed a lightning
beam
> from the highest ether ...
> But the cloud fell, and is still falling ...
> Oh, great Father Indra, god of gods, what regions have I
> come to?
> Why is it so close,
> so hard to breathe?

INDRA'S VOICE: You have left the second world and entered a
third.
> Far from Śukra, the Morning Star,
> you have come to a circle of vapors called Earth.
> Mark there the seventh house of the sun,
> Libra, where the star of day lights the balance scale of au-
> tumn
> and day and night weigh the same ...

INDRA'S DAUGHTER: You speak of the Earth, is that this dark and
heavy world lit by the moon?

INDRA'S VOICE: It is the densest and heaviest of the spheres that
wander space.

INDRA'S DAUGHTER: Does the sun never shine there?

INDRA'S VOICE: Of course the sun shines there, but not all the
time ...

INDRA'S DAUGHTER: My cloud is opening and I can see what's
there ...

INDRA'S VOICE: What do you see, child?

INDRA'S DAUGHTER: I see . . . that it is fair . . . with green forests, blue waters, white mountains, and golden fields . . .

INDRA'S VOICE: Yes it is fair, as is all Brahmā created . . .
> but it was fairer still
> once, in the dawn of time.
> Then something happened,
> a disturbance in the orbit, perhaps something else,
> an act of disobedience followed by crimes, which had to be
> suppressed . . .

INDRA'S DAUGHTER: Now I hear sounds from down below . . .
What kind of creatures dwell there?

INDRA'S VOICE: Descend and see . . . I'll not slander the Creator's children.
> What you hear is their speech.

INDRA'S DAUGHTER: It sounds like . . . There's no happiness in it.

INDRA'S VOICE: Yes, I know. Complaining
> is their mother tongue!
> They're an ungrateful race,
> impossible to please . . .

INDRA'S DAUGHTER: Don't say that, now I hear shouts of joy,
> and shots and boomings, see lightning flashes,
> now bells are ringing, fires are lit,
> and a thousand times a thousand voices
> sing praise and thanks to heaven . . .
> (*pause*)
> You judge them too hard, oh Father . . .

INDRA'S VOICE: Descend and see, listen and return.
> Tell me then if they have cause and reason
> for complaints and lamentations . . .

INDRA'S DAUGHTER: So be it. I'll descend, but come with me, Father!

INDRA'S VOICE: No, I cannot breathe there . . .

INDRA'S DAUGHTER: My cloud is descending. The air is close; I'm suffocating . . .
> What I breathe is not air, but smoke and water . . .
> So heavy, it draws me down, down,
> and now I can feel it turning and rolling.

This third world is surely not the best ...
INDRA's VOICE: Not the best, but not the worst.
    This globe of dust spins around like all the others,
    and so its creatures sometimes suffer a dizziness
    bordering between foolishness and madness ———
    Have courage, my child, this is but a trial.
INDRA's DAUGHTER (*on her knees as the cloud descends*): I'm fall-
ing!
    (*The backdrop now represents a forest of giant hollyhocks in bloom: white, pink, sulphur-yellow, violet. Above them rises the gilded roof of a castle topped by a crown-shaped flower bud. Spread out below the foundation walls of the castle are piles of straw, covering manure from the castle stables. On the wings, which remain in place for the entire play, are stylized paintings representing a mixture of interiors, exteriors, and landscapes. The* GLAZIER *and the* DAUGHTER *enter.*)
DAUGHTER: The castle keeps growing up out of the earth ... Fa-
ther, do you see how much it's grown since last year?
GLAZIER (*to himself*): I have never seen this castle before ... have
never heard of a castle growing ... but ——— (*to the* DAUGH-
TER *with strong conviction*) Yes, it's grown seven and a half
feet, but that's because it's been fertilized ... and if you look
closely, you'll see that a wing has sprouted on the sunny side.
DAUGHTER: It should bloom soon since we're past midsummer.
GLAZIER: Don't you see the flower up there?
DAUGHTER: Oh, yes, I see it! (*clapping her hands*) Tell me, why
do flowers grow up out of filth?
GLAZIER (*gently*): They don't like the filth, and so they hurry out
of it as fast as they can, up toward the light, to bloom and die.
DAUGHTER: Do you know who lives in the castle?
GLAZIER: I used to know, but I forgot.
DAUGHTER: I think there's a prisoner inside ... and I'm sure he's
waiting for me to set him free.
GLAZIER: But at what price?
DAUGHTER: You don't bargain about what you have to do. Let's
go in the castle! ...
GLAZIER: Yes, let's go!
    (*They cross toward the backdrop, which slowly divides to re-*

veal a simple, bare room with a table and a few chairs. On one of the chairs sits an OFFICER, *wearing a very unusual contemporary military uniform. He is rocking in the chair and striking the table with a saber. The* DAUGHTER *crosses to him and slowly takes the saber out of his hand.*)

DAUGHTER: No, no, you mustn't do that!

OFFICER: Oh, please, Agnes, let me keep my saber!

DAUGHTER: No, you're chopping the table to pieces. (*to the* GLAZIER) Father, you go down to the harness room and replace the windowpane. We'll see each other later. (*He leaves.*) You're a prisoner in your own room. I've come to set you free.

OFFICER: I guess I've been expecting this, but I wasn't sure you'd want to.

DAUGHTER: The castle is strong, with seven walls, but it can be done . . . Do you want to or not?

OFFICER: To be honest, I don't know. Either way I'll suffer. You have to pay for every joy in life with twice the sorrow. It's hard sitting here, but if I have to buy my freedom, I'll suffer threefold. ———— Agnes, I'd just as soon put up with it, as long as I can see you.

DAUGHTER: What do you see in me?

OFFICER: The beauty that gives harmony to the universe. ———— I see in you lines I find only in the orbits of the solar system, in a lovely chord of music, in the vibrations of light. ———— You are a child of heaven . . .

DAUGHTER: So are you.

OFFICER: Then why do I have to look after horses? Clean stables and shovel manure?

DAUGHTER: So that you'll long to get out of here.

OFFICER: I do, but it's so hard to tear myself away.

DAUGHTER: But everyone has an obligation to seek freedom in the light.

OFFICER: Obligation? What about life's obligations to me?

DAUGHTER: You feel life has wronged you?

OFFICER: Yes. It's been unjust . . .

(*Voices are heard from behind a screen, which divides the stage. The screen is drawn aside. The* OFFICER *and the* DAUGHTER *look in that direction, then freeze in place. The* MOTHER, *sickly, sits at a table. In front of her burns a tallow candle, and she trims the wick from time to time with a pair of snuffers. On the table are piles of newly sewn shirts, which she is marking with marking ink and a quill pen. A brown wardrobe stands to the left. The* FATHER *brings her a silk shawl.*)

FATHER (*gently*): Don't you want it?

MOTHER: A silk shawl for me? What use is that, dear? I'll soon be dead.

FATHER: Then you believe what the doctor said?

MOTHER: Yes, that too, but mostly I believe the voice I hear inside me.

FATHER (*sorrowfully*): Then it really is serious . . . And you're thinking of your children, first and last.

MOTHER: They've been my whole life, my reason for being . . . my joy, and my sorrow . . .

FATHER: Kristina, forgive me . . . for everything.

MOTHER: For what? Forgive me, dear. We've tormented each other . . . and why? Neither of us knows. We couldn't do otherwise . . . Anyway, here are the children's new shirts . . . See that they change twice a week, Wednesdays and Sundays, and that Louisa washes them . . . all over . . . Are you going out?

FATHER: I have to be up at school at eleven.

MOTHER: Ask Alfred to come in before you go.

FATHER (*pointing to the* OFFICER): But sweetheart, he's standing right here.

MOTHER: My eyesight is going too . . . It's getting so dark . . . (*trims the candle*) Alfred, come here! (*The* FATHER, *nodding good-bye, walks out through the wall. The* OFFICER *crosses to the* MOTHER.)

MOTHER: Who is that girl?

OFFICER (*whispering*): That's Agnes.

MOTHER: Oh, so that's Agnes. Do you know what they're saying? . . . That she's the daughter of the god Indra, and that she asked to come down to Earth to feel what it's like to be a human being . . . But don't say anything . . .

OFFICER: She's a divine creature, that's for certain.

MOTHER (*aloud*): Alfred, my dear, I'm soon going to leave you and your brothers and sisters . . . There's something I want you to remember for the rest of your life.

OFFICER (*sadly*): Of course, Mother.

MOTHER: Just one thing: never quarrel with God!

OFFICER: What do you mean, Mother?

MOTHER: You mustn't go around feeling that life has wronged you.

OFFICER: But I've been treated unjustly.

MOTHER: You're still brooding about the time you were punished for stealing a coin which was later found.

OFFICER: Yes. That injustice warped my whole life ...

MOTHER: I see! Now go over to the wardrobe ...

OFFICER (*ashamed*): So, you know. It's ...

MOTHER: The copy of *The Swiss Family Robinson* ... that ...

OFFICER: Don't say any more! ...

MOTHER: That your brother got punished for ... when it was *you* who tore it up and hid the pieces.

OFFICER: Imagine! That wardrobe is still standing there after more than twenty years ... And we moved so many times, and my mother died ten years ago!

MOTHER: What difference does that make? Why must you always question everything and spoil the best that life has to offer? ... Look, there's Lina!

LINA (*enters*): Ma'am, I'm very grateful, but I can't go to the christening ...

MOTHER: Why not, child?

LINA: I have nothing to wear.

MOTHER: You can borrow my shawl.

LINA: That's very kind, but I couldn't do that.

MOTHER: I don't understand you. I'll never be able to use it again myself.

OFFICER: What will Father say? It's a present from him ...

MOTHER: What small minds you all have ...

FATHER (*sticking his head in*): Are you lending my present to one of the maids?

MOTHER: Don't talk like that ... Remember, I was a servant once myself ... Why must you hurt an innocent person?

FATHER: Why must you hurt me, your husband? ...

MOTHER: Oh, what a world! You try to do the right thing and there's always someone who thinks it's wrong. ... If you help one person, you hurt another. What a world! (*She trims the* candle so that it goes out. *The stage is darkened, and the screen is drawn again.*)

DAUGHTER: Human beings are to be pitied.

OFFICER: You think so?

DAUGHTER: Yes, life is hard, but love conquers all! Come and see! (*They cross upstage.*)

(*The backdrop is raised to reveal a new backdrop which represents an old, dirty, free-standing fire wall. In the middle of the wall a gate opens on an alley, which leads to a brightly lit green area where a giant blue monkshood [aconitum] can be seen. To the left of the gate, in front of a booth, sits the* STAGE DOORKEEPER, *a woman with a shawl over her head and shoulders. She is crocheting a star-patterned comforter. To the right a gas lamp hangs over a billboard which the* BILLPOSTER *is cleaning. Beside him stands a fishing net with a green handle. Farther to the right is a door with an air hole in the shape of a four-leaf clover. To the left of the gate stands a small linden tree with a pitch-black trunk and several pale green leaves. Next to it is a cellar air vent.*)

DAUGHTER (*crossing to the* DOORKEEPER): Isn't the star comforter finished yet?

DOORKEEPER: No, dear child. Twenty-six years is no time at all for a piece of work like this.

DAUGHTER: And your young man never came back?

DOORKEEPER: No, but it wasn't his fault. He just *had* to leave . . . poor man. That was thirty years ago.

DAUGHTER (*to the* BILLPOSTER): She was a ballet dancer, wasn't she? Up there, in the opera?

BILLPOSTER: She was the prima ballerina there . . . but when *he* left, it was as if he took her dancing with him . . . She never got any more parts . . .

DAUGHTER: Everyone complains, with their eyes if not with their voices . . .

BILLPOSTER: Oh, I don't complain much any more . . . not since I got a scoop net and green fish box.

DAUGHTER: And that makes you happy?

BILLPOSTER: Yes, very happy, very . . . It was my childhood dream and now it's come true. Of course, I just turned fifty . . .

DAUGHTER: Fifty years for a net and a fish box ...

BILLPOSTER: A *green* fish box ... a *green* one ...

DAUGHTER (*to the* DOORKEEPER): Give me the shawl now, so I can sit and watch the children of man. But you must stand behind me and tell me about them. (*puts on the shawl and sits down by the gate*)

DOORKEEPER: It's the last performance of the season today and the opera is closing ... Now they find out if they're rehired ...

DAUGHTER: What happens to those who aren't?

DOORKEEPER: Lord Jesus, you'll see ... I always pull the shawl over my head ...

DAUGHTER: Poor people!

DOORKEEPER: Look, here comes one! ... She's not among the chosen ones ... Do you see how she's crying? ... (*The* SINGER *rushes out through the gate, her handkerchief covering her eyes. She stops for a moment outside the gate and leans her head against the wall. Then she runs off.*)

DAUGHTER: Human beings are to be pitied! ...

DOORKEEPER: But look: here's the way a happy person looks!

(*The* OFFICER *comes down the alley wearing a frock coat and top hat. He is carrying a bouquet of roses and looks radiantly happy.*)

DOORKEEPER: He's going to marry Miss Victoria! ...

OFFICER (*downstage, looks up and sings*): Victoria!

DOORKEEPER: She'll be right down.

OFFICER: Fine! I've got the carriage waiting, the table set, and the champagne on ice ... May I embrace you, ladies? (*embraces the* DOORKEEPER *and the* DAUGHTER; *sings*) Victoria!

WOMAN'S VOICE (*singing from above*): I'm here!

OFFICER (*begins to stroll around*): Well, I'm waiting!

DAUGHTER: Don't you know me?

OFFICER: No, I know only one woman ... Victoria! For seven years I've been walking here and waiting for her ... at noon, when the sun reaches the chimney tops, and in the evening, when darkness begins to fall ... Look at the pavement here, worn down by a faithful lover. Hurrah! She's mine! (*sings*) Victoria! (*There is no answer.*) Oh well, she's probably getting dressed. (*to the* BILLPOSTER) I see you have a fishing net. Everybody at the Opera is crazy about fishing nets ... or rather, fish!

That's because fish can't sing! . . . What does a thing like that cost?

BILLPOSTER: It's pretty expensive.

OFFICER (*sings*): Victoria! . . . (*shakes the linden tree*) Look, it's getting new leaves again! For the eighth time! . . . (*sings*) Victoria! . . . Now she's fixing her hair! . . . (*to the* DAUGHTER) Ma'am, can I go up and fetch my bride? . . .

DOORKEEPER: No one is allowed on stage!

OFFICER: Seven years I've been walking up and down here. Seven times three hundred and sixty-five makes two thousand five hundred and fifty-five! (*stops and pokes at the door with the clover-shaped hole*) . . . And I've looked at this door two thousand five hundred and fifty-five times without finding out where it leads to. And this cloverleaf opening to let in light . . . light for whom? Is there someone inside? Does anyone live there?

DOORKEEPER: I don't know. I've never seen it opened . . .

OFFICER: It looks like a pantry door I saw when I was four years old and one Sunday afternoon went off with the maid. Off to other houses, other maids. But I never got beyond the kitchen, and I sat between the water barrel and the salt tub. I've seen so many kitchens in my day, and the pantry was always in the entry hall, with round bored holes and a cloverleaf in the door . . . But how can the Opera have a pantry when it has no kitchen? (*sings*) Victoria! . . . Listen, she can't leave by any other way, can she, ma'am?

DOORKEEPER: No, there's no other way out.

OFFICER: Good, then I can't miss her. (*Theatre people come rushing out, scrutinized by the* OFFICER.) She's got to come out soon! . . . Ma'am, that blue monkshood out there. I saw one like that when I was a child . . . Could it be the same flower? . . . I remember it in a minister's garden when I was seven. There were usually two doves, blue doves, under the hood. . . . But that time a bee came and went into the hood, and I thought: "Now I've got you," and I squeezed the flower. But the bee stung me, right through it, and I cried. And the minister's wife came and put some wet dirt on it. . . . Then we got wild strawberries and milk for supper! . . . I think it's getting dark already ——— (*to the* BILLPOSTER) Where are you going?

BILLPOSTER: Home for supper.

OFFICER (*rubbing his eyes*): Supper? At this time of day? ———
Say ... can I go in for a moment and phone the Growing Castle?

DAUGHTER: What for?

OFFICER: I want to tell the Glazier to put in double windows. It's
winter soon and I'm really freezing. (*goes past the* DOORKEEPER
into her booth)

DAUGHTER: Who is Miss Victoria?

DOORKEEPER: She's his beloved.

DAUGHTER: Of course, I see! What she is to other people doesn't
interest him. All she is is what she means to him ... (*It suddenly
grows dark.*)

DOORKEEPER (*lights the gas lamp*): It's getting dark quickly today.

DAUGHTER: For the gods a year is like a minute.

DOORKEEPER: And for human beings a minute can be as long as a
year. (*The* OFFICER *enters again. He looks dusty; his roses have
wilted.*)

OFFICER: She hasn't come yet?

DOORKEEPER: No.

OFFICER: She'll come, all right! ... *She'll* come! (*strolls around*)
But maybe it would be wise to phone and cancel lunch, anyway
... since it's already evening ... Yes, I'll do that. (*goes in to telephone*)

DOORKEEPER (*to the* DAUGHTER): Can I have my shawl back
now?

DAUGHTER: No, my friend, you rest a while longer. I'll do your
work ... I want to know about people and life, to find out if it's
as hard as they say.

DOORKEEPER: But they don't let you sleep on this job, never
sleep, day or night ...

DAUGHTER: Not sleep at night?

DOORKEEPER: Well, if you can, with a bell cord tied to your arm.
You see, there are night watchmen on the stage, and they're
relieved every three hours ...

DAUGHTER: But that must be torture ...

DOORKEEPER: Maybe you think so, but we're happy to get jobs
like this. If you knew how envied I am ...

DAUGHTER: Envied? People envy someone who's tortured?

DOORKEEPER: Yes ... But do you know what's worse than night work and drudgery and drafts and cold and dampness? Having to listen, as I do, to all the stories of unhappiness up there ... They all come to me. Why? Maybe they see the lines of suffering in my face and read sympathy there ... Hidden in this shawl, my dear, are thirty years of anguish, mine and others'! ...

DAUGHTER: It's heavy too, and it stings like nettles ...

DOORKEEPER: Wear it as long as you like ... When it gets too heavy, call me, and I'll come and relieve you.

DAUGHTER: Good-bye. If you could stand it, surely I can.

DOORKEEPER: We'll see ... But be kind to my little friends and be patient with their complaining. (*She disappears down the alley.*)

(*Blackout. When the lights come up, the setting is changed: the linden tree has lost its leaves, the blue monkshood is almost withered, and the green area at the end of the alley is autumn brown. The* OFFICER *enters. He now has gray hair and a gray beard. His clothes are dilapidated, his collar black and limp. Only a few petals are left in the bouquet of roses. He strolls around.*)

OFFICER: All the signs are that summer is over and autumn is near. —— I see that from the linden tree and the monkshood ... (*strolling*) But autumn is my *spring* because that's when the theatre reopens. And then she must come. Ma'am, would you please let me sit in that chair for awhile.

DAUGHTER: You sit, my friend, I'll stand.

OFFICER (*sits*): If only I could sleep a little, I'd feel better ... (*He dozes off for a moment, then jumps up and continues strolling, stopping before the door with the cloverleaf opening and poking at it.*) This door won't give me any peace ... What's behind it? There must be something! (*Soft music sounds from above in dance rhythm.*) Oh! Rehearsals have begun! (*The lights flash on and off as if the stage were illuminated by a lighthouse beacon.*) What's this? (*in time with the flashes*) Light and dark; light and dark?

DAUGHTER (*imitating him*): Day and night, day and night! ... A merciful Providence wants to shorten your waiting. And so the days fly by, chasing the nights! (*The lights remain on again.*

The BILLPOSTER *enters, carrying his net and posting equip-ment.*)

OFFICER: There's the Billposter, with his net . . . Has the fishing been good?

BILLPOSTER: Oh, yes! The summer was hot and a bit long . . . The net was pretty good, but not *quite* as I imagined . . .

OFFICER (*stressing the words*): Not quite as I imagined! . . . That's very well put. Nothing is ever as I imagined it! . . . It's always greater in my imagination, better than it turns out to be . . . (*strolls around striking the walls with the bouquet so that the last petals fall*)

BILLPOSTER: Hasn't she come yet?

OFFICER: No, not yet, but she'll come soon! . . . Do you know what's behind that door?

BILLPOSTER: No, I've never seen that door open.

OFFICER: I'm going to phone for a locksmith to come and open it. (*He goes in to phone. The* BILLPOSTER *pastes up a poster and starts exiting right.*)

DAUGHTER: What's wrong with the net?

BILLPOSTER: Wrong? Well, there's nothing really wrong . . . It's just not as I imagined it, and so I didn't enjoy it quite as much as . . .

DAUGHTER: How did you imagine the net?

BILLPOSTER: How? . . . I can't say exactly . . .

DAUGHTER: Maybe I can . . . It was different in your imagination. It was green, but not *that* green!

BILLPOSTER: Yes, you understand, you do! You know every-thing—and that's why everyone comes to you with their trou-bles . . . maybe you'd listen to me too, sometime . . .

DAUGHTER: Of course I will . . . Come over here and tell me what's bothering you . . . (*She goes in her booth. The* BILLPOST-ER *stands outside and speaks to her through the window.*)

(*Blackout. When the lights come up, the linden tree has leaves again, the monkshood is in flower, and the open area at the end of the alley shines green in the sun. The* OFFICER *en-ters. He is now old and white-haired. His clothes are tattered and his shoes worn out. The bouquet is a handful of twigs. He*

still strolls around, but slowly, like an old man. He reads a post-
er. A BALLET DANCER *enters right.*)

OFFICER: Has Miss Victoria gone?

BALLET DANCER: No, she hasn't.

OFFICER: Then I'll wait. She's coming soon, isn't she?

BALLET DANCER (*earnestly*): I'm sure she will.

OFFICER: Don't go, you'll be able to see what's behind this door.
I've sent for the locksmith.

BALLET DANCER: It'll really be interesting to see that door
opened. The door and the Growing Castle. Do you know the
Growing Castle?

OFFICER: Do I? ——— I was a prisoner there.

BALLET DANCER: No, was that you? Say, why did they have so
many horses there?

OFFICER: It was a horse castle, of course . . .

BALLET DANCER (*painfully*): How stupid of me. I should have
known. (*A* SINGER *enters right.*)

OFFICER: Has Miss Victoria gone?

SINGER (*earnestly*): No, she hasn't gone. She never goes.

OFFICER: That's because she loves me! . . . Don't leave before the
locksmith gets here. He's going to open the door.

SINGER: Oh, is the door going to be opened? What fun! . . . I just
want to ask the Doorkeeper something. (*The* PROMPTER *enters*
right.)

OFFICER: Prompter, has Miss Victoria gone?

PROMPTER: No, not that I know.

OFFICER: You see! Didn't I say she was waiting for me? ———
Don't go. The door's going to be opened.

PROMPTER: What door?

OFFICER: Is there more than one door?

PROMPTER: Oh, I know: the one with the cloverleaf . . . I'll have to
stay for that! Just want to have a little word with the Doorkeeper. (*The* BALLET DANCER, *the* SINGER, *and the* PROMPTER *gath-*
er around the BILLPOSTER *outside the* DOORKEEPER's *window,*
where they take turns speaking to the DAUGHTER. *The* GLA-
ZIER *enters through the gate.*)

OFFICER: Are you the locksmith?

GLAZIER: No, the locksmith had company. A glazier will do just as well.

OFFICER: Certainly . . . of course. You brought your diamond, didn't you?

GLAZIER: Naturally! Did you ever hear of a glazier without his diamond?

OFFICER: Never! ——— Let's get to work! (*He claps his hands. Everyone gathers in a circle around the door. Singers in costumes for* Die Meistersinger *and female dancers from* Aïda *enter right and join them.*) Locksmith—uh, rather, Glazier—do your duty! (*The* GLAZIER *advances with his diamond.*) There aren't many moments like this in a person's life. And so, dear friends, I beg you . . . consider carefully . . .

POLICEMAN (*entering*): In the name of the law I forbid the opening of this door!

OFFICER: Oh, God, what a fuss there is when you try to do something new and important! . . . We'll take it to court! . . . Let's go to the Lawyer! We'll see what the law has to say! ——— To the Lawyer!

(*The scene changes, in full view of the audience, to the* LAWYER's *office: the gate remains and now functions as the gate in an office railing, which extends across the entire stage. The* DOORKEEPER's *booth turns to open toward the audience and becomes the niche for the* LAWYER's *desk. The linden tree, leafless, is a clothes tree. The billboard is hung with royal proclamations and court decisions. The door with the four-leaf clover opening is now part of a filing cabinet.*

The LAWYER, *in white tie and tails, is seated on the left inside the railing at a high desk covered with papers. His face bears witness to extraordinary suffering; it is chalk-white, lined, and with purple shadows. He is ugly and his face reflects all the crime and vice his profession has compelled him to come in contact with. He has two* CLERKS, *one of whom has only one arm, the other one eye.*

The people who assembled to observe "the opening of the door" remain but are now clients waiting for the LAWYER *and seem to have been standing there forever. The* DAUGHTER [*in her shawl*] *and the* OFFICER *are standing downstage.*)

LAWYER (*crossing to the* DAUGHTER): Sister, may I take your shawl? . . . I'll hang it in here until I get a fire going in the stove. Then I'll burn it with all its sorrows and miseries . . .

DAUGHTER: Not yet, my brother, I want it to be quite full first, and more than anything I want to be able to gather in all your pain, all the confidences you've had to share about crime and vice and unjust imprisonment, about slander and libel . . .

LAWYER: Your shawl wouldn't be big enough, my child. Look at these walls! Doesn't it seem as if the wallpaper is stained with every kind of sin? Look at these papers: the records I keep of injustice. Look at *me* . . . I never see any smiles on the people who come here, nothing but angry looks, bared teeth, clenched fists . . . And they spit out all their anger, envy, and suspicions on me . . . You see how black my hands are? I can never get them clean. You see how they're cracked and bleeding . . . I can never wear the same clothes for more than a day or two; they stink of other people's crimes . . . Sometimes I try fumigating the place with smoking sulphur, but it doesn't help. I sleep in the next room and dream of nothing but crimes . . . I have a murder case right now, but as terrible as that is, do you know what's worse? . . . Separating husbands and wives! ———— It's as if heaven and earth cried out against the betrayal—betrayal of Nature, virtue, love . . . And do you know, after all the mutual accusations have filled reams of paper, and someone sympathetic finally grabs one of the parties by the ear, pulls him or her aside, and in a friendly way asks the simple question: "What have you actually got against your husband or wife?"—they just stand there speechless. They don't know. Oh yes, in one case the trouble started with an argument over a salad. Another time it was a single word, or something equally trivial. But the pain, the suffering! These I have to bear! . . . Look at me! And tell me if you believe that I could win a woman's love with this criminal's face! Or that anyone would even want to be friends with the person responsible for collecting all the unpaid debts in town! . . . You try to act like a human being and you get nothing but misery in return!

DAUGHTER: Human beings are to be pitied.

LAWYER: That they are! And what they live on is a mystery to me. They get married on an income of two thousand crowns when they need four thousand . . . Which means they borrow, of course, everybody borrows! They live from hand to mouth till the day they die. And they always leave debts behind them. Who will pay the final reckoning? Tell me that.

DAUGHTER: He who feeds the birds.

LAWYER: Yes. But if He who feeds the birds would come down to the earth He made and see what wretches human beings are, maybe He would have some compassion . . .

DAUGHTER: They are to be pitied.

LAWYER: They are indeed. (*to the* OFFICER) What can I do for you?

OFFICER: I just wanted to ask if Miss Victoria has gone.

LAWYER: No, she hasn't. You can rest assured of that. Why are you poking at my filing cabinet?

OFFICER: I was thinking that this door resembles . . .

LAWYER: No, it doesn't! Absolutely not! (*Church bells can be heard.*)

OFFICER: Is there a funeral in town?

LAWYER: No, it's a commencement exercise. Doctoral degrees will be awarded. I was just going over to receive my doctorate in law. Would you like to get a degree and a laurel wreath?

OFFICER: Sure, why not? I could use a little diversion . . .

LAWYER: It's an impressive ceremony, and we should probably leave for it right away. ——— Just go and change your clothes.

(*The* OFFICER *exits. Blackout. The setting is changed to a church chancel. The office railing remains but now serves as the balustrade in front of the high altar. The billboard becomes the announcement board for psalms. The linden/clothes tree becomes a candelabra. The* LAWYER's *desk becomes the* CHAN- CELLOR's *lectern. The door with the cloverleaf opening now leads to the vestry . . . The* CHORUS *from* Die Meistersinger *become* HERALDS *with staffs, and the* DANCERS *carry laurel wreaths. The rest of the people are spectators. The backdrop rises, and the new backdrop represents a giant organ; above the keyboard is a mirror. Music sounds. At the sides stand repre- sentatives of the four faculties:* PHILOSOPHY, THEOLOGY, MEDI- CINE, *and* LAW. *The stage is empty for a moment. The* HER-

ALDS *enter right, followed by the* DANCERS, *holding their laurel wreaths out before them. The three* CANDIDATES *enter left, one after the other, are crowned by the* DANCERS, *and exit right. The* LAWYER *advances to receive his wreath. The* DANCERS *turn away, refusing to crown him, and leave. The* LAWYER, *shaken, leans against a pillar. Everyone else exits, leaving him alone. The* DAUGHTER *enters with a white veil over her head and shoulders.*)

DAUGHTER: Look, I've washed the shawl ... But why are you standing here? Didn't you get your wreath?

LAWYER: No, I wasn't worthy.

DAUGHTER: Why not? Because you defended poor people, spoke up for prisoners' rights, lightened the burdens of the guilty, won reprieves for the condemned ... Oh, these human beings ... They're no angels; they are pitiful creatures.

LAWYER: Don't speak badly of them. I can plead their case.

DAUGHTER (*leaning against the organ*): But why must they hurt their own friends so?

LAWYER: They don't know any better.

DAUGHTER: Then we'll enlighten them, you and I, together. Shall we?

LAWYER: They won't accept enlightenment ... If only our complaints could reach the gods in heaven ...

DAUGHTER: They shall reach the throne ... (*at the organ*) Do you know what I see in this mirror? ... The world as it really is! ... Before it got turned around.

LAWYER: How did it get turned around?

DAUGHTER: When the copy was made ...

LAWYER: Of course, that's it! The copy ... I've always felt that this was a false copy ... and when I began to sense what the original must have been like, I became dissatisfied with everything ... People called me malcontent and troublemaker and worse ...

DAUGHTER: It is a crazy world! Take those representatives of the four university faculties, for example! ... The government is afraid of change, so it supports all four: theology, the study of God's truth, is always being attacked and ridiculed by philosophy, which claims to be wisdom itself! And medicine, which always challenges philosophy and calls theology not an academic discipline but a superstition . . . And they all sit together on a council which is supposed to teach young people respect—for the university. It's nothing but a madhouse! And heaven help the first persons to see the truth!

LAWYER: That'll be the theologians. They begin their studies with philosophy, which teaches them that theology is nonsense. Later, in theology, they learn that philosophy is nonsense. Madmen, right?

DAUGHTER: And then there's law, the servant of all, except those who serve it.

LAWYER: All for the sake of justice, in whose name terrible wrongs are committed! . . . By the just, who are so often unjust!

DAUGHTER: That's the way you've arranged things, you children of man! Yes, *children!* ———— Come, I'll give you a wreath . . . one that'll suit you better. (*puts a crown of thorns on his head*) Now I'll play for you. (*She sits at the organ and plays a "kyrie," but instead of organ tones, human voices are heard.*)

CHILDREN'S VOICES: Eternal One! Eternal One! (*The last note is held.*)

WOMEN'S VOICES: Have mercy upon us! (*The last note is held.*)

MEN'S VOICES (*tenors*): Save us, for Thy sake!

MEN'S VOICES (*basses*): Spare Thy children, Lord, and be not wrathful against us!

ALL: Have mercy upon us! Hear us! Pity us mortals! ———— Eternal One, why art Thou so far from us? . . . Out of the depths we call: mercy, Eternal One! Make not the burden too heavy for Thy children! Hear us! Hear us!

(*The lights fade. The* DAUGHTER *rises and approaches the* LAWYER. *The lights transform the organ into Fingal's Grotto. The sea swells in between basalt pillars, producing a sound ensemble, a harmony of wind and waves.*)

LAWYER: Where are we, sister?

DAUGHTER: What do you hear?

LAWYER: I hear drops falling . . .

DAUGHTER: Those are tears, human tears . . . What else do you hear?

LAWYER: Sighing . . . moaning . . . wailing . . .

DAUGHTER: The complaints of mortals have reached this far . . . but no further. Why this eternal complaining? Has life no joy to offer?

LAWYER: Yes, the sweetest which is also the bitterest, love! Wife and home; the best things and the worst.

DAUGHTER: Let me try it!

LAWYER: You mean with me?

DAUGHTER: With you! You know the pitfalls, the stumbling blocks. We can avoid them.

LAWYER: But I'm poor.

DAUGHTER: What does that matter, as long as we love each other? And a little beauty doesn't cost anything.

LAWYER: Maybe the things I like you'll dislike.

DAUGHTER: Then we'll compromise.

LAWYER: And if we tire of each other?

DAUGHTER: Then a child will come and bring us delights that are always new!

LAWYER: And you'll have me, an outcast: poor and ugly and despised?

DAUGHTER: Yes! Let us join our destinies!

LAWYER: So be it, then.

(*A very simple room adjoining the* LAWYER'S *office. To the right a large curtained double bed near a window. To the left an iron stove with cooking utensils.* KRISTINE *is pasting over all the cracks between the window and its sash. A door upstage leads to the office, where poor people can be seen waiting to see the* LAWYER. *The* DAUGHTER, *pale and worn, sits by the stove.*)

KRISTINE: I'm pasting, I'm pasting!

DAUGHTER: You're cutting off all the air. I'm suffocating . . .

KRISTINE: There's only one little crack left.

DAUGHTER: Let in some air! I can't breathe!

KRISTINE: I'm pasting, I'm pasting!

LAWYER: That's right, Kristine. Heat costs money.

DAUGHTER: Oh, it's as if you're pasting my mouth shut!

LAWYER (*in the doorway with a paper in his hand*): Is the baby asleep?

DAUGHTER: Yes, finally.

LAWYER (*gently*): Its crying is scaring away my clients.

DAUGHTER (*sympathetically*): What can we do about it?

LAWYER: Nothing.

DAUGHTER: We'll have to get a larger apartment.

LAWYER: We can't afford it.

DAUGHTER: Can't I open the window? This bad air is suffocating me.

LAWYER: Then the heat will escape and we'll freeze.

DAUGHTER: This is dreadful . . . Can we scrub the office then?

LAWYER: You don't have the strength to scrub, neither do I, and Kristine has to paste. She has to paste every crack in the place, ceilings, floors, and walls.

DAUGHTER: I was prepared to be poor, not filthy.

LAWYER: Poverty and filth go together.

DAUGHTER: This is much worse than I dreamed.

LAWYER: It could be a lot worse. We still have food in the house.

DAUGHTER: But what food! . . .

LAWYER: Cabbage is cheap, nourishing and good.

DAUGHTER: For people who like cabbage. To me it's disgusting.

LAWYER: Why haven't you said that before?

DAUGHTER: Because I loved you. I was willing to make a sacrifice.

LAWYER: Then I'll have to give up cabbage. Sacrifices must be mutual.

DAUGHTER: What'll we eat then? Fish? You hate fish.

LAWYER: And it's expensive.

DAUGHTER: This is much harder than I expected.

LAWYER (*sympathetically*): You see how hard it is? . . . And the child, who should have been a blessing, a bond that brought us together . . . is only driving us apart.

DAUGHTER: Dearest! I'm dying in this air, in this room, with its window that looks out on nothing but a backyard, with its endless nights where I lie awake listening to a child crying, and with those people out there, always moaning and quarreling and accusing . . . I'm dying in here.

LAWYER: My poor little flower, with no light, no air . . .

DAUGHTER: And you say there are those who have it harder.

LAWYER: I'm among the most envied people in the neighborhood.

DAUGHTER: I could manage if only I had a little beauty in my home.

LAWYER: You mean a flower, don't you, maybe a heliotrope? But it costs one and a half crowns. That's six liters of milk or a half bushel of potatoes.

DAUGHTER: If I could have my flower, I'd gladly do without food.

LAWYER: There's one kind of beauty that doesn't cost anything, and when that's absent in a home, it's pure torture for someone with any sense of beauty.

DAUGHTER: What is that?

LAWYER: If I tell you, you'll get angry.

DAUGHTER: We agreed not to get angry.

LAWYER: We did agree ... All right, Agnes, providing we can avoid getting snide or sarcastic ... You know what I mean, don't you?

DAUGHTER: We won't use harsh tones.

LAWYER: Not if it's up to me.

DAUGHTER: Now tell me!

LAWYER: Well, when I come into a home, the first thing I look for is how the curtains are draped ... (*crosses to the window curtains and straightens them*) ... If they hang like a string or a rag ... I leave right away ... Then I glance at the chairs ... If they're placed properly, I stay ... (*straightens a chair against the wall*) After that I look at the candles ... If they're leaning over instead of standing straight, the house is crooked ... (*straightens a candle on the bureau*) That, my dear, is the beauty that doesn't cost anything!

DAUGHTER (*bowing her head*): Not that harsh tone, Axel!

LAWYER: It wasn't harsh!

DAUGHTER: Yes, it was!

LAWYER: Goddamn it! ...

DAUGHTER: What sort of language is that?

LAWYER: Forgive me, Agnes. But I've suffered as much from your untidiness as you have from the dirt. And I didn't dare straighten up things myself, because you'd take it as criticism and get angry ... Ugh! Shall we stop now?

DAUGHTER: It's terribly hard to be married ... harder than anything else. I think you have to be an angel.

LAWYER: Yes, I think so too.

DAUGHTER: I'm starting to hate you after all this.

LAWYER: God help us! Let's try to prevent hatred. I promise never again to comment on your housekeeping . . . even though it's torture for me.

DAUGHTER: And I'll eat cabbage, even thought it's a torment for me.

LAWYER: And so living together is a torment. One person's pleasure is another's pain.

DAUGHTER: Human beings are to be pitied!

LAWYER: You realize that?

DAUGHTER: Yes. But in God's name, now that we know the pitfalls so well, let's try to avoid them!

LAWYER: Let's do that! After all, we're enlightened and considerate people. We can forgive and forget.

DAUGHTER: And we can smile at trifles.

LAWYER: Yes, we can, of course we can . . . Do you know, I read in the newspaper today . . . By the way—where is the paper?

DAUGHTER (*embarrassed*): Which paper?

LAWYER (*harshly*): Do I get more than one paper?

DAUGHTER: Try to smile, and don't speak harshly . . . I started the fire with your paper . . .

LAWYER (*violently*): Goddamn it!

DAUGHTER: Remember, smile! . . . I burned it because it ridiculed the things I believe in . . .

LAWYER: And that I don't believe in. Well! . . . (*smashes his fist in his hand furiously*) Oh, I'll smile. I'll smile so hard every tooth will show . . . I'll be considerate and keep my opinions to myself, and be evasive and hypocritical. So, you've burned up my newspaper! Well! (*adjusts the hanging on the bedpost*) You see! Here I am tidying up again, and making you angry! . . . Agnes, this is simply impossible!

DAUGHTER: Of course it is!

LAWYER: And yet we must put up with it, not because of our vows, but for the sake of the child.

DAUGHTER: That's true. For the child. Oh! ——— Oh! . . . We must put up with it!

LAWYER: I have to go out to my clients. Listen to them: buzzing impatiently! They can't wait to tear at each other, to have each other fined and imprisoned . . . lost souls.

DAUGHTER: Poor, poor human beings! And this pasting! (*She bows her head in silent despair.*)

KRISTINE: I'm pasting. I'm pasting. (*The* LAWYER *stands at the door, twisting the doorknob nervously.*)

DAUGHTER: Oh, how the doorknob screeches. It's as if you were twisting a knife in my heart . . .

LAWYER: I'm twisting, I'm twisting . . .

DAUGHTER: Please, don't!

LAWYER: I'm twisting . . .

DAUGHTER: No!

LAWYER: I'm . . .

OFFICER (*inside the office, grasps the doorknob*): May I?

LAWYER (*releasing the doorknob*): Of course! After all, you've got your doctorate.

OFFICER: The whole world is mine! All roads are open to me. I've climbed Parnassus. The laurel wreath is won. Immortality, honor, it's all mine!

LAWYER: But what will you live on?

OFFICER: Live on?

LAWYER: Aren't you going to have a home, clothes, food?

OFFICER: That's no problem, as long as you have someone who loves you.

LAWYER: Oh, naturally, of course . . . Of course! Paste, Kristine! Paste! Until no one can breathe! (*He backs out, nodding.*)

KRISTINE: I'm pasting, I'm pasting! Until no one can breathe!

OFFICER: Are you coming along now?

DAUGHTER: Right away! But where?

OFFICER: To Fairhaven! A summer resort where the sun is shining and there are young people, children, and flowers! With singing and dancing, parties, and feasting!

DAUGHTER: That's where I want to go!

OFFICER: Come on!

LAWYER (*entering again*): And I'll return to my first hell . . . this was the second . . . and the worst! The sweetest of all but the worst hell . . . Look, she's dropped hairpins on the floor again! . . . (*picks one up*)

OFFICER: Oh, that's nothing!

LAWYER: Isn't it? . . . Look at it! Two prongs, but one pin. It's two, but it's one. If I straighten it out, it's a single piece. If I bend it, it's two, without ceasing to be one. "And the two shall become as one." But if I break it—like this—then the two are two. (*breaks the hairpin and throws away the pieces*)

OFFICER: What a wonderful image! . . . But in order for you to break it, the prongs have to diverge. If they converge, they hold together!

LAWYER: But if they're parallel, they never meet, never come together . . . It's like ice on water that neither bears nor breaks.

OFFICER: The hairpin must be the most perfect thing ever created: both a straight line and two parallel lines at the same time!

LAWYER: A lock that fastens when it is open!

OFFICER: Fastening open a braid of hair which remains open when it is fastened . . .

LAWYER: Like this door. When I close it, I open the way out, for you, Agnes! (*withdraws and closes the door*)

DAUGHTER: And now?

(*Scene change: the bed and canopy are transformed into a tent; the iron stove remains; the backdrop rises. In the foreground to the right charred hills are visible, covered with red heather and tree stumps left black and white after a forest fire; red pigsties and outhouses. Below this is an open-air gymnasium for hospital patients who exercise on machines resembling instruments of torture. In the foreground to the left a section of the quarantine station complex: open sheds with furnaces, boilers, and pipes. Beyond the foreground is a strait of water. The backdrop depicts another island: a beautiful wooded shoreline with flag-bedecked piers where white boats are moored, some with sails hoisted, some not. Between the trees on the shore small country estates with gazebos, kiosks, and marble statues can be seen.*

On the shore of the island in the foreground the QUARANTINE MASTER, *dressed as a Moor, is walking. The* OFFICER *crosses to him and shakes his hand.*)

OFFICER: If it isn't old Bombast! So you ended up here.

MASTER: Yes, I did. I'm the Quarantine Master here.

OFFICER: This is Fairhaven, isn't it?

MASTER: No, that's over there. This is Foulport.

OFFICER: Then we came to the wrong place!

MASTER: We? ———— Aren't you going to introduce me?

OFFICER: Oh, I couldn't do that. (*whispering*) She's Indra's own daughter!

MASTER: Indra's? And I thought it was the god Varuṇa himself! ... Aren't you surprised that I'm wearing a black mask?

OFFICER: My son, I'm over fifty, so nothing surprises me any more ... I just assumed you were going to a masquerade this afternoon.

MASTER: You're absolutely right. And I hope you'll come along.

OFFICER: Certainly, for there's nothing very ... appealing about this place. What sort of people do you have staying here?

MASTER: Sick people. Healthy people are over on the other island.

OFFICER: Nothing but poor people here, eh?

MASTER: On the contrary, they're all rich. You see that one being stretched on the rack? He's eaten so much goose liver with truffles and drunk so much burgundy that his feet are curling up on themselves.

OFFICER: Curling up?

MASTER: Yes, he's got curly feet ... And that one over there—lying on the guillotine—he's drunk so much cognac we have to pull him through rollers to straighten his back out.

OFFICER: And that's no fun, I bet.

MASTER: Everyone staying on this island has something terrible to hide. Take that one coming now, for example. (*An* Attendant *rolls an elderly* DANDY *in a wheelchair, accompanied by a gaunt, ugly, sixty-year-old* COQUETTE, *dressed in the latest fashion. She is attended by a forty-year-old male* "FRIEND.")

OFFICER: Why that's the Major! He was in school with us.

MASTER: Don Juan! And he's still in love with that scarecrow who's with him. He doesn't see that she's grown old, that she's ugly, unfaithful, cruel.

OFFICER: That's true love! I never would've believed someone that fickle could be capable of loving so deeply and seriously.

MASTER: What a beautiful way to look at it.

OFFICER: I've been in love myself with Victoria ... Yes, I still wait for her in the alley outside the Opera.

MASTER: So, you're the one who waits in the alley?

OFFICER: That's me!

MASTER: And have you gotten the door open yet?

OFFICER: No, the case is still pending... The Billposter is out fishing with his new net, you see, so he hasn't testified yet... Meanwhile, the Glazier has put in window panes in the castle, which has grown half a story... It's been an unusually good year... warm and humid.

MASTER: Not as warm as it is here with me!

OFFICER: How hot does it get in those ovens?

MASTER: When we disinfect people suspected of carrying cholera, the temperature is 140 degrees.

OFFICER: Is cholera going around again?

MASTER: Didn't you know?...

OFFICER: Yes, of course I did, but I so often forget what I know.

MASTER: I often wish I could forget what I know, especially about myself. That's why I'm always on the lookout for masquerades, fancy dress balls, and spectacular parties.

OFFICER: What've you been up to?

MASTER: If I talk about it, people say I'm boasting. If I keep my mouth shut, they call me a hypocrite.

OFFICER: So that's why you've blackened your face?

MASTER: Yes. A little blacker than I really am.

OFFICER: Who's that coming?

MASTER: Oh, he's a poet, come for his mud bath. (*The* POET *enters, staring up at the sky and carrying a bucket of mud.*)

OFFICER: What? Shouldn't someone like that be bathing in light and air?

MASTER: No, he spends so much time on higher planes that he gets homesick for the mud... Wallowing in mire makes his skin as tough as a pig's. Then he can't feel the stings of the critics.

OFFICER: What a strange world of contradictions.

POET (*ecstatically*): Out of clay the creator god Ptah made man on a potter's wheel, a lathe, ——— (*skeptically*) ——— or some other damned thing!... (*ecstatically*) Out of clay the sculptor creates his more or less immortal masterpieces ——— (*skeptically*) ——— which are mostly junk! (*ecstatically*) Out of clay are manufactured those vessels so necessary in the kitchen and pantry, and which we call jars and plates, —— (*skeptically*) —— though I don't give a damn what they're called! (*ecstatically*) This is clay! In its liquid state it's called mud —— *C'est mon affaire!* (*shouting*) Lina! (LINA *enters carrying a bucket.*) Lina, let Miss Agnes see you . . . She met you ten years ago, when you were a young, happy, and, let's say, pretty girl . . . Look at her now! Five children and a house full of drudgery, screaming, beatings, and starvation. Do you see how her beauty has faded, her joy disappeared? All drained away by duties and responsibilities that should have made her feel fulfilled.

MASTER (*putting his hand over the* POET'S *mouth*): That's enough, shut up!

POET: That's what they all say! And if you do keep quiet, they tell you to speak out! These impossible human beings!

DAUGHTER (*crossing to* LINA): Tell me your troubles.

LINA: No, I don't dare to! Things would only get worse!

DAUGHTER: Who could be that cruel?

LINA: I don't dare talk about it! They'd beat me!

POET: She's right. But I'll talk about it, even if the Moor tries to knock my teeth out! . . . I'll tell how unjust things can be sometimes . . . Agnes, daughter of the gods! Do you hear that music and dancing up there on the hill? . . . Well, that's for Lina's sister, who's come home from town, where she . . . went astray, if you know what I mean . . . Now they're slaughtering the fatted calf for her, while Lina, who stayed at home, has to carry buckets to feed the pigs! . . .

DAUGHTER: But there's rejoicing there, not just because a child came home, but because someone who went astray found the right path again! Don't you see?

POET: Then make it festive every night for this poor woman who never went astray! Do that! . . . But no one will. When Lina has any time off, she goes to prayer meeting where she's scolded for not being perfect! Is that justice?

DAUGHTER: Your questions are so hard to answer . . . Problems I never expected . . .

POET: That's what he said, too—Harun the Just, Caliph of Baghdad! . . . He just sat calmly, up there on his throne, too remote from the troubles of the common people. Finally, their complaints reached his exalted ear. One fine day he stepped down, disguised himself, and walked unnoticed among his subjects to see how justice was being kept.

DAUGHTER: You don't think I'm like Harun the Just, do you?

OFFICER: Let's talk about something else! . . . Here come visitors! (*From the left a white ship shaped like a dragon glides in, with a light blue silk sail flying from a golden yard and a rose-colored pennant flapping on a golden mast.* HE *and* SHE *sit at the helm with their arms around each other.*) Look at them! There's perfect happiness for you, bliss without limits, the triumph of young love! (*The stage becomes brighter.*)

HE (*rises in the boat and sings*):
> Hail to thee, fair bay,
> where the springtimes of my youth were spent,
> where I dreamed those early, rosy dreams!
> You have me back again,
> but no longer alone!
> Greet her,
> groves and bays,
> sea and sky!
> My love, my bride!
> My sun, my life!

(*The flags on Fairhaven's piers dip in greeting; white handkerchiefs wave from the estates and the beaches, and a chord played on harps and violins sounds over the strait.*)

POET: See how radiant they are! Listen to that sound across the water! . . . Eros!

OFFICER: It's Victoria!

MASTER: Well, what are you going to do about it?

OFFICER: He has his Victoria and I have mine! And mine no one may see! . . . Hoist the quarantine flag, and I'll haul in the net! (*The* QUARANTINE MASTER *waves a yellow flag. The* OFFICER *pulls on a line, and the boat turns toward Foulport.*) Heave to there! (HE *and* SHE *now notice the dreadful landscape and are horrified.*)

MASTER: Oh yes! You have to pay the price! Anyone and everyone coming from a contaminated area has to stop here!

POET: How can you treat them like that, even talk like that to people in love? Leave them alone! Interfering with love is high treason! . . . Alas! Everything beautiful is dragged down, down in the mud. (HE *and* SHE *come ashore, sad and ashamed.*)

HE: Have pity on us! What have we done?

MASTER: You don't need to have done anything to be contaminated by life's little troubles.

SHE: Must joy and happiness be so brief?

HE: How long must we stay here?

MASTER: Forty days and forty nights.

SHE: We'd rather throw ourselves in the sea!

HE: Live here, among charred hills and pigsties?

POET: Love conquers all, even sulphur fumes and carbolic acid! (*The* QUARANTINE MASTER *lights the oven. Blue sulphur fumes rise.*)

MASTER: I've lit the sulphur! You're welcome to step in!

SHE: Oh! My blue dress will lose its color.

MASTER: And turn white! Your red roses will also turn white.

HE: And your cheeks too. In forty days.

SHE (*to the* OFFICER): This must please you.

OFFICER: No, it doesn't! . . . It's true that your happiness caused me suffering, but . . . it doesn't matter—I have my doctorate now and a job on that other island . . . Oh yes, I do. This autumn I'll be working in a school there . . . teaching boys the same lessons I had to learn all the time I was growing up, all the time, over and over. And now it'll be the same lessons again, for the rest of my life, the same lessons. How much is two times two? How many times does two go evenly into four? . . . Until I retire, on a pension, with—nothing to do but wait around for meals and newspapers—until finally they carry me out to the crematorium to be burned up . . . Have you got any retired people here? The worst thing I know next to two times two is four is having to begin school again when you already have your doctorate. Asking the same questions over and over until you die . . . (*An elderly man walks past, his hands behind his back.*) Look, there goes a retired person, waiting away his life. He's probably a captain who never made major, or a law clerk who never became a judge—many are called, but few are chosen . . . Nothing to do but wait for his lunch . . .

RETIRED MAN: No, for the paper! The morning paper!

OFFICER: And he's only fifty-four years old. He can go on for another twenty-five years waiting for meals and newspapers ... Isn't that awful?

RETIRED MAN: Tell me what isn't awful! Go ahead, tell me!

OFFICER: Yes, whoever can! ... Now I'll have to teach boys that two and two are four! How many times does two go evenly into four? (*He scratches his head in despair.*) And Victoria, whom I loved and therefore wished the greatest happiness on earth ... Now she has that happiness, more than she's ever known, and I'm suffering ... suffering, suffering!

SHE: Do you think I can be happy when I see you suffering? How can you believe that? Maybe it'll ease your pain that I'll be a prisoner here for forty days and nights. It will, won't it?

OFFICER: Yes and no! How can I enjoy your suffering? Oh!

HE: And do you think I can build my happiness on your anguish?

OFFICER: We're all to be pitied—all of us! (ALL *stretch their hands toward heaven and utter a cry of pain that sounds like a dissonant chord:* "Oh!")

DAUGHTER: Eternal One, hear them! Life is evil! Human beings are to be pitied! (ALL *cry out again:* "Oh!")

(*The stage grows completely dark for a moment, during which everyone either leaves or changes places. When the lights come up again, Fairhaven's beach is visible in the foreground, but lies in shadow. Beyond the foreground is the strait of water and beyond that Foulport; both are brightly lit. To the right a corner of the resort's clubhouse; through its open windows couples can be seen dancing. Standing on an empty box outside are three MAIDS, their arms about each other's waists, watching the dancing. On the terrace of the building is a bench where UGLY EDITH is sitting, bareheaded and sad, her massive head of hair tousled. In front of her is a piano, its keyboard open. To the left a yellow frame house. Outside, two children in summer clothes are throwing a ball.*

At the rear of the foreground is a pier with white boats and flags flying from flagpoles. Out in the strait is a white, square-rigged warship with gunports.

But the landscape itself is winter-clad, with snow on the bare trees and ground. The DAUGHTER *and the* OFFICER *enter.*)

DAUGHTER: It's vacation time, with everyone relaxed and happy! All work has stopped and there's a party every day. Everyone's dressed in holiday finery and there's music and dancing, even in the mornings. (*to the* MAIDS) Why don't you girls go in and dance?

FIRST MAID: Us?

OFFICER: But they're servants!

DAUGHTER: That's true! ... But why is Edith sitting there instead of dancing? (EDITH *hides her face in her hands.*)

OFFICER: Leave her alone! She's been sitting there for three hours and no one has asked her ... (*He enters the yellow house to the left.*)

DAUGHTER: What a cruel game! (EDITH's MOTHER, *in a décolleté dress, comes out of the clubhouse and crosses to her daughter.*)

MOTHER: Why haven't you gone in as I told you to?

EDITH: Because ... I can't just invite myself. No one wants to dance with me because I'm ugly, I know that. I don't have to be reminded of it! (*She begins to play J. S. Bach's "Toccata and Fugue" No. 10 on the piano.*)

(*The waltz being played inside the clubhouse can be heard only faintly at first. Then it grows louder, as if to challenge the Bach Toccata. But* EDITH's *playing subdues the waltz music. Clubhouse guests appear in the doorway to hear her play. Everyone on stage listens raptly.*

Then a NAVAL OFFICER *grabs* ALICE, *one of the clubhouse guests, around the waist, and leads her down to the pier.)*

NAVAL OFFICER: Come quickly! (EDITH *breaks off playing, rises and watches them, her heart broken. She remains standing, as if turned to stone.)*

(*The wall on the yellow house now rises to reveal the interior.* SCHOOLBOYS *sit on three benches. In among them is the* OFFICER, *who looks ill at ease and troubled. The* SCHOOLMASTER, *wearing glasses, and with chalk and a cane in his hands, stands before them.)*

SCHOOLMASTER (*to the* OFFICER): Well, my boy, can you tell me how much two times two is? (*The* OFFICER *remains seated, struggling painfully but unsuccessfully to remember the answer.)* Stand up when you're asked a question!

OFFICER (*rises, tormented*): Two ... times two ... Let me see! ... It's two twos.

SCHOOLMASTER: I see! You haven't done your homework!

OFFICER (*ashamed*): Yes, I have, but ... I know what it is, but I can't say it ...

SCHOOLMASTER: Don't try that with me, boy! You know it, but can't *say* it! Maybe I can help you! (*He pulls the* OFFICER's *hair.*)

OFFICER: Ow, this is awful, awful!

SCHOOLMASTER: Yes, it is awful that a big boy like you has no ambition ...

OFFICER (*in agony*): A *big* boy! Yes, I *am* big, much bigger than the others here. I'm grown up. I've finished school ... (*as if awakening*) ... Why, I have my doctorate ... Then what am I doing here? Didn't I get my doctorate?

SCHOOLMASTER: Yes, of course, but you'll sit here until you're mature, do you understand? You've got to mature ... That's only right, isn't it?

OFFICER (*clutching his forehead*): Yes, yes, it's only right. You have to mature ... Two times two ... is two! And I can prove it by an analogy, the highest form of proof! Listen! One times one is one, therefore two times two is two! What applies to one, applies to the other!

SCHOOLMASTER: Your proof follows the laws of logic precisely, but the answer is wrong!

OFFICER: Something that follows the laws of logic can't be wrong. Here's another proof: one goes into one once, therefore two goes into two twice!

SCHOOLMASTER: Absolutely correct, according to the proof of analogy. But then how much is one times three?

OFFICER: Three!

SCHOOLMASTER: Then consequently two times three is also three!

OFFICER (*contemplating*): No, that can't be right . . . it can't be . . . otherwise . . . (*sits down in despair*) No, I'm not mature yet!

SCHOOLMASTER: No, you're not, far from it . . .

OFFICER: But then how long will I have to sit here?

SCHOOLMASTER: How long? Do you think time and space exist? . . . If time does exist, you should be able to tell me what it is. What is time?

OFFICER: Time . . . (*thinking*) I can't say, but I know what it is: ergo, I *can* know how much two times two is and still not be able to say it! Can you tell me what time is, sir?

SCHOOLMASTER: Certainly I can!

ALL THE BOYS: Tell us then!

SCHOOLMASTER: Time? . . . Let me see! (*standing motionless, his finger alongside his nose*) While we speak, time flies. Therefore, time is something that flies while I speak.

A BOY (*rising*): The teacher is speaking, and while he speaks, I fly. Therefore, I am time! (*flees*)

SCHOOLMASTER: That's absolutely correct, according to the laws of logic.

OFFICER: But then the laws of logic must be crazy! Nils can't be time just because he's flying off!

SCHOOLMASTER: That's also absolutely correct according to the laws of logic. Although you're right, it is crazy.

OFFICER: Then logic is crazy!

SCHOOLMASTER: It really looks that way. But if logic is crazy, then the whole world is crazy . . . And I'll be damned if I stand here teaching you such nonsense! . . . If someone will buy us all a drink, we'll go for a swim!

OFFICER: But that's a *posterus prius* or turned-around world. You're supposed to swim first and then have a drink! You old fogey!

SCHOOLMASTER: Don't get arrogant, *Doctor!*

OFFICER: Officer, if you please! I'm an officer, and I can't understand why I have to sit here among schoolboys and be scolded . . .

SCHOOLMASTER (*raising his finger*): Because we've got to mature!
  (*The* QUARANTINE MASTER *enters.*)

MASTER: The quarantine is beginning!

OFFICER: Oh, it's you! Can you imagine, this man has me sitting on a school bench, even though I have my doctorate!

MASTER: Well, why don't you get up and leave?

OFFICER: Listen to that! . . . Leave? It's not so easy.

SCHOOLMASTER: No, I bet it isn't. Try!

OFFICER (*to the* QUARANTINE MASTER): Save me! Save me from his eyes!

MASTER: Come on! . . . Come on and help us dance . . . We have to dance before the plague breaks out! We have to!

OFFICER: Then the naval ship is leaving?

MASTER: Yes, it's the first to leave . . . That'll mean a lot of weeping, of course.

OFFICER: Always weeping: when it arrives and when it leaves . . . Let's go! (*They exit. The* SCHOOLMASTER *continues his lesson. The* MAIDS, *who were standing at the clubhouse window, now move sadly down toward the pier.* EDITH, *who had been standing by the piano as if turned to stone, follows them slowly.*)

DAUGHTER (*to the* OFFICER): Isn't there a single happy human being in this paradise?

OFFICER: Yes, those newlyweds! Listen to them! (*The newlyweds enter.*)

HUSBAND (*to his* WIFE): My happiness is so great at this moment I wish I could die . . .

WIFE: Why die?

HUSBAND: Because in the midst of happiness grows a seed of unhappiness. Happiness consumes itself like a flame. It can't burn forever; sooner or later it must die. And that knowledge destroys the joy for me, right at its peak.

WIFE: Let us die together then, right now!

HUSBAND: Die? Very well. I'm afraid of happiness. It's deceitful!
  (*They cross toward the sea.*)

DAUGHTER (*to the* OFFICER): Life is cruel. Human beings are to be pitied!

OFFICER: Do you see that man coming now? He is the most envied person on the island. (*The* BLIND MAN *is led in.*) He owns all the hundred country estates here. All these bays, inlets, beaches, and woods are his, all the fish in the water, the birds in the air, the game in the woods. These thousand people are *his* tenants, and the sun rises on *his* sea and sets on *his* lands . . .

DAUGHTER: And does he complain too?

OFFICER: Yes, and with good reason. He can't see.

MASTER: He's blind . . .

DAUGHTER: The most envied person of all.

OFFICER: He's come to see the ship sail. His son is on board.

BLIND MAN: I can't see, but I can hear! I hear the claw of the anchor tearing at the clay at the bottom of the sea. It's like when you pull the hook out of a fish's throat and the heart follows with it . . . My son, my only child, will travel to foreign lands on the great wide sea. I can only follow him with my thoughts . . . Now I hear the anchor chain screeching . . . and . . . something snapping and flapping like wash hanging on a line . . . wet handkerchiefs perhaps . . . And I hear sobbing and sniffling, like people crying . . . Is it the waves lapping at the ship's planking or the girls on the shore? . . . the abandoned ones . . . inconsolable . . . I once asked a child why the ocean was salty. And the child, whose father was away on a long voyage, answered without hesitation: "The ocean is salty because sailors cry so much." "And why do sailors cry so much?" I asked. "Well," he answered, "because they always have to go away . . . And that's why they always dry their handkerchiefs up in the masts!" . . . "Why do people cry when they're sad?" I continued . . . "Well," he said, "because sometimes you have to wash the windows of your eyes to see more clearly!" . . . (*The ship has set sail and glides away. The girls on the shore alternate waving good-bye with their handkerchiefs and drying their tears. On the foremast the signal "yes" is hoisted, a red ball on a white field.* ALICE *waves joyfully in response.*)

DAUGHTER (*to the* OFFICER): What does that flag mean?

OFFICER: It means "yes." The Lieutenant is affirming his love in red, as red as the blood in his heart, etched against the blue of the sky.

DAUGHTER: And what does "no" look like?

OFFICER: Blue, as blue as the unclean blood in his veins ... Look how jubilant Alice is!

DAUGHTER: While Edith weeps! ...

BLIND MAN: Meeting each other and leaving each other. Leaving and meeting. That's what life is! I met his mother. And then she left. But I still had my son, and now he's gone!

DAUGHTER: He'll come back, you'll see!

BLIND MAN: Who's that speaking to me? I've heard that voice before; in my dreams, in my youth when summer holidays began, then when I got married, and when my child was born. Every time life smiled I heard that voice, like the murmur of the south wind, like a chord of music from above when the angels greet Christmas ... (*The* LAWYER *enters, crosses to the* BLIND MAN, *and whispers something to him.*)

BLIND MAN: Is that right?

LAWYER: Yes, it is. (*crossing to the* DAUGHTER) You've seen just about everything, but you haven't experienced the worst thing of all.

DAUGHTER: What could that be?

LAWYER: The endless repetitions ... Doing the same things over and over ... Learning the same lessons again and again ... Come!

DAUGHTER: Where?

LAWYER: Back to your duties.

DAUGHTER: What are they?

LAWYER: Everything you dread doing. Whatever you don't want to do but must! It means giving up things, denying yourself, going without, leaving behind ... It's everything unpleasant, disgusting, painful ...

DAUGHTER: Are there no pleasant duties?

LAWYER: Only those that are already done ...

DAUGHTER: And no longer exist ... So duty is everything unpleasant. What's pleasant then?

LAWYER: What's pleasant is what's sinful.

DAUGHTER: Sinful?

LAWYER: And so must be punished. Yes. If I have a really pleasant day and evening, a guilty conscience makes me suffer the pangs of hell the next day.

DAUGHTER: How strange!

LAWYER: Yes, I wake up in the morning with a headache and have to relive the whole experience, only this time totally differently. What was beautiful, witty, and enjoyable the night before, seems ugly, stupid, and disgusting the morning after. It's as if the pleasure turned sour, and the joy dissolved. What people call success is only preparation for the next failure. All the successes in my life have contributed to my ruin. It's human instinct to dread someone else becoming prosperous. People think it's unjust of fate to favor one person over another. So they try to restore the balance by putting obstacles in the paths of others. To have talent can cost you your life, for you can easily starve to death! . . . Anyway, it's either return to your duties or I take you to court, and, if necessary, appeal the case to the highest level!

DAUGHTER: Return? To the iron stove and the cabbage pot, the baby's clothes . . .

LAWYER: That's right. In fact, there's a big load of laundry today. All the handkerchiefs have to be washed . . .

DAUGHTER: Oh, and I have to do all that again?

LAWYER: That's all life is: doing the same things over and over again . . . take the new schoolteacher here . . . He got his doctorate yesterday, with a laurel wreath and the firing of cannon. He ascended Parnassus and was embraced by the king . . . Today he starts back in the schoolhouse again, asking how much two and two are, and will continue until he dies . . . Anyway, come back, to your home!

DAUGHTER: I'd rather die than that!

LAWYER: Die? It's not allowed! First of all, suicide is against the law; second, it means the loss of God's grace—it's a mortal sin!

DAUGHTER: It's never easy being a human being!

ALL: True!

DAUGHTER: I won't return with you to humiliation and filth! . . . I want to go back where I came from, but . . . first, the door must be opened so that I'll know the secret . . . I want the door to be opened!

LAWYER: Then you'll have to retrace your steps, take the same road back, put up with all the horrors of a courtroom trial: reliving and repeating everything, over and over . . .

DAUGHTER: So be it, but first I must seek seclusion in the wilderness to find myself once more. We'll meet again. (*to the* POET) Come with me! (*Cries of woe sound from Foulport in the distance.*) What was that?

LAWYER: Those are the lost souls in Foulport.

DAUGHTER: But why are they complaining more than usual today?

LAWYER: Because the sun is shining over here, because there's music, dancing, and young people. It makes their suffering so much worse.

DAUGHTER: We must set them free!

LAWYER: Go ahead and try. There was once someone else who wanted to set mankind free, but they hung Him on a cross.

DAUGHTER: Who did?

LAWYER: All the right-thinking people.

DAUGHTER: Who are they?

LAWYER: You mean you don't know who the right-thinking people are? We'll have to introduce you.

DAUGHTER: Were they the ones who denied you your degree?

LAWYER: Yes.

DAUGHTER: Then I know who they are.

(*The Riviera. To the left in the foreground is a white wall above which the tops of fruit-laden orange trees can be seen. Upstage are estates and a casino with a terrace. To the right a large pile of coal with two wheelbarrows. To the right upstage a blue strip of the sea.*

Two COAL HEAVERS, *naked to the waist, their faces, hands, and other exposed parts of their bodies blackened, sit on their wheelbarrows in despair. The* DAUGHTER *and the* LAWYER *appear upstage.*)

DAUGHTER: This is paradise!

1ST COAL HEAVER: This is hell!

2ND COAL HEAVER: It's a hundred and fifteen in the shade!

1ST COAL HEAVER: Shall we cool off in the water?

2ND COAL HEAVER: The police'll come. You're not allowed to swim here.

1ST COAL HEAVER: What about picking one of those oranges?

2ND COAL HEAVER: No, the police would come then too.

1ST COAL HEAVER: But I can't work in this heat. I'm walking out.

2ND COAL HEAVER: Then you'll get arrested ... (*pause*) ... and they'll put you on bread and water ...

1ST COAL HEAVER: Bread and water! We work the hardest and get the least to eat! ... And the rich people, who don't do anything, get the most! ... If the truth be known, I call that unjust ... What does the daughter of the gods think?

DAUGHTER: I don't know what to say ... What have you done that you should have to work so hard and get so dirty?

1ST COAL HEAVER: What have we done? We were born poor, and our parents weren't very respectable ... And maybe we got arrested a couple of times.

DAUGHTER: Arrested?

1ST COAL HEAVER: That's right ... The ones who didn't get arrested are sitting up there in the casino, eating eight-course dinners with wine.

DAUGHTER (*to the* LAWYER): Can that be true?

LAWYER: For the most part, yes! ...

DAUGHTER: Do you mean that everyone has at least once in his life done something to be arrested for?

LAWYER: Yes.

DAUGHTER: You too?

LAWYER: Yes.

DAUGHTER: Is it true that these poor people can't swim in the sea here?

LAWYER: Yes, not even with their clothes on. Only people caught trying to drown themselves get away without paying a fine. But I hear the police beat them up later in the station house.

DAUGHTER: Why don't they go where the beaches aren't private?

LAWYER: All the beaches are private.

DAUGHTER: But I mean outside of town, in the country, where the land doesn't belong to anyone.

LAWYER: It all belongs to someone.

DAUGHTER: Even the sea? The great, open ...

LAWYER: Everything! If you're out on the sea in a boat, you can't even come ashore without getting permission and paying a fee. Beautiful, isn't it?

DAUGHTER: This is no paradise!

LAWYER: No, it isn't, I promise you.

DAUGHTER: Why don't people do something to reform things? . . .

LAWYER: Oh, they do. But all reformers end up in prison or the madhouse . . .

DAUGHTER: Who puts them in prison?

LAWYER: All the right-thinking people, all those honorable . . .

DAUGHTER: Who puts them in the madhouse?

LAWYER: Their own despair, when they realize how hopeless their efforts are.

DAUGHTER: Hasn't anyone ever thought that there might be a hidden reason why things are as they are?

LAWYER: That's exactly what the people who have it good believe.

DAUGHTER: That things are good as they are? . . .

1ST COAL HEAVER: And yet we're the foundations of society. Without the coal we deliver, everything would die out or ground to a halt: the stove in the kitchen, the furnace in the basement, the machine in the factory, the lights on the streets, in the stores, in the homes. Cold and darkness would descend over everything . . . And so we sweat like hell to bring you that black coal . . . What do you give us in return?

LAWYER (*to the* DAUGHTER): Help them . . . (*pause*) I can understand that there can't be absolute equality for everyone, but does there have to be this much inequality? (*A* GENTLEMAN *and his* WIFE *cross the stage.*)

WIFE: Are you going to come and play cards?

GENTLEMAN: No, I have to take a walk to work up an appetite.

1ST COAL HEAVER: Work up an appetite?

2ND COAL HEAVER: Work up an . . . ? (*Children enter and scream in terror when they see the* HEAVERS.)

1ST COAL HEAVER: They scream when they see us! They scream . . .

2ND COAL HEAVER: Damn it to hell! . . . It's time to bring out the guillotines and chop away the corruption . . .

1ST COAL HEAVER: You said it! Goddamn it! (*spits in disgust*)

LAWYER (*to the* DAUGHTER): It's all so crazy! But it's not people who are bad . . . it's . . .

DAUGHTER: What? . . .

LAWYER: The way they're forced to live . . .

DAUGHTER (*covering her face as she leaves*): This is no paradise!

COAL HEAVERS: No, it's hell, that's what it is!

(*Fingal's Grotto. Long green waves roll slowly into the cave. In the foreground a red bell buoy bobs on the waves; during the scene it sounds only in the places indicated. The music of the winds. The music of the waves. The* DAUGHTER *and the* POET *enter.*)

POET: Where have you led me?

DAUGHTER: Far from the murmur and moaning of the children of man, to the ends of the ocean, to this grotto we call the Ear of Indra since they say that the Lord of Heaven listens here to the lamentations of mortals.

POET: Here? How?

DAUGHTER: Don't you see how the grotto is shaped like a sea-shell? Yes, of course you do. Don't you realize that your ear is shaped like a seashell? You do, but you haven't thought about it. (*She picks up a shell from the beach.*) Didn't you ever as a child hold a seashell to your ear and listen . . . listen to the buzz-ing of your heart's blood, the murmur of thoughts in your brain, the bursting of thousands of tiny threads in the fabric of your body . . . These things you could hear in a little shell, imagine what you'll hear in one this big!

POET (*listening*): I hear nothing but the sighing of the wind . . .

DAUGHTER: Then I'll interpret it for you! Listen! The lamentation of the winds. (*reciting to soft music*)

> Born under heaven's clouds
> we were chased by Indra's thunderbolts
> down to this dusty earth . . .
> The mud of the fields soiled our feet.
> We suffered
> the smoke of the highways,
> the soot of the cities,
> the pungent smells of food and wine
> and human breath . . .
> So we raced out across the open sea
> to clean our lungs,
> shake our wings,

wash our feet.
Indra, Lord of Heaven,
hear us!
Hear us when we sigh!
The earth is not clean,
life is not good,
human beings are not evil,
nor are they good.
They live as best they can,
one day at a time.
Sons of dust in dust they wander,
of dust they were born
to dust they return.
Instead of wings,
they have only feet to plod with.
If they become dusty,
is the fault theirs
or thine?

POET: This is familiar . . .

DAUGHTER: Hush! The winds sing on! (*reciting to soft music*)
We winds, children of the air,
sing the lamentations of men.
Have you heard our song
on autumn nights
in oven doors,
in window cracks,
in the weeping of the rain on the roof tiles,
or on a winter night
in a snowy wood?
Have you heard on a wind-blown sea
the weeping and wailing
in the tackle and sails? . . .
It is we, the winds,
children of the air.
Men breathed us in
and taught us
these songs of pain . . .
In the sickroom, on the battlefield,

but mostly in the nursery,
where the newborn cry
and wail and scream
from the pain of being.
It is we, we, the winds,
who whine and wail
woe! woe! woe!

POET: I'm sure I've heard this ...

DAUGHTER: Hush! The waves are singing now. (*reciting to soft music*)

It is we, we, the waves,
who rock the winds
to sleep!
Green cradles, we waves.
Wet we are, and salt;
flaming up like fire,
wet flames are we.
Quenching, burning,
bathing, cleansing,
begetting, bearing.
We, we, the waves,
that rock the winds
to sleep!

False waves and faithless. Everything on earth that isn't burned is drowned—in the waves. ———— Look here. (*pointing to a heap of flotsam*) See what the sea has plundered and smashed ... All that's left of these sunken ships are their figureheads ... and their names: Justice, Friendship, Golden Peace, Hope—this is all that's left of hope ... deceitful hope! ... Spars, oarlocks, bailers! And look: the lifebuoy ... it saved itself and let those in distress perish!

POET (*searching in the flotsam*): Here's the nameboard for the Justice. That was the ship that left Fairhaven with the Blind Man's son. Now it's sunk. And Alice's fiancé was on board: Edith's hopeless love.

DAUGHTER: The Blind Man? Fairhaven? I must have dreamed these things. And Alice's fiancé, ugly Edith, Foulport and the quarantine station, the sulphur and carbolic acid, the commencement in the church, the lawyer's office, the stage door alley and Victoria, the Growing Castle and the Officer . . . All these things were in my dreams . . .

POET: All these things were in my poems . . .

DAUGHTER: Then you know what poetry is . . .

POET: Then I know what dreams are . . . What is poetry?

DAUGHTER: Not reality, but more than reality . . . not dreams, but waking dreams, reveries . . .

POET: And the children of man think we only play . . . only make-believe!

DAUGHTER: It's just as well, my friend. Otherwise nothing would ever get done in this world. If people took you seriously, they would only lie on their backs and look up at the sky. No one would touch a plow or a shovel, a pick or a hoe.

POET: What do you know of these things, Daughter of Indra? You're from another world.

DAUGHTER: You're right to reproach me. I've stayed too long down here, bathing in mud, like you . . . My thoughts no longer soar: they have clay on their wings, earth on their feet . . . and I ——— (*lifting her arms*) ——— feel myself sinking, sinking . . . Help me, Father, Lord of Heaven! (*silence*) I can't hear his answers any more! The ether no longer carries the sound from his lips to the shell of my ear . . . the silver thread has snapped . . . Alas! I am earthbound!

POET: Then you intend to return . . . soon?

DAUGHTER: As soon as I have burned away this mortal clay . . . for the waters of the ocean cannot make me clean. Why do you ask?

POET: Because I . . . I have a prayer . . . a petition . . .

DAUGHTER: What kind of petition? . . .

POET: A petition from mankind to the ruler of the world, drawn up by a dreamer . . .

DAUGHTER: To be presented by . . . ?

POET: By Indra's Daughter . . .

DAUGHTER: Can you speak the words?

POET: I can.

DAUGHTER: Then speak them.

POET: Better that you should.

DAUGHTER: Where can I read them?

POET: In my thoughts, or here! (*hands her a scroll*)

DAUGHTER (*takes the scroll but reads aloud without looking at it*):
Very well, then I'll speak them.
> "Child of man, why must you be born in pain?
> Why must you hurt your mother so
> to bring her the joy of motherhood,
> joy of joys?
> Why do you awaken to life
> and greet the light
> with a scream of outrage and pain?
> Why don't you smile at life,
> child of man, since the gift of life
> is happiness itself?
> Why are we born like animals,
> we descendents of gods and men?
> The spirit craves other garb
> than this of blood and filth!
> If we are made in God's own image,
> why must we endure this form? . . ."
> . . . Hush! Inquisitive one . . .
> a creation shouldn't find fault with its Creator!
> The riddle of life has yet to be solved! . . .
> "And thus the pilgrimage begins
> over thorns, stones and thistles.
> The beaten path, you'll find,
> is closed to you.
> If you pick a flower, you learn
> it belongs to someone else.
> If your road is blocked by a field,
> and you must go on,
> you'll trample others' crops
> as others will trample yours
> to even the score.
> Every happiness you enjoy
> brings sorrow to others,
> but your sorrow makes no one happy,
> because sorrow begets only sorrow.

And when the journey ends in one man's death,
its purpose seems to give another man breath."
Son of mortal clay, is this the way you intend
to approach the All Highest . . . ?

POET: How can a son of mortal clay find
words luminous, pure and airy enough
to rise from the earth?
Child of the gods, will you translate
our lament into language
the Immortal One understands?

DAUGHTER: I will.

POET (*indicating the buoy*): What's that floating there? . . . A buoy?

DAUGHTER: Yes.

POET: It looks like a lung with a windpipe.

DAUGHTER: It's the watchman of the sea. When danger threatens, it sings.

POET: The sea seems to be rising, and the waves are beginning to . . .

DAUGHTER: Yes, you're right!

POET: Oh! What's that? It's a ship . . . beyond the reef.

DAUGHTER: What ship is it?

POET: I think it's the ghost ship.

DAUGHTER: What's that?

POET: The Flying Dutchman.

DAUGHTER: Him? Why is he punished so severely, and why does he never come ashore?

POET: Because he had seven unfaithful wives.

DAUGHTER: Must he be punished for that?

POET: Yes! All the right-thinking people condemned him . . .

DAUGHTER: Strange world! . . . How can he be set free from the curse?

POET: Free? You have to be careful about setting people free . . .

DAUGHTER: Why?

POET: Because . . . No, it's not the Dutchman! It's just an ordinary ship in distress! . . . Why doesn't the buoy cry out? . . . Look, the sea is rising, the waves getting higher. We'll soon be trapped in this grotto! . . . The ship's bell is ringing! ———— We'll soon

have another figurehead . . . Cry out, buoy! Do your duty,
watchman! . . . (*The buoy sounds a four-part chord in fifths and
sixths, resembling a foghorn's signal.*) . . . The crew is waving to
us . . . but we ourselves are perishing!

DAUGHTER: Don't you want to be set free?

POET: Yes, of course, of course I do, but not now . . . and not by
water!

THE CREW (*singing in four-part*): Christ Kyrie!

Christ   Ky - ri - - e!

POET: They're calling and the sea is calling. But no one hears.

THE CREW (*as before*): Christ Kyrie!

DAUGHTER: Who's that coming there?

POET: Walking on the water? There's only One who walks upon
the water. ——— It couldn't be Peter, the rock, for he sank like
a stone . . . (*A shimmering white light appears out on the water.*)

THE CREW: Christ Kyrie!

DAUGHTER: Is it He?

POET: It is He, the one they crucified . . .

DAUGHTER: Why—tell me, why was He crucified?

POET: Because He tried to set men free . . .

DAUGHTER: I've forgotten—who crucified Him?

POET: All the right-thinking people.

DAUGHTER: What a strange world!

POET: The sea is rising! It's getting dark . . . The storm's getting
worse . . . (THE CREW *screams.*) The crew is screaming in horror
now that they see their Savior . . . And . . . they're jumping over-
board, in terror of the Redeemer . . . (THE CREW *screams again.*)

Now they're screaming because they're going to die! They
scream when they're born, and they scream when they die!
(*The rising waves in the grotto threaten to drown them.*)

DAUGHTER: If I were sure it was a ship . . .

POET: Actually . . . I don't think it is a ship . . . It's a two-story
house with trees outside it . . . and . . . a telephone tower . . . a
tower reaching into the clouds . . . It's a modern Tower of Babel,
sending wires upward—to communicate with those above . . .

DAUGHTER: Child, human thought needs no wires to travel on . . .
The prayers of the faithful penetrate all worlds . . . It's definitely
not the Tower of Babel. If you want to storm heaven, do it with
your prayers!

POET: No, it's not a house . . . not a telephone tower either . . . Do
you see?

DAUGHTER: What do you see?

POET: I see a snow-covered heath, a drill field . . . The winter sun
is shining behind a church on a hill, and the church tower casts
a long shadow on the snow . . . A troop of soldiers is marching
across the heath. They're marching across the tower's shadow,
toward the top of the spire. Now they're on the cross, and I
sense that the first one to step on the weathercock will die . . .
They're getting closer . . . The corporal is in the lead . . . Aha! A
cloud is moving over the heath, blotting out the sun, of course
. . . Now everything is gone . . . the water of the cloud has
quenched the fire of the sun! ———— The sun's rays created the
dark shadow of the tower, but the dark shadow of the cloud
smothered the tower . . . (*During the* POET's *speech, the setting
has changed back to the stage door alley.*)

DAUGHTER (*to the* DOORKEEPER): Has the Chancellor of the university come yet?

DOORKEEPER: No.

DAUGHTER: What about the Deans?

DOORKEEPER: No.

DAUGHTER: Then call them at once because the door is going to
be opened . . .

DOORKEEPER: Is it that urgent?

DAUGHTER: Yes, it is. People think that the solution to the riddle
of the world is hidden there . . . So, call the Chancellor and the

Deans of the four faculties! (*The* DOORKEEPER *blows a whistle.*)
And don't forget the Glazier and his diamond. Without him we
can't do anything. (*Theatre people enter from left as in the beginning of the play. The* OFFICER *enters from upstage wearing a
frock coat and a top hat. He is carrying a bouquet of roses and
looks radiantly happy.*)

OFFICER: Victoria!

DOORKEEPER: She's coming soon!

OFFICER: Fine! I've got the carriage waiting, the table set, and the
champagne on ice . . . May I embrace you, ma'am? (*embraces
the* DOORKEEPER) Victoria!

WOMAN'S VOICE (*singing from above*): I'm here!

OFFICER (*begins to stroll around*): Well, I'm waiting!

POET: I think I've been through this before . . .

DAUGHTER: Me too.

POET: Maybe it was a dream.

DAUGHTER: Or a poem.

POET: Or a poem.

DAUGHTER: Then you know what poetry is.

POET: Then I know what dreams are.

DAUGHTER: It seems to me we said these words before, somewhere else.

POET: Then you'll soon know what reality is.

DAUGHTER: Or dreams.

POET: Or poetry. (*The* CHANCELLOR *enters with the* DEANS *of*
THEOLOGY, PHILOSOPHY, MEDICINE, *and* LAW.)

CHANCELLOR: It's this business about the door, of course! ———
What do you think about it, as Dean of Theology?

DEAN OF THEOLOGY: Speaking theologically, I don't think, I believe . . . *credo* . . .

DEAN OF PHILOSOPHY: Speaking philosophically, I consider . . .

DEAN OF MEDICINE: Speaking medically, I know . . .

DEAN OF LAW: Speaking legally, I withhold judgment until I've
seen the evidence and heard the witnesses.

CHANCELLOR: They're starting to fight again . . . Let me hear first
from theology.

DEAN OF THEOLOGY: I believe this door must not be opened since
it conceals dangerous truths.

DEAN OF PHILOSOPHY: The truth is never dangerous.

DEAN OF MEDICINE: What is truth?

DEAN OF LAW: Whatever can be proven by the testimony of two witnesses.

DEAN OF THEOLOGY: With two false witnesses anything can be proven—by a crooked lawyer.

DEAN OF PHILOSOPHY: Truth is wisdom, and wisdom and knowledge are the core of philosophy ... Philosophy is the science of sciences, the sum of all learning, and all other sciences are its servants.

DEAN OF MEDICINE: The only science is natural science. Philosophy is not a science. It's only empty speculations.

DEAN OF THEOLOGY: Bravo!

DEAN OF PHILOSOPHY (*to the* DEAN OF THEOLOGY): So, you say bravo! And what are you? You're the archenemy of all learning, the very opposite of science. You are ignorance and darkness ...

DEAN OF MEDICINE: Bravo!

DEAN OF THEOLOGY (*to the* DEAN OF MEDICINE): Look who's shouting bravo now! Someone who can't see beyond the end of his nose except through a magnifying glass! Someone who believes only what his deceptive senses tell him: your eye, for example, which could be far-sighted, near-sighted, bleary-eyed, cross-eyed, one-eyed, color-blind, red-blind, green-blind, just plain blind ...

DEAN OF MEDICINE: Idiot!

DEAN OF THEOLOGY: Jackass! (*They begin to fight.*)

CHANCELLOR: Stop that! I won't have my deans squabbling among themselves.

DEAN OF PHILOSOPHY: If I had to choose between the two—theology or medicine—it would be neither!

DEAN OF LAW: And if I were the judge in a case involving the three of you, I'd find against you all! ... You can't agree on a single thing and never could ... Back to the business at hand! Chancellor, what is your opinion about this door and whether it should be opened?

CHANCELLOR: Opinion? I don't have any opinions. I was appointed by the government only to see to it that you educate students instead of breaking each other's arms and legs in committee meetings. Opinions? No, I'm very careful about holding opinions. I once had some opinions, which I debated, but my opponent immediately refuted them... Perhaps now we can open the door, even at the risk that it conceals dangerous truths.

DEAN OF LAW: What is truth? Where is it?

DEAN OF THEOLOGY: I am the truth and the life...

DEAN OF PHILOSOPHY: I am the science of all sciences...

DEAN OF MEDICINE: I am exact science...

DEAN OF LAW: And I object! (*They begin to fight.*)

DAUGHTER: Shame on you! Shame! Teachers of the young!

DEAN OF LAW: Chancellor, as representative of the government and head of the faculty, it's up to you to bring charges against this woman! To say "shame on you" to us is libel, and that sneering way she calls us "teachers of the young" amounts to defamation of character.

DAUGHTER: Poor students.

DEAN OF LAW: By pitying the students, she's accusing us! Chancellor, bring charges!

DAUGHTER: Yes, I accuse you, all of you, of sowing doubt and dissension in the minds of the young.

DEAN OF LAW: Listen to her! She's raising doubts herself in the young about our authority and then accuses us of raising doubts. I ask you—all right-thinking people—is this not a criminal action?

ALL THE RIGHT-THINKING PEOPLE: Yes, it's criminal.

DEAN OF LAW: All the right-thinking people have condemned you! ———— Go in peace with your gains. Otherwise...

DAUGHTER: My gains? ———— Otherwise? Otherwise what?

DEAN OF LAW: Otherwise you'll be stoned.

POET: Or crucified.

DAUGHTER: I'm going. Come with me and learn the answer to the riddle.

POET: What riddle?

DAUGHTER: What did he mean by my "gains"?...

POET: Probably nothing. That's what we call chatter. He was chattering.

DAUGHTER: But that hurt me more than anything!

POET: That's why he said it, I guess... Human beings are like that.

ALL THE RIGHT-THINKING PEOPLE: Hurray! The door is opened!

CHANCELLOR: What was concealed behind it?

GLAZIER: I can't see anything.

CHANCELLOR: You can't? Well, that's not surprising . . . Deans! What was concealed behind the door?

DEAN OF THEOLOGY: Nothing! That's the solution to the riddle of the world . . . In the beginning God created Heaven and Earth out of nothing.

DEAN OF PHILOSOPHY: Out of nothing comes nothing.

DEAN OF MEDICINE: Nonsense! That's what nothing is.

DEAN OF LAW: I'm suspicious. This looks like fraud to me. I appeal to all the right-thinking people.

DAUGHTER (*to the* POET): Who are the right-thinking people?

POET: Good question. It depends on which way the wind is blowing. Today the right-thinking people are me and mine, tomorrow they're you and yours. ———— It's something you're nominated for, or rather, you nominate yourself for.

ALL THE RIGHT-THINKING PEOPLE: We've been cheated!

CHANCELLOR: Who cheated you?

ALL THE RIGHT-THINKING PEOPLE: Indra's Daughter!

CHANCELLOR (*to the* DAUGHTER): Will you kindly tell us what you intended by having the door opened?

DAUGHTER: No, my friends! If I told you, you wouldn't believe it.

DEAN OF MEDICINE: But there's nothing.

DAUGHTER: That's it exactly. ———— But you haven't understood it.

DEAN OF MEDICINE: She's talking nonsense.

ALL THE RIGHT-THINKING PEOPLE: Nonsense!

DAUGHTER (*to the* POET): I pity them.

POET: Are you serious?

DAUGHTER: Always serious.

POET: You pity the right-thinking people too?

DAUGHTER: Maybe them most of all.

POET: And the four deans of the faculty?

DAUGHTER: Even them, and not the least. Four heads, four minds, on one body. Who made this monster?

ALL THE RIGHT-THINKING PEOPLE: She won't answer about the door!

CHANCELLOR: Then stone her!

DAUGHTER: I did answer you.

CHANCELLOR: Listen, she's answering.

ALL THE RIGHT-THINKING PEOPLE: Stone her! She's answering!

DAUGHTER: It's "stone her" if I answer and "stone her" if I don't!
... Come, poet and seer, I'll tell you the answer to the riddle,
but far from here, out in the wilderness, where no one can hear
us, or see us! Because ...

LAWYER (*coming forward to take the* DAUGHTER *by the arm*):
Have you forgotten your duties?

DAUGHTER: Oh, God, no! But I have higher duties.

LAWYER: And your child?

DAUGHTER: My child! What about it?

LAWYER: Your child is calling for you.

DAUGHTER: My child! Alas! I am earthbound! ... And this pain in
my breast, this anguish ... what is it?

LAWYER: Don't you know?

DAUGHTER: No!

LAWYER: The pangs of conscience.

DAUGHTER: The pangs of conscience?

LAWYER: Yes. You feel them after every neglected duty, after every pleasure, even the most innocent, if there is such a thing as
an innocent pleasure, which is doubtful. And you feel them after every suffering you've caused to those closest to you.

DAUGHTER: And there's no cure?

LAWYER: Yes, but only one: to do your duty without hesitation ...

DAUGHTER: You look like a demon when you say that word
"duty"! —————— But what if a person has two duties, as I have?

LAWYER: First do one and then the other!

DAUGHTER: Then the highest one first ... Will you look after my
child, so I can fulfill my duty? ...

LAWYER: Your child misses you terribly ... Can you let another
human being suffer because of you?

DAUGHTER: Suddenly my soul can find no peace ... It's torn in
two directions!

LAWYER: Life's little problems will do that.

DAUGHTER: But they're tearing me apart!

POET: If you had any idea how much disappointment and grief I
caused by fulfilling my highest duty—my calling—you wouldn't
want to take my hand!

DAUGHTER: How could that be?

POET: My father placed all his hopes in me, his only son. I was to take over his business ... But I ran away from business school, and he ... worried himself to death. My mother wanted me to be religious ... but I couldn't ... She disowned me ... I had a friend who helped me through hard times ... but he exploited the very people whose cause I was pleading in my poems. To save my soul I was forced to strike down my friend and benefactor. Since then I've had no peace. People call me traitor and scum of the earth. It doesn't help when my conscience tells me I was right because the next moment it tells me I was wrong. Such is life.

DAUGHTER: Come with me into the wilderness!

LAWYER: But your child!

DAUGHTER (*indicating everyone around her*): Here are my children. Individually they are good and kind, but when they get together, they fight and turn into demons ... Farewell!

(*Outside the castle. The setting is the same as the earlier scene, but the ground at the foot of the castle is now covered with flowers [blue monkshood, aconite]. Atop a small tower on the roof of the castle is a chrysanthemum bud ready to burst into bloom. The castle windows are illuminated by candles. The* POET *and the* DAUGHTER *appear.*)

DAUGHTER: The moment is near when I shall rise again into the ether with the help of fire ... This is what mortals call death and which you approach with fear.

POET: Fear of the unknown.

DAUGHTER: Which you know.

POET: Who knows it?

DAUGHTER: Everyone! Why won't you believe your prophets?

POET: Prophets have never been believed. I wonder why? ———— And "if God has spoken, why will the people then not believe?" His power to persuade should be irresistible.

DAUGHTER: Have you always doubted?

POET: No! I've had certainty often, but after a time it would vanish, like a dream when you wake up.

DAUGHTER: It's not easy to be a human being.

POET: You really know that now, don't you? ...

DAUGHTER: Yes.

POET: Tell me, wasn't it Indra who once sent his Son to earth to hear the complaints of mankind?

DAUGHTER: Yes, it was. How was He received?

POET: To answer with a question: did He accomplish His mission?

DAUGHTER: To answer with another: weren't conditions improved for mankind after His visit to earth? Answer truthfully!

POET: Improved? ... Yes, a little. Very little! ... But instead of all these questions: will you tell me the answer to the riddle?

DAUGHTER: Yes, but what good will it do? You won't believe me.

POET: I want to believe you, for I know who you are.

DAUGHTER: Very well, I'll tell you.

In the dawn of time, before the sun shone, Brahman, the divine primal force, allowed itself to be seduced by Māyā, the world mother, into propagating. This contact between divine and earthly substances was heaven's original sin. And so the world, life and human beings are only an illusion, a phantom, a dream image ...

POET: My dream!

DAUGHTER: A dream become reality! ... But to be set free from this earthly substance, Brahman's descendents seek self-denial and suffering. ... There you have suffering as liberator ... But this yearning for suffering comes in conflict with the desire for pleasure, or love ... Do you understand then why love is sublime joy and the greatest pain, the sweetest and the bitterest? Do you understand then what woman is? Woman, through whom sin and death entered life?

POET: I understand! ... And the outcome? ...

DAUGHTER: What you already know ... A struggle between the torment of pleasure and the suffering that brings release ... the pangs of remorse and the joys of sensuality ...

POET: Nothing but struggle?

DAUGHTER: Struggle between opposites generates power, as when fire and water make steam ...

POET: But what of peace? Rest?

DAUGHTER: Hush, you mustn't ask any more and I mustn't answer! ... The altar is already decked for the sacrifice ... The flowers stand watch, the candles are lit ... Death is near ...

POET: You say this so calmly, as if suffering didn't exist for you.

DAUGHTER: Not exist? . . . I've suffered all your suffering, but a hundredfold, because my senses were sharper . . .

POET: Tell me your sorrows!

DAUGHTER: Poet, could you tell me yours so completely that every word counted? Have you ever found words equal to the moment?

POET: No, you're right. I've always thought of myself as a deaf mute. Whenever my songs were admired, they seemed only noise to me . . . That's why I always blushed when people praised me.

DAUGHTER: And yet you want *me* to . . .? Look into my eyes.

POET: I can't bear to . . .

DAUGHTER: How then could you bear my words, if I were to speak in my own language?

POET: Tell me anyway, before you go: what did you suffer most from here?

DAUGHTER: From just—being alive: from sensing my vision dimmed by my eyes, my hearing muffled by my ears, and my thoughts, my bright, airy thoughts trapped in that labyrinth of fatty coils in my brain. You've seen a brain . . . those devious turns, those secret paths . . .

POET: So that's why all the right-thinking people think so deviously.

DAUGHTER: That was cruel, always cruel, but so are you all! . . .

POET: How can we be otherwise?

DAUGHTER: First I must shake the dust from my feet . . . the earth, the clay . . . (*She takes off her shoes and puts them in the fire.*)

DOORKEEPER (*enters and puts her shawl in the fire*): Perhaps I may burn my shawl too? (*exits*)

OFFICER (*enters*): And I my roses . . . only the thorns are left. (*exits*)

BILLPOSTER (*enters*): The posters can go, but never my scoop net! (*exits*)

GLAZIER (*enters*): The diamond that opened the door. Good-bye. (*exits*)

LAWYER (*enters*): The trial proceedings from great cases involving the Pope's beard or the depleted water supply at the sources of the river Ganges. (*exits*)

QUARANTINE MASTER (*enters*): A small contribution: the black mask that made me a blackamoor against my own will. (*exits*)

VICTORIA (*enters*): My beauty, my sorrow. (*exits*)

EDITH (*enters*): My ugliness, my sorrow. (*exits*)

THE BLIND MAN (*enters and sticks his hand in the fire*): A hand for an eye! (*exits*)

DON JUAN (*enters in his wheelchair with the* COQUETTE *and her* "FRIEND"): Hurry up, hurry up, life is short! (*They exit.*)

POET: I've read that when life is ending, everything and everyone passes in review . . . Is this the end?

DAUGHTER: For me, yes. Farewell!

POET: Won't you say a parting word?

DAUGHTER: No, I can't. Do you still believe that words can express your thoughts?

DEAN OF THEOLOGY (*enters, raging*): I've been abandoned by God, persecuted by men, rejected by the government, and scorned by my colleagues! How can I have faith when no one else has faith . . . How can I defend a God who won't defend His own people? It's all nonsense! (*throws a book in the fire and exits*)

POET (*snatching the book from the fire*): Do you know what this is? . . . A Book of Martyrs, a calendar with a martyr for each day in the year.

DAUGHTER: A martyr?

POET: Yes, someone tortured and killed for his faith. Tell me why! Do you think everyone who's tortured suffers and that everyone who's killed feels pain? Isn't suffering redemption and death deliverance?

KRISTINE (*enters with strips of paper*): I paste, I paste till there's nothing more to paste . . .

POET: And if the dome of heaven itself cracked, you'd try to paste that together too . . . Go!

KRISTINE: Are there no double windows in the castle?

POET: No, Kristine, not in there.

KRISTINE (*exiting*): Then I'll go.

DAUGHTER: Our parting time has come and the end approaches.
      Farewell, you child of man, you dreamer,
      you poet, who understands best how to live.
      Hovering on your wings above the world,

you plunge to earth from time to time,
but just to brush against it, not be trapped by it!

— — — — — — — — — — — — — — — — — — — —

Now as I go ... in the moment of parting,
leaving behind a friend, a place,
how great I feel the loss of all I loved
how great the regret for all I offended ...
Oh, now I know all the pain of being,
this is what it's like to be human ...
You miss even things you didn't value,
regret even wrongs you didn't commit ...
You want to go, and you want to stay ...
And so the heart is divided,
as if wild horses were pulling it apart,
torn by contradiction, indecision, uncertainty ...

— — —

Farewell! Tell my brothers and sisters I shall remember
    them
where I now go, and their lament
I shall bear in your name to the throne.
Farewell!
(*She goes into the castle. Music can be heard! The backdrop
is illuminated by the burning castle and reveals a wall of human
faces, questioning, grieving, despairing ... As the castle burns,
the flower bud on the roof bursts open into a giant chrysanthemum.*)

The Ghost Sonata

(1907)

Characters

THE OLD MAN, *Director Hummel*
THE STUDENT, *Arkenholz*
THE MILKMAID, *an apparition*
THE SUPERINTENDENT'S WIFE
THE SUPERINTENDENT
THE DEAD MAN, *a Consul*
THE LADY IN BLACK, *daughter of the Dead Man and the Super-intendent's wife*
THE COLONEL
THE MUMMY, *the Colonel's wife*
THE YOUNG LADY, *the Colonel's daughter, but actually the Old Man's daughter*
BARON SKANSKORG, *engaged to the Lady in Black*
JOHANSSON, *Hummel's servant*
BENGTSSON, *The Colonel's footman*
THE FIANCÉE, *a white-haired old woman, formerly engaged to Hummel*
THE COOK
BEGGARS
A MAID

265

Scene 1

(Outside a fashionable apartment building. Only a corner and the first two floors are visible. The ground floor ends in the Round Room; the floor above ends in a balcony with a flagpole.

When the curtains are drawn up in the Round Room, a white marble statue of a young woman can be seen, surrounded by palms and lit brightly by the sun. In the window to the left are potted hyacinths in blue, white, and pink.

Hanging on the railing of the balcony are a blue silk quilt and two white pillows. The windows to the left are draped with white sheets [in Sweden the indication that someone has died]. It is a clear Sunday morning.

Standing in front of the house downstage is a green bench.

Downstage right is a public fountain, downstage left a free-standing column covered with posters and announcements.

In the house façade upstage left is the entrance. The steps leading up to the door are of white marble, the railings of mahogany with brass fittings. Flanking the steps on the sidewalk are laurels in tubs.

The corner of the house with the Round Room faces a side street which runs upstage.

To the left of the entrance door a mirror is mounted outside a window [enabling the occupant of that apartment to observe, without being seen, what is happening in the street].

As the curtain rises, church bells can be heard in the distance.

All the doors visible in the house are open. A woman dressed in black stands motionless on the steps.

The SUPERINTENDENT'S WIFE *in turn sweeps the vestibule, polishes the brass on the front door, and waters the laurels.*

The OLD MAN *sits reading a newspaper in a wheelchair near the poster column. He has white hair, a beard and wears glasses.*

The MILKMAID *enters from around the corner carrying bottles in a wire basket. She is wearing a summer dress, with brown shoes, black stockings, and a white cap. She takes off her cap and hangs it on the fountain, wipes the sweat from her brow, takes a drink from a dipper in the fountain, washes her hands, and arranges her hair, using the water as a mirror.*

A steamboat's bell can be heard, and from time to time the bass notes of an organ in a nearby church penetrate the silence.

The silence continues for a few moments after the MILKMAID *has finished her toilet. Then the* STUDENT *enters left, sleepless and unshaven, and crosses directly to the fountain. Pause)*

STUDENT: Can I borrow the dipper? (*The* MILKMAID *hugs the dipper to her.*) Aren't you through using it? (*She stares at him in terror.*)

OLD MAN (*to himself*): Who is he talking to? ——— I don't see anyone! ——— Is he crazy? (*continues to stare at them in amazement*)

STUDENT (*to the* MILKMAID): Why are you staring? Do I look so frightening? ——— Well, I didn't sleep last night and I guess you think I've been out carousing . . . (*the* MILKMAID *as before*) Think I've been drinking, huh? ——— Do I smell of whiskey? (*the* MILKMAID *as before*) I didn't shave, I know that . . . Give me a drink of water, girl, I've earned it! (*pause*) All right, I suppose I have to tell you. All night I've been bandaging wounds and tending injured people. I was there, you see, when the house collapsed last night . . . Now you know. (*The* MILKMAID *rinses the dipper and gives him a drink.*) Thanks! (*The* MILKMAID *stands motionless. The* STUDENT *continues slowly.*) Would you do me a big favor? (*pause*) The thing is, my eyes are inflamed, as you can see. Since my hands have been touching the injured and the dead, I don't dare bring them near my eyes . . . Would you take my clean handkerchief, moisten it in fresh water, and bathe my poor eyes? ——— Would you? ——— Would you be a good Samaritan? (*The* MILKMAID *hesitates but does as he asks.*) Thank you, friend! (*He takes out his wallet. She makes a gesture of refusal.*) Forgive me, that was thoughtless, but I'm not really awake . . .

OLD MAN (*to the* STUDENT): Excuse me, but I heard you say that you were at the accident last night . . . I was just reading about it in the paper . . .

STUDENT: Is it already in the paper?

OLD MAN: Yes, the whole story. And your picture too. But they regret they couldn't learn the name of the very able student . . .

STUDENT (*looking at the paper*): Really? Yes, that's me! Well!

OLD MAN: Whom were you talking to just now?

STUDENT: Didn't you see? (*pause*)

OLD MAN: Would you think me rude if I . . . asked your name?

STUDENT: What for? I don't want any publicity. ——— First comes praise, then criticism. ——— Slandering people has become a fine art nowadays. ——— Besides, I didn't ask for any reward . . .

OLD MAN: You're wealthy, eh?

STUDENT: Not at all . . . on the contrary. I'm penniless.

OLD MAN: You know . . . there's something familiar about your voice. I've only met one other person who pronounces things the way you do. Are you possibly related to a wholesale merchant by the name of Arkenholz?

STUDENT: He was my father.

OLD MAN: Strange are the ways of fate . . . I saw you when you were little, under very painful circumstances . . .

STUDENT: Yes, they say I came into the world in the middle of a bankruptcy proceedings . . .

OLD MAN: That's right.

STUDENT: Can I ask what your name is?

OLD MAN: My name is Hummel.

STUDENT: Are you . . .? Yes, I remember . . .

OLD MAN: You've heard my name mentioned often in your family?

STUDENT: Yes!

OLD MAN: And probably mentioned with a certain ill will? (*The* STUDENT *remains silent.*) Yes, I can imagine! ——— I suppose you heard that I was the one who ruined your father? ——— People who ruin themselves through stupid speculation always blame the one person they couldn't fool for their ruin. (*pause*) The truth is that your father swindled me out of seventeen thousand crowns—my whole life savings at the time.

STUDENT: It's amazing how a story can be told in two such different ways.

OLD MAN: You don't think I'm lying, do you?

STUDENT: What else can I think? My father never lied!

OLD MAN: That's very true. A father never lies . . . but I too am a father, and consequently . . .

STUDENT: What are you trying to say?

OLD MAN: I saved your father from disaster, and he repaid me with all the terrible hatred of a man who feels obliged to be grateful. He taught his family to speak ill of me.

STUDENT: Maybe you made him ungrateful by poisoning your charity with unnecessary humiliations.

OLD MAN: All charity is humiliating, young man.

STUDENT: What do you want of me?

OLD MAN: I'm not asking for money. If you would perform a few services for me, I'd be well repaid. As you can see, I'm a cripple. Some people say it's my own fault; others blame my parents. Personally, I believe life itself is to blame, waiting in ambush for us, and if you avoid one trap, you walk straight into another. However—I can't run up and down stairs or ring doorbells. And so, I'm asking you: help me!

STUDENT: What can I do?

OLD MAN: First of all, push my chair so that I can read those posters. I want to see what's playing tonight ...

STUDENT (*pushing the wheelchair*): Don't you have a man to help you?

OLD MAN: Yes, but he's away on an errand ... be back soon ... Are you a medical student?

STUDENT: No, I'm studying languages. But I really don't know what I want to be ...

OLD MAN: Aha. ——— How are you at mathematics?

STUDENT: Fairly good.

OLD MAN: Fine. ——— Would you like a job?

STUDENT: Sure, why not?

OLD MAN: Good! (*reading the posters*) They're giving a matinée of *The Valkyrie* ... That means the Colonel and his daughter will be there. And since he always sits on the aisle in the sixth row, I'll put you next to them. Would you go into that telephone booth and reserve a ticket for seat number eighty-two in the sixth row?

STUDENT: You want me to go to the opera in the middle of the day?

OLD MAN: Yes. You do as I tell you, and you'll be well rewarded. I want you to be happy, rich, and respected. Your debut yesterday as a courageous rescuer will make you famous overnight. Your name will be really worth something.

STUDENT (*crossing to the booth*): What an amusing adventure . . .

OLD MAN: Are you a gambler?

STUDENT: Yes, unfortunately . . .

OLD MAN: We'll make that "fortunately"! ——— Make the call! (*He reads his newspaper. The* LADY IN BLACK *has come out on the sidewalk to speak to the* SUPERINTENDENT's WIFE; *the* OLD MAN *listens to them, but the audience hears nothing. The* STUDENT *returns.*) Is it all arranged?

STUDENT: It's all arranged.

OLD MAN: Have you ever seen this house before?

STUDENT: I certainly have! . . . I walked by here yesterday when the sun was blazing on its windows—and could picture all the beauty and luxury there must be inside. I said to my friend: "Imagine owning an apartment there, four flights up, a beautiful young wife, two lovely little children, and an independent income of 20,000 crowns a year . . ."

OLD MAN: Did you say that? *Did you say that?* Well! I too love that house . . .

STUDENT: You speculate in houses?

OLD MAN: Mmm, yes. But not in the way you think . . .

STUDENT: Do you know the people who live here?

OLD MAN: All of them. At my age you know everyone, their fathers and forefathers before them, and we're all kin, in some way or another. ——— I just turned eighty—but no one knows me, not really. ——— I take an interest in people's destinies . . . (*The curtains in the Round Room are drawn up. The* COLONEL *can be seen inside, dressed in civilian clothes. After looking at the thermometer, he crosses away from the window to stand in front of the statue.*) Look, there's the Colonel you'll sit next to this afternoon . . .

STUDENT: Is that—the Colonel? I don't understand any of this. It's like a fairy tale . . .

OLD MAN: My whole life is like a book of fairy tales, young man. But although the tales are different, a single thread joins them together, and the same theme, the leitmotif, returns again and again, like clockwork.

STUDENT: Is that statue of someone?

OLD MAN: It's his wife, of course . . .

STUDENT: Was she that wonderful?

OLD MAN: Uh, yes. Yes!

STUDENT: Tell me, really!

OLD MAN: It's not for us to judge other people, my boy! ———— If I were to tell you that she left him, that he beat her, that she returned and remarried him and now sits in there like a mummy, worshipping her own statue, you'd think I was crazy.

STUDENT: What? I don't understand!

OLD MAN: I can well believe it. ———— Then we have the hyacinth window. That's his daughter's room . . . She's out riding, but she'll be home soon . . .

STUDENT: Who's the dark lady talking to the caretaker?

OLD MAN: Well, you see, that's a little complicated. It has to do with the dead man, up there, where you see the white sheets hanging . . .

STUDENT: Who was he?

OLD MAN: He was a human being, like the rest of us. But the most conspicuous thing about him was his vanity . . . If you were a Sunday child, you'd soon see him come out the front door to look at the consulate flag flying at half-mast in his honor. ———— He was a consul, you see, and adored coronets, lions, plumed hats, and colored ribbons.

STUDENT: You mentioned a Sunday child—I'm told I was born on a Sunday . . .

OLD MAN: No! Were you . . .? I might have known it . . . I saw it in the color of your eyes . . . but then you can see what others can't see. Have you ever noticed that?

STUDENT: I don't know what others see, but sometimes . . . Well, things like that you don't talk about.

OLD MAN: I was almost certain of it! But you can talk about them with me . . . because I—understand such things . . .

STUDENT: Yesterday, for example . . . I was drawn to that secluded street where the house later collapsed . . . I walked down it and stopped in front of a building I'd never seen before . . . Then I noticed a crack in the wall, and heard the floorboards breaking. I ran forward and snatched up a child who was walking under the wall ... The next moment the house collapsed ... I was rescued, but in my arms, where I thought I held the child, there was nothing ...

OLD MAN: Amazing ... And I thought that ... Tell me something: why were you gesturing just now by the fountain? And why were you talking to yourself?

STUDENT: Didn't you see the milkmaid I was talking to?

OLD MAN (*terrified*): Milkmaid?

STUDENT: Yes, certainly. The girl who handed me the dipper.

OLD MAN: Is that right? So, that's what it was ... Well, even if I can't see, there are other things I can do ... (*A white-haired woman sits down at the window with the mirror.*) Look at that old woman in the window! Do you see her? ———— Good! She was once my fiancée, sixty years ago ... I was twenty then. ———— Don't be alarmed, she doesn't recognize me. We see each other every day, but I feel nothing, despite that we swore to be true to each other then—for ever!

STUDENT: How indiscreet your generation was! Young people don't talk like that nowadays.

OLD MAN: Forgive us, young man. We didn't know any better! ———— But can you see that that old woman was once young and beautiful?

STUDENT: It doesn't show. Though I like the way she looks around, but I can't see her eyes. (*The* SUPERINTENDENT's WIFE *comes out of the house and hangs a funeral wreath on the front door.*)

OLD MAN: That's the Superintendent's Wife. ———— The Lady in Black over there is her daughter by the dead man upstairs. That's why her husband got the job as superintendent ... but the Lady in Black has a lover, an aristocrat with grand expectations. He's in the process of getting a divorce, and his wife is giving him a mansion to get rid of him. This aristocratic lover is son-in-law to the dead man whose bedclothes you see being aired up there on the balcony ... As I said, it's all very complicated.

STUDENT: It's damned complicated!

OLD MAN: Yes, but that's the way it is, internally and externally. Though it looks simple.

STUDENT: Yes, but then who was the dead man?

OLD MAN: You just asked me and I told you. If you could see around the corner, by the service entrance, you'd notice a crowd of poor people, whom he used to help . . . when he felt like it . . .

STUDENT: So he was a kind man, then?

OLD MAN: Yes . . . sometimes.

STUDENT: Not always?

OLD MAN: No! . . . That's the way people are. Oh, young man, push my wheelchair a little, into the sun! I'm so terribly cold. When you never get to move around, the blood congeals. ——— I'm going to die soon, I know that. But before I do, I have a few things to take care of. ——— Take my hand and feel how cold I am.

STUDENT: Yes, incredibly! (*He tries in vain to free his hand.*)

OLD MAN: Don't leave me. I'm tired, I'm lonely, but I haven't always been like this, you know. I have an infinitely long life behind me—infinitely. ——— I've made people unhappy, but they've made me unhappy. The one cancels out the other. Before I die, I want to see you happy . . . Our destinies are intertwined through your father—and in other ways too . . .

STUDENT: But let go of my hand! You're draining my strength, you're freezing me. What do you want of me?

OLD MAN: Patience, and you'll see and understand . . . Here comes the young lady . . .

STUDENT: The Colonel's daughter?

OLD MAN: Yes! "His daughter"! Look at her! ——— Have you ever seen such a masterpiece?

STUDENT: She's like the marble statue in there . . .

OLD MAN: Well, that is her mother!

STUDENT: You're right. ——— Never have I seen such a woman of woman born. ——— Happy the man who leads her to the altar and his home.

OLD MAN: You *can* see it! ——— Not everyone recognizes her beauty . . . Well, so it is written. (*The* YOUNG LADY *enters left, wearing an English riding habit. She crosses slowly, without looking at anyone, to the front door, where she stops and says a few words to the* SUPERINTENDENT's WIFE. *She then enters the house. The* STUDENT *covers his eyes with his hand.*) Are you crying?

STUDENT: In the face of what's hopeless there can only be despair!

OLD MAN: But I can open doors and hearts if I but find a hand to do my will . . . Serve me and you shall prevail!

STUDENT: Is this some kind of pact? Do I have to sell my soul?

OLD MAN: Sell nothing! ——— You see, all my life I have *taken.* Now I have a desperate longing to be able to give! give! But no one will accept . . . I am rich, very rich, but I have no heirs, except for a good-for-nothing who plagues the life out of me . . . Be like a son to me. Be my heir while I'm still alive. Enjoy life while I'm here to see it, even if just from a distance.

STUDENT: What am I to do?

OLD MAN: First, go and listen to *The Valkyrie.*

STUDENT: As good as done. What else?

OLD MAN: Tonight you shall sit in there, in the Round Room.

STUDENT: How do I get there?

OLD MAN: By way of *The Valkyrie!*

STUDENT: Why have you chosen me as your medium? Did you know me before?

OLD MAN: Yes, of course! I've had my eyes on you for a long time . . . But look, up on the balcony. The maid is raising the flag to half-mast for the Consul . . . and she's turning the bedclothes . . . Do you see that blue quilt? ——— Once two people slept un-der it, but now only one . . . (*The* YOUNG LADY, *her clothes changed, appears at the window to water the hyacinths.*) Ah, there's my little girl. Look at her, look! ——— She's talking to the flowers. Isn't she like a blue hyacinth herself? . . . She's giv-ing them drink, just ordinary water, and they transform the wa-ter into color and fragrance . . . Here comes the Colonel with a newspaper! ——— He's showing her the story about the house collapsing . . . He's pointing out your picture! She's interested . . . she's reading about your bravery . . . I think it's getting cloudy. What if it should rain? I'll be in fine fix if Johansson doesn't come back soon . . . (*It grows cloudy and dark. The old woman at the mirror closes her window.*) My fiancée is closing her win-dow . . . seventy-nine years old . . . That mirror is the only mir-ror she uses, because she can't see herself in it, just the outside world in two different directions. But the world can see her, and that she didn't think of . . . A beautiful little old lady though . . . (*The* DEAD MAN, *in his winding-sheet, comes out the front door.*)

STUDENT: Oh my God!

OLD MAN: What's the matter?

STUDENT: Don't you see? There, in the doorway, the dead man!

OLD MAN: I see nothing, but I expected this! Go on ...

STUDENT: He's going out into the street ... (*pause*) Now he's turning his head to look at the flag.

OLD MAN: What did I tell you? Now he'll count the funeral wreaths and read the names on the cards ... God help those who are missing!

STUDENT: Now he's turning the corner ...

OLD MAN: He's gone to count the poor people at the service entrance ... They'll add a nice touch to his obituary: "Accompanied to his grave by the blessings of ordinary citizens." Well, he won't have my blessing! ——— Just between us, he was a great scoundrel ...

STUDENT: But charitable ...

OLD MAN: A charitable scoundrel, who always dreamed of a beautiful funeral ... When he felt that the end was near, he fleeced the government of fifty thousand crowns! ... Now his daughter is having an affair with another woman's husband and wondering if she's in his will ... The scoundrel can hear every word we say, and he deserves it! ——— Ah, here's Johansson! (JOHANSSON *enters from left.*) Report! (JOHANSSON *speaks but the audience cannot hear.*) Not at home, eh? You're an ass! ——— Any telegrams? ——— Nothing at all! ... Go on, go on! ... Six o'clock this evening? That's fine! ——— An extra edition? ———And his name in full! Arkenholz, student, born ... parents ... splendid ... I think it's starting to rain ... What did he have to say? ... Is that right? ——— He doesn't want to? ——— Well, he'll just have to! ——— Here comes the aristocratic lover! ——— Push me around the corner, Johansson, I want to hear what the poor people are saying ... Arkenholz, you wait for me here ... do you understand? ——— Hurry up, hurry up! (JOHANSSON *pushes the chair around the corner. The* STUDENT *remains behind, watching the* YOUNG LADY, *who is loosening the soil around the flowers.* BARON SKANSKORG *enters, wearing mourning, and speaks to the* LADY IN BLACK, *who has been walking up and down the sidewalk.*)

BARON SKANSKORG: Well, what can we do about it? ——— We'll

simply have to wait!

LADY IN BLACK: But I can't wait!

BARON SKANSKORG: Really? Better leave town then!

LADY IN BLACK: I don't want to.

BARON SKANSKORG: Come over here, otherwise they'll hear what
we're saying. (*They cross to the poster column and continue
their conversation, unheard by the audience.* JOHANSSON *enters
right and crosses to the* STUDENT.)

JOHANSSON: My master asks you not to forget the other matter,
sir.

STUDENT (*carefully*): Listen—first tell me: who is your master?

JOHANSSON: Oh, he's a lot of things, and he's been everything.

STUDENT: Is he sane?

JOHANSSON: Yes, and what is *that*, eh? ——— He says all his life
he's been looking for a Sunday child, but maybe it's not true ...

STUDENT: What does he want? Money?

JOHANSSON: He wants power ... All day long he rides around in
his chariot, like the great god Thor ... He looks at houses, tears
them down, widens streets, builds over public squares. But he
also breaks into houses, crawls through windows, destroys people's lives, kills his enemies, and forgives nothing. ——— Can
you imagine that that little cripple was once a Don Juan? Although he always lost his women.

STUDENT: That doesn't make sense.

JOHANSSON: Well, you see, he was so cunning that he got the
women to leave once he tired of them ... However, now he's
like a horse thief, only with people. He steals them, in all kinds
of ways ... He literally stole me out of the hands of justice ... I
had committed a ... blunder that only he knew about. Instead
of turning me in, he made me his slave, which is what I do, just
for my food, which is nothing to brag about ...

STUDENT: What does he want to do in this house?

JOHANSSON: Well, I wouldn't want to say. It's so complicated.

STUDENT: I think I'd better get out of here ... (*The* YOUNG LADY
drops her bracelet through the window.)

JOHANSSON: Look, the young lady's dropped her bracelet through
the window ... (*The* STUDENT *crosses slowly to the bracelet,
picks it up and hands it to the* YOUNG LADY, *who thanks him*

stiffly. The STUDENT *crosses back to* JOHANSSON.) So, you were thinking about leaving, eh? . . . It's not as easy as you think, once the old man's dropped his net over your head . . . And he's afraid of nothing between heaven and earth . . . well, except for one thing, or rather one person . . .

STUDENT: Wait, I think I know who!

JOHANSSON: How could you know that?

STUDENT: I'm guessing! ———— Is it . . . a little milkmaid that he's afraid of?

JOHANSSON: He always turns away when he sees a milk wagon . . . and then he talks in his sleep. You see, he was once in Hamburg . . .

STUDENT: Can anyone believe this man?

JOHANSSON: You can believe him—capable of anything!

STUDENT: What is he doing around the corner?

JOHANSSON: Listening to the poor people . . . Planting ideas here and there, pulling out bricks, one at a time, until the house collapses . . . metaphorically speaking . . . You see, I'm an educated man; I was once a bookseller . . . Are you going to leave now?

STUDENT: I don't want to seem ungrateful . . . The man saved my father once, and now he's only asking a small favor in return . . .

JOHANSSON: What's that?

STUDENT: I'm going to see *The Valkyrie* . . .

JOHANSSON: That's beyond me . . . He's always coming up with a new idea . . . Look, now he's talking to the police. He's always close with the police. He uses them, involves them in his schemes, binds them hand and foot with false hopes and promises. All the while he pumps them for information. ————
You'll see—before the day is over he'll be received in the Round Room.

STUDENT: What does he want there? What is there between him and the Colonel?

JOHANSSON: Well, I have my suspicions, but I'm not sure. You'll just have to see for yourself when you get there . . .

STUDENT: I'll never get in there . . .

JOHANSSON: That depends on you. ———— Go to *The Valkyrie* . . .

STUDENT: Is that the way?

JOHANSSON: If he said it was. ———— Look, look at him, in his war chariot, drawn in triumph by beggars who get nothing for their pains but the vague promise of a handout at his funeral! (*The* OLD MAN *enters standing in his wheelchair, drawn by one of the* BEGGARS, *and followed by others.*)

OLD MAN: Hail the noble youth, who at the risk of his own life, rescued so many in yesterday's accident! Hail, Arkenholz! (*The* BEGGARS *bare their heads but do not cheer. At the window the* YOUNG LADY *waves her handkerchief. The* COLONEL *stares out his window. The* OLD WOMAN *rises at her window. The* MAID *on the balcony raises the flag to the top.*) Clap your hands, my fellow citizens! It's Sunday, it's true, but the ass in the well and the stalk in the field give us absolution. Even though I'm not a Sunday child, I have both the spirit of prophecy and the gift of healing, for once I brought a drowned person back to life ... Yes, it was in Hamburg on a Sunday afternoon just like this one ... (*The* MILKMAID *enters, seen only by the* STUDENT *and the* OLD MAN. *She reaches out with her arms, like someone drowning, and stares at the* OLD MAN, *who sits down and shrinks back in terror.*) Johansson! Push me out of here! Quickly ――― Arkenholz, don't forget *The Valkyrie!*

STUDENT: What is all this?

JOHANSSON: We'll have to wait and see! We'll just have to wait and see!

Scene 2

(*The Round Room. Upstage is a white porcelain tile stove, studded with mirrors and flanked by a pendulum clock and a candlelabra. To the right the entrance hall, through which can be seen a green room with mahogany furniture. To the left a wallpaper-covered door leading to a closet. Further left the statue, shadowed by potted palms; it can be concealed by draperies. Upstage left is the door to the Hyacinth Room, where the* YOUNG LADY *sits reading. The* COLONEL *is visible, his back to the audience, writing in the green room.*

BENGTSSON, *the footman, dressed in livery, enters from the hall with* JOHANSSON, *who is dressed as a waiter.*)

BENGTSSON: Johansson, you'll do the serving, and I'll take their clothes. You've done this sort of thing before, haven't you?

JOHANSSON: As you know, I push that war chariot around during the day, but in the evenings I work as a waiter at receptions. Besides, it's always been my dream to come into this house . . . They're peculiar people, aren't they?

BENGTSSON: Well, yes, a little unusual, you might say.

JOHANSSON: Is it going to be a musical evening, or what?

BENGTSSON: Just the usual ghost supper, as we call it. They drink tea and never say a word, or else the Colonel does all the talking. And they nibble on cookies, all at the same time, so that it sounds like rats nibbling in an attic.

JOHANSSON: Why is it called a ghost supper?

BENGTSSON: They look like ghosts . . . And this has been going on for twenty years, always the same people, saying the same things, or else too ashamed to say anything.

JOHANSSON: Isn't there a lady of the house too?

BENGTSSON: Oh yes, but she's queer in the head. She sits in a closet, because her eyes can't stand the light . . . She's right in there . . . (*points to the wallpaper-covered door*)

JOHANSSON: In there?

BENGTSSON: Well, I told you they were a little unusual . . .

JOHANSSON: How does she look?

BENGTSSON: Like a mummy . . . Do you want to see her? (*opens the door*) See, there she is!

JOHANSSON: Oh, Jesus . . .

MUMMY (*like a baby*): Why did you open the door? Haven't I told you to keep it shut? . . .

BENGTSSON (*using baby talk*): Ta, ta, ta, ta! Sweetums must be good, then you'll get something nice!———Pretty polly!

MUMMY (*like a parrot*): Pretty polly! Is Jacob there? Awwk!

BENGTSSON: She thinks she's a parrot, and who knows?, maybe she is . . . (*to the* MUMMY) Polly, whistle a little for us. (*She whistles.*)

JOHANSSON: I've seen lots in my life, but this beats everything!

BENGTSSON: You see, when a house gets old, it gets moldy. And when people sit around tormenting each other for so long, they get crazy. Now the madam here—quiet Polly!—this mummy has been sitting here for forty years—same husband, same furniture, same relatives, same friends ... (*closes the wallpaper-covered door*) Even I don't know everything that's gone on in this house ... Do you see this statue? ... that's the madam when she was young!

JOHANSSON: Oh, my God! ———— Is that the Mummy?

BENGTSSON: Yes! ———— It's enough to make you cry! ———— And somehow or other—the power of imagination, maybe— she's taken on some of the qualities of a real parrot. ———— For instance, she can't stand cripples or sick people ... That's why she can't stand the sight of her own daughter ...

JOHANSSON: Is the young lady sick?

BENGTSSON: Didn't you know that?

JOHANSSON: No! ... And the Colonel, who is he?

BENGTSSON: You'll have to wait and see!

JOHANSSON (*looking at the statue*): It's terrible to think that ... How old is the madam now?

BENGTSSON: No one knows ... but they say that when she was thirty-five, she looked nineteen, and convinced the Colonel that she was ... In this house ... Do you know what that black Japanese screen is for, there, next to the chaise longue? ———— It's called the death screen, and when someone is dying, it's put up around them, just like in a hospital ...

JOHANSSON: What a horrible place! ... And the student wants to come here because he thinks it's a paradise ...

BENGTSSON: What student? Oh, him! The one who's coming here this evening ... The Colonel and the young lady met him at the opera and were taken by him ... Hm! ... Now it's my turn to ask questions: who is your master? the businessman in the wheelchair?

JOHANSSON: Yes. ———— Is he coming here too?

BENGTSSON: He's not invited.

JOHANSSON: If necessary, he'll come uninvited ... (*The* OLD MAN *appears in the hallway, dressed in a frock coat. He steals forward on his crutches to eavesdrop.*)

BENGTSSON: I hear he's an old crook!

JOHANSSON: Full blown!

BENGTSSON: He looks like the devil himself!

JOHANSSON: And he must be a magician too!—for he can go through locked doors . . .

OLD MAN (*crosses and grabs* JOHANSSON *by the ear*): Rascal! —— You watch your step! (*to* BENGTSSON) Announce me to the Colonel!

BENGTSSON: Yes, but we're expecting guests . . .

OLD MAN: I know that! But my visit is as good as expected, if not exactly looked forward to . . .

BENGTSSON: Is that so? And what was the name? Director Hummel!

OLD MAN: Precisely! (BENGTSSON *crosses to the hallway and enters the green room, closing the door behind him. The* OLD MAN *turns to* JOHANSSON.) Disappear! (JOHANSSON *hesitates.*) Disappear! (JOHANSSON *disappears into the hallway. The* OLD MAN *inspects the room, stopping in front of the statue in great astonishment.*) Amalia! . . . It's she! . . . She! (*He wanders about the room fingering things; he straightens his wig in front of the mirror, and returns to the statue.*)

MUMMY (*from within the closet*): Pretty polly!

OLD MAN (*wincing*): What was that? Is there a parrot in the room? I don't see one!

MUMMY: Is Jacob there?

OLD MAN: The place is haunted!

MUMMY: Jaaaacob!

OLD MAN: I'm scared . . . So, these are the secrets they've been hiding in this house! (*He looks at a painting, his back turned to the closet.*) There he is! . . . He! (*The* MUMMY *comes out of the closet, goes up to him from behind, and yanks on his wig.*)

MUMMY: Squir-rel! Is it Squir-rel?

OLD MAN (*badly frightened*): Oh my God! —— Who are you?

MUMMY (*in a normal voice*): Is it you, Jacob?

OLD MAN: As a matter of fact, my name is Jacob . . .

MUMMY (*moved*): And my name is Amalia.

OLD MAN: Oh, no, no, no . . . Lord Je . . .

MUMMY: Yes, this is how I look! —— And (*pointing to the statue*) that's how I *used* to look! Life teaches us so much. —— I stay in the closet mostly, both to avoid seeing people, and being seen . . . But what do you want here, Jacob?

OLD MAN: My child! Our child . . .

MUMMY: She's in there.

OLD MAN: Where?

MUMMY: There, in the hyacinth room.

OLD MAN (*looking at the* YOUNG LADY): Yes, there she is. (*pause*) What does her father say? The Colonel? Your husband?

MUMMY: Once, when I was angry at him, I told him everything . . .

OLD MAN: And?

MUMMY: He didn't believe me. He just said: "That's what all wives say when they want to murder their husbands." ——— Even so, it was a terrible crime. Everything in his life is a forgery, his family tree too. Sometimes when I look at the List of the Nobility, I think to myself: "Why that woman has a false birth certificate, like a common servant girl. People get sent to prison for that."

OLD MAN: Many people do that. I seem to remember you falsified your age . . .

MUMMY: My mother made me . . . it wasn't my fault! . . . But in our crime you were most responsible . . .

OLD MAN: No, your husband provoked the crime when he stole my fiancée away from me! ——— I was born unable to forgive until I've punished! I saw it as a compelling duty . . . and still do!

MUMMY: What are you looking for in this house? What do you want? How did you get in? ——— Is it my daughter? If you touch her, you'll die!

OLD MAN: I want what's best for her.

MUMMY: But you must spare her father!

OLD MAN: No!

MUMMY: Then you shall die. In this room. Behind that screen . . .

OLD MAN: That may be . . . but once I sink my teeth into something, I can't let go . . .

MUMMY: You want to marry her off to that student. Why? He has nothing and is nothing.

OLD MAN: He'll become rich, through me!

MUMMY: Were you invited here this evening?

OLD MAN: No, but I intend to get an invitation to the ghost supper.

MUMMY: Do you know who's coming?

OLD MAN: Not exactly.

MUMMY: The Baron . . . who lives upstairs and whose father-in-law was buried this afternoon . . .

OLD MAN: The one who's getting divorced so he can marry the superintendent's daughter . . . The one who was once your—lover!

MUMMY: Another guest will be your former fiancée, whom my husband seduced . . .

OLD MAN: What an elegant gathering . . .

MUMMY: God, if only we could die! If *only* we could die!

OLD MAN: Then why do you associate with each other?

MUMMY: Crimes and secrets and guilt bind us together! ———— We've broken up and gone our separate ways an endless number of times, but we're always drawn back together again . . .

OLD MAN: I think the Colonel's coming . . .

MUMMY: Then I'll go in to Adèle . . . (*pause*) Jacob, mind what you do! Spare him . . . (*pause; she leaves.*)

COLONEL (*entering; cool, reserved*): Won't you sit down? (*The* OLD MAN *sits down slowly; pause; the* COLONEL *stares at him.*) Are you the one who wrote this letter?

OLD MAN: Yes.

COLONEL: Your name is Hummel?

OLD MAN: Yes. (*pause*)

COLONEL: Since I know you bought up all my unpaid promissory notes, it follows that I am at your mercy. What is it you want?

OLD MAN: Payment of one kind or another.

COLONEL: What kind did you have in mind?

OLD MAN: A very simple one—but let's not talk about money. ———— Just tolerate me in your house as a guest.

COLONEL: If that's all it takes to satisfy you . . .

OLD MAN: Thank you.

COLONEL: Anything else?

OLD MAN: Fire Bengtsson!

COLONEL: Why should I do that? My trusted servant, who's been with me for a generation—who wears the national medal for loyal and faithful service? Why should I do that?

OLD MAN: All his beautiful virtues exist only in your imagination. ———— He's not the man he appears to be.

COLONEL: But who is?

OLD MAN (*winces*): True! But Bengtsson must go!

COLONEL: Are you trying to run my house?

OLD MAN: Yes! Since I own everything here: furniture, curtains, dinner service, linen . . . and other things!

COLONEL: What other things?

OLD MAN: Everything! I own everything! It's all mine!

COLONEL: Very well, it's all yours. But my family's coat of arms, and my good name—they remain mine!

OLD MAN: No, not even those! (*pause*) You're not a nobleman.

COLONEL: How dare you?

OLD MAN (*taking out a paper*): If you read this extract from the Book of Noble Families, you'll see that the name you bear died out a hundred years ago.

COLONEL (*reading*): I've certainly heard such rumors, but the name I bear was my father's . . . (*reading*) It's true, you're right . . . I'm not a nobleman! —— Not even that remains! —— Then I'll take off my signet ring. —— It too belongs to you . . . Here, take it!

OLD MAN (*pocketing the ring*): Now we'll continue! —— You're not a colonel either.

COLONEL: I'm not?

OLD MAN: No! You were a former temporary colonel in the American Volunteers, but when the army was reorganized after the Spanish-American War, all such ranks were abolished . . .

COLONEL: Is that true?

OLD MAN (*reaching into his pocket*): Do you want to read about it?

COLONEL: No, it's not necessary! . . . Who are you, that you have the right to sit there and strip me naked like this?

OLD MAN: We'll see! But speaking about stripping . . . do you know who you really are?

COLONEL: Have you no sense of shame?

OLD MAN: Take off your wig and look at yourself in the mirror! Take out your false teeth too, and shave off your mustache! We'll have Bengtsson unlace your corset, and we'll see if a certain servant, Mr. XYZ, won't recognize himself: a man who was once a great sponger in a certain kitchen . . . (*The* COLONEL *reaches for the bell on the table but is stopped by the* OLD

MAN.) Don't touch that bell! If you call Bengtsson in here, I'll have him arrested ... Your guests are arriving. ——— You keep calm and we'll continue to play our old roles a while longer!

COLONEL: Who are you? I recognize that expression in your eyes and that tone in your voice ...

OLD MAN: No more questions! Just keep quiet and do as you're told!

STUDENT (*enters and bows to the* COLONEL): Good evening, sir!

COLONEL: Welcome to my home, young man! Everyone is talking about your heroism at that terrible accident, and it's an honor for me to greet you ...

STUDENT: Colonel, my humble origin ... Your brilliant name and noble background ...

COLONEL: Let my introduce you: Director Hummel, Mr. Arkenholz ... Would you go in and join the ladies? I have to finish my conversation with the director ... (*The* STUDENT *is shown into the Hyacinth Room, where he remains visible, engaged in shy conversation with the* YOUNG LADY.) A superb young man, musical, sings, writes poetry ... If he were a nobleman and our equal socially, I would have nothing against ... yes ...

OLD MAN: Against what?

COLONEL: My daughter ...

OLD MAN: *Your* daughter? ——— By the way, why does she always sit in there?

COLONEL: Whenever she's at home, she feels compelled to sit in the Hyacinth Room. It's a peculiar habit she has ... Ah, here comes Miss Beate von Holsteinkrona ... a charming old lady ... Very active in the church and with a modest income from a trust ...

OLD MAN (*to himself*): My old fiancée! (*The* FIANCÉE *enters; she is white-haired and looks crazy.*)

COLONEL: Director Hummel, Miss Holsteinkrona ... (*She curtsies and sits. The* BARON *enters, dressed in mourning and looking as if he is hiding something; he sits.*) Baron Skanskorg ...

OLD MAN (*to himself, without rising*): If it isn't the jewel thief ... (*to the* COLONEL) Call in the Mummy, and the party will be complete ...

COLONEL (*at the door to the Hyacinth Room*): Polly!

MUMMY (*entering*): Squir-rel!

COLONEL: Should the young people be in here too?

OLD MAN: No! Not the young people! They'll be spared . . . (*They all sit in silence in a circle.*)

COLONEL: Can we have the tea served?

OLD MAN: What for? No one here likes tea, so there's no use pretending we do. (*pause*)

COLONEL: Shall we talk then?

OLD MAN (*slowly, with long pauses*): About what: the weather, which we all know? Ask about each other's health, which we also know. I prefer silence. Then you can hear thoughts and see into the past. In silence you can't hide anything . . . as you can in words. The other day I read that the reason different languages developed was because primitive tribes tried to keep secrets from each other. And so languages are codes, and whoever finds the key will understand them all. But there are certain secrets that can be exposed without a key, especially when it comes to proving paternity. But proving something in a courtroom is something else. That takes two false witnesses, providing their stories agree. But on the kinds of expeditions I'm thinking of, witnesses aren't taken along. Nature itself plants in human beings an instinct for hiding that which should be hidden. Nevertheless, we stumble into things without intending to, and sometimes the opportunity presents itself to reveal the deepest of secrets, to tear the mask off the imposter, to expose the villain . . . (*pause; all watch each other without speaking.*) How quiet it's become! (*long silence*) Here, for instance, in this honorable house, in this lovely home, where beauty, culture and wealth are united . . . (*long silence*) All of us know who we are . . . don't we? . . . I don't have to tell you . . . And you know me, although you pretend ignorance . . . In there is my daughter, *mine!* You know that too . . . She had lost the desire to live, without knowing why . . . because she was withering away in this atmosphere of crime, deceit and falseness of every kind . . . That's why I looked for a friend for her in whose company she could sense the light and warmth of a noble deed . . . (*long silence*) And so my mission in this house was to pull up the weeds, expose the crimes, settle all accounts, so that those young people might start anew in a home that I had given them! (*long silence*) Now I'm going to give you a chance to leave, under safe-conduct, each of you, in your own time. Whoever stays, I'll have arrested! (*long silence*) Listen to the clock ticking, like a deathwatch beetle in the wall! Do you hear what it says? "Times-up! Times-up! —— —— ——" In a few moments it'll strike and your time will be up. Then you may go, but not before. But it sounds a threat before it strikes. —— Listen! There's the warning: "The clock-can-strike." —— —— —— I too can strike... (*He strikes the table with his crutch.*) Do you hear? (*silence; the* MUMMY *crosses to the clock and stops it.*)

MUMMY (*clearly and seriously*): But I can stop time in its course. —— I can wipe out the past, undo what has been done. Not with bribes, not with threats—but through suffering and repentance —— —— —— (*crosses to the* OLD MAN) We are only wretched human beings, we know that. We have trespassed and we have sinned, like all the rest. We are not what we seem, for deep down we are better than ourselves, since we detest our faults. But that you, Jacob Hummel, with your false name, can sit here and judge us, proves that you are worse than us miserable creatures! You too are not what you seem! —— You're a thief who steals souls. You stole mine once with false promises. You murdered the Consul who was buried today; you strangled him with debts. You stole the Student by binding him to a debt you pretended was left by his father, who never owed you a penny... (*During her speech, the* OLD MAN *has tried to rise and speak, but has fallen back in his chair, crumpling up more and more as she continues.*) But there's a dark spot in your life. I've long suspected what it is, but I'm not sure... I think Bengtsson knows. (*rings the bell on the table*)

OLD MAN: No, not Bengtsson! Not him!

MUMMY: Ah, then he *does* know! (*She rings again. The little* MILKMAID *appears in the hallway door, unseen by everyone except the* OLD MAN, *who becomes terrified. The* MILKMAID *disappears as* BENGTSSON *enters.*)

MUMMY: Bengtsson, do you know this man?

BENGTSSON: Yes, I know him, and he knows me. Life has its ups and downs, as we all know. I was once in his service; another time he was in mine. For two whole years he was a sponger who used to flirt with the cook in my kitchen. ———— Because he had to get away by three o'clock, dinner was ready by two. And so we had to eat the warmed-over leavings of that ox! ———— And he also drank the soup stock, which the cook then filled up with water. He was like a vampire, sucking the marrow out of the house and turning us all into skeletons. ———— And he almost got us put in prison when we called the cook a thief. Later, I met him in Hamburg under another name. This time he was a usurer, a bloodsucker. And he was accused of having lured a girl out onto the ice to drown her, because she had witnessed a crime he was afraid would be discovered . . . (*The* MUMMY *passes her hand across the* OLD MAN'S *face.*)

MUMMY: This is you! Now give me the notes and the will! (JO-HANSSON *appears in the hallway door and watches the proceedings with great interest, knowing that he will shortly be freed from his slavery. The* OLD MAN *takes out a bundle of papers and throws them on the table. The* MUMMY *strokes him on the back.*) Polly! Is Jacob there?

OLD MAN (*like a parrot*): Ja-cob is there! ———— Kakadora! Dora!

MUMMY: Can the clock strike?

OLD MAN (*clucking*): The clock can strike! (*imitating a cuckoo clock*) Cuck-oo, cuck-oo, cuck-oo! . . .

MUMMY (*opens the closet door*): Now the clock has struck! ———— Get up and go into that closet, where I've spent twenty years grieving our mistake. ———— There's a rope hanging in there. Let it stand for the one you used to strangle the Consul upstairs, and with which you intended to strangle your benefactor . . . Go! (*The* OLD MAN *goes into the closet. The* MUMMY *closes the door.*) Bengtsson! Put out the screen! The death screen! (BENGTSSON *puts out the screen in front of the door.*) It is finished! ———— May God have mercy on his soul!

ALL: Amen! (*long silence; in the Hyacinth Room the* YOUNG LADY *can be seen accompanying the* STUDENT *on the harp as he recites.*)

STUDENT: (*after a prelude*):
     I saw the sun, and seemed to see

what was hidden.
You cannot heal with evil
deeds done in anger.
Man reaps as he sows;
blessed is the doer of good.
Comfort him you have grieved
with your goodness, and you will have healed.
No fear has he who has done no ill;
goodness is innocence.

Scene 3

(*The Hyacinth Room. The style of the décor is somewhat bizarre, with oriental motifs. Hyacinths of every color everywhere. On top of the porcelain tiled stove is a large statue of a seated Buddha. In his lap is a bulb, out of which the stalk of a shallot has shot up, bearing its globe-shaped cluster of white, starlike flowers.*

Upstage right the door to the Round Room, where the COLONEL *and the* MUMMY *sit silently, doing nothing. A portion of the death screen is also visible. To the left the door to the pantry and the kitchen.*

The STUDENT *and the* YOUNG LADY, *Adèle, are near a table, she with the harp, he standing.*)

YOUNG LADY: Sing for my flowers!

STUDENT: Is the hyacinth the flower of your soul?

YOUNG LADY: The one and only. Do you love the hyacinth?

STUDENT: I love it above all others—its virginal figure rising so slim and straight from the bulb, floating on the water and sending its pure white roots down into the colorless fluid. I love its colors: the snow-white of innocence, the honey-gold of sweetness and pleasure, the rosy-pink of youth, the scarlet of maturity, but above all the blue, the blue of deep eyes, of dew, of faithfulness ... I love its colors more than gold and pearls, have loved them since I was a child, have worshipped them because they possess all the virtues I lack ... And yet ...

YOUNG LADY: What?

STUDENT: My love is not returned, for these lovely blossoms hate me . . .

YOUNG LADY: How do you mean?

STUDENT: Their fragrance—strong and pure as the early winds of spring that have passed over melting snow—it confuses my senses, deafens me, crowds me out of the room, dazzles me, shoots me with poisoned arrows that wound my heart and set my head on fire. Don't you know the legend of this flower?

YOUNG LADY: Tell me.

STUDENT: But first its meaning. The bulb, whether floating on water or buried in soil, is our earth. The stalk shoots up, straight as the axis of the world, and above, with its six-pointed star flowers, is the globe of heaven.

YOUNG LADY: Above the earth—the stars! How wonderful! Where did you learn to see things this way?

STUDENT: Let me think! —— In your eyes! —— And so this flower is a replica of the universe . . . That's why the Buddha sits brooding over the bulb of the earth in his lap, watching it grow outwards and upwards, transforming itself into a heaven. —— This wretched earth aspires to become heaven! That's what the Buddha is waiting for!

YOUNG LADY: Now I see—aren't snowflakes also six-pointed, like hyacinth lilies?

STUDENT: You're right! —— Then snowflakes are falling stars . . .

YOUNG LADY: And the snowdrop is a snow star . . . rising from the snow.

STUDENT: And the largest and most beautiful of all the stars in the firmament, the red and gold Sirius, is the narcissus, with its red and gold chalice and six white rays . . .

YOUNG LADY: Have you ever seen the shallot in bloom?

STUDENT: I certainly have! —— It too bears its flowers in a ball, a sphere like the globe of heaven, strewn with white stars . . .

YOUNG LADY: Yes! God, how magnificent! Whose idea was this?

STUDENT: Yours!

YOUNG LADY: Yours!

STUDENT: Ours! —— Together we have given birth to something. We are wed . . .

YOUNG LADY: Not yet . . .

STUDENT: What else remains?

YOUNG LADY: The waiting, the trials, the patience!

STUDENT: Fine! Try me! (*pause*) Tell me, why do your parents sit so silently in there, without saying a word?

YOUNG LADY: Because they have nothing to say to each other, because neither believes what the other says. As my father puts it: "What's the point of talking, when we can't fool each other?"

STUDENT: What a terrible thing to believe . . .

YOUNG LADY: Here comes the Cook . . . Oh, look at her, she's so big and fat . . .

STUDENT: What does she want?

YOUNG LADY: She wants to ask me about dinner. I run the house, you see, while my mother is ill . . .

STUDENT: Why should we bother about the kitchen?

YOUNG LADY: We have to eat . . . You look at her, I can't bear to . . .

STUDENT: Who is this monstrous woman?

YOUNG LADY: She belongs to the Hummel family of vampires. She's devouring us . . .

STUDENT: Why don't you get rid of her?

YOUNG LADY: She won't go! We have no control over her. She is punishment for our sins . . . Can't you see that we're wasting away, withering? . . .

STUDENT: You mean you don't get enough to eat?

YOUNG LADY: Oh yes, we get lots to eat, but nothing nourishing. She boils the meat until there's nothing left but gristle and water, while she drinks the stock herself. And when there's a roast, she first cooks out all the goodness and drinks the gravy and broth. Everything she touches shrivels up and dries out. It's as if she can drain you with her eyes. She drinks the coffee and we get the grounds. She drinks from the wine and fills the bottles with water . . .

STUDENT: Drive her out of the house!

YOUNG LADY: We can't!

STUDENT: Why not?

YOUNG LADY: We don't know! She won't go! No one has any control over her! ———— She's taken all our strength!

STUDENT: May I send her away?

YOUNG LADY: No! Things must be as they are! ———— Now she's here. She'll ask what we'll have for dinner. I'll answer this and that. She'll object and get her own way.

STUDENT: Then let her decide the meals.

YOUNG LADY: She won't do that!

STUDENT: This *is* a strange house. It's bewitched!

YOUNG LADY: Yes. ———— Oh, she turned away when she saw you.

COOK (*in the door*): No, that wasn't why. (*She sneers, her teeth showing.*)

STUDENT: Get out, woman!

COOK: When I'm good and ready. (*pause*) Now I'm ready. (*disappears*)

YOUNG LADY: Don't lose your temper! ———— You must be patient. She's one of the trials we have to endure in this house. Another is the maid—we have to clean up after her.

STUDENT: I feel myself sinking down! *Cor in aethere!* Music!

YOUNG LADY: Wait!

STUDENT: Music!

YOUNG LADY: Patience! ———— This room is called the room of trials. ———— It's beautiful to look at, but it's full of imperfections . . .

STUDENT: I can't believe that! But we'll have to overlook them. It is beautiful, but it feels cold. Why don't you have a fire?

YOUNG LADY: Because it smokes.

STUDENT: Can't you have the chimney cleaned?

YOUNG LADY: It doesn't help! . . . Do you see that writing table?

STUDENT: It's very beautiful.

YOUNG LADY: But it wobbles! Every day I put a piece of cork under that leg, but the maid takes it away when she sweeps, and I have to cut a new one. Every morning the penholder is covered with ink, and so is the inkstand. As sure as the sun rises, I'm always cleaning up after that woman. (*pause*) What chore do you hate most?

STUDENT: Separating dirty laundry. Ugh!

YOUNG LADY: That's what I have to do. Ugh!

STUDENT: What else?

YOUNG LADY: Be awakened from a sound sleep to lock a window ... which the maid left rattling.

STUDENT: What else?

YOUNG LADY: Climb a ladder to fix the damper on the stove after the maid pulled the cord loose.

STUDENT: What else?

YOUNG LADY: Sweep after her, dust after her, light the stove after her—she'll only put the wood in! Open the damper, wipe the glasses dry, *re*set the table, uncork the wine bottles, open the windows to air the rooms, *re*make my bed, rinse the water pitcher when it gets green with algae, buy matches and soap, which we're always out of, wipe the lamp chimneys, and trim the wicks to keep the lamps from smoking. And to be sure they won't go out when we have company, I have to fill them myself ...

STUDENT: Music!

YOUNG LADY: Wait! ——— First, the drudgery, the drudgery of keeping the filth of life at a distance.

STUDENT: But you're well off. You've got two servants.

YOUNG LADY: It wouldn't help if we had three. It's so difficult just to live, and sometimes I get so tired ... Imagine if there were a nursery too!

STUDENT: The greatest joy of all ...

YOUNG LADY: And the most expensive ... Is life worth this much trouble?

STUDENT: That depends on what you want in return ... I would do anything to win your hand.

YOUNG LADY: Don't talk like that! ——— You can never have me.

STUDENT: Why not?

YOUNG LADY: You mustn't ask. (*pause*)

STUDENT: But you dropped your bracelet out of the window ...

YOUNG LADY: Because my hand has grown so thin ... (*pause; the* COOK *appears carrying a bottle of Japanese soy sauce.*) It's she, who's devouring me, devouring us all.

STUDENT: What's she got in her hand?

YOUNG LADY: The Japanese bottle with the lettering like scorpions! It's soy sauce to turn water into broth. She uses it instead of gravy when she cooks cabbage and makes mock turtle soup.

STUDENT: Get out!

COOK: You suck the juices out of us, and we out of you. We take the blood and give you back water—with coloring. This is colored water! ——— I'm going now, but I'm staying in this house, as long as I want! (*exits*)

STUDENT: Why did Bengtsson get a medal?

YOUNG LADY: For his great merits.

STUDENT: Has he no faults?

YOUNG LADY: Oh yes, terrible ones, but you don't get medals for them. (*They smile.*)

STUDENT: You have many secrets in this house . . .

YOUNG LADY: Like everyone else . . . Let us keep ours! (*pause*)

STUDENT: Don't you like frankness?

YOUNG LADY: Yes, within reason.

STUDENT: Sometimes I get a raging desire to say exactly what I think. But I know that if people were really frank and honest, the world would collapse. (*pause*) I was at a funeral the other day . . . in the church. ——— It was very solemn and beautiful.

YOUNG LADY: For Director Hummel?

STUDENT: Yes, my false benefactor! ——— At the head of the coffin stood an old friend of the dead man, carrying the funeral mace. I was especially impressed by the minister because of his dignified manner and moving words. ——— Yes, I cried, we all cried. ——— Afterwards we went to a restaurant . . . There I learned that the man with the mace had been in love with the dead man's son . . . (*The* YOUNG LADY *stares at him questioningly.*) And that the dead man had borrowed money from his son's . . . admirer . . . (*pause*) The next day the minister was arrested for embezzling church funds! ——— Pretty story, isn't it?

YOUNG LADY: Oh! (*pause*)

STUDENT: Do you know what I'm thinking now about you?

YOUNG LADY: Don't tell me, or I'll die!

STUDENT: I must, or I'll die! . . .

YOUNG LADY: It's only in asylums that people say everything they think . . .

STUDENT: Yes, exactly! ——— My father ended up in a madhouse . . .

YOUNG LADY: Was he ill?

STUDENT: No, he was well, but he was crazy. The madness broke out one day, when things became too much for him . . . Like the rest of us, he had a circle of acquaintances, which, for the sake of convenience, he called friends. Naturally, they were a miserable bunch, as most people are. But he needed them because he couldn't bear to be alone. Well, he didn't ordinarily tell people what he thought of them, any more than anyone else does. He certainly knew how false they were, what treachery they were capable of! . . . However, he was a prudent man, and well brought up, and so he was always polite. But one day he gave a big party. —— It was in the evening, and he was tired, tired after the day's work, and tired from the strain of wanting to keep his mouth shut and having to talk nonsense with his guests . . . (*The* YOUNG LADY *shrinks back in horror.*) Anyway, at the dinner table, he rapped for silence, raised his glass, and began to talk . . . Then something loosed the trigger, and in a long speech he stripped everybody naked, one after another, exposing all their falseness! Exhausted, he sat down in the middle of the table and told them all to go to hell!

YOUNG LADY: Oh!

STUDENT: I was there, and I'll never forget what happened next! . . . My father and mother fought, and the guests rushed for the door . . . My father was taken to a madhouse, where he died. (*pause*) When we keep silent for too long, stagnant water starts to form, and everything rots! And that's the way it is in this house too! There's something rotting here! And I thought this was a paradise the first time I saw you enter here . . . On that Sunday morning I stood outside and looked in. I saw a colonel who wasn't a colonel. I had a noble benefactor who was a bandit and had to hang himself. I saw a mummy who was not a mummy, and a maiden—which reminds me: where is virginity to be found? Where is beauty? Only in Nature or in my mind when it's dressed up in Sunday best. Where are honor and faith? In fairy tales and children's games. Where is anything that fulfills its promise? . . . In my imagination! —— Do you see? Your flowers have poisoned me, and now I've given the poison back to you. —— I begged you to be my wife and share our home. We made poetry, sang and played, and then in came the Cook

... *Sursum Corda!* Try once more to strike fire and splendor from the golden harp ... try, I beg you, I command you on my knees! ... Very well, then I'll do it myself! (*takes the harp and plucks the strings, but there is no sound*)

It's deaf and dumb! Why is it that the most beautiful flowers are so poisonous, the most poisonous? Damnation hangs over the whole of creation ... Why wouldn't you be my bride? Because you're sick at the very source of life ... I can feel that vampire in the kitchen beginning to drain me. I think she's a Lamia who sucks the blood of children. It's always in the kitchen that a child's seed leaves are nipped, its growth stunted, if it hasn't already happened in the bedroom ... There are poisons that blind you, and poisons that open your eyes. ———— I must have been born with the second kind in my veins, for I can't see beauty in ugliness or call evil good, I can't! Jesus Christ descended into hell. That was his pilgrimage on this earth: to this madhouse, this dungeon, this morgue of a world. And the madmen killed him when he tried to set them free, but they let the bandit go. It's always the bandit who gets the sympathy! ———— Alas! Alas for us all! Savior of the World, save us, we are perishing! (*The* YOUNG LADY, *apparently dying, lies crumpled in her chair. She rings and* BENGTSSON *enters.*)

YOUNG LADY: Bring the screen! Quickly—I'm dying! (BENGTSSON *exits and returns with the screen, which he unfolds and sets up around the* YOUNG LADY.)

STUDENT: He's coming to set you free! Welcome, you pale and gentle deliverer! ———— Sleep, my beautiful one, lost and innocent, blameless in your suffering. Sleep without dreaming. And when you awaken again ... may you be greeted by a sun that does not burn, in a home without dust, by friends who cause no pain, by a love without flaw ... You wise and gentle Buddha, sitting there waiting for a heaven to rise up out of the earth, grant us patience in the time of testing, and purity of will, so that your hope may not be in vain! (*The strings of the harp make a murmuring sound. The room is filled with white light.*)

I saw the sun, and thought I saw
what was hidden.
You cannot heal with evil

deeds done in anger.
Man reaps as he sows;
blessed is the doer of good.
Comfort him you have grieved
with your goodness, and you will have healed.
No fear has he who has done no ill;
goodness is innocence.
(*A whimpering can be heard from behind the screen.*) You poor little child, child of this world of illusion, guilt, suffering, and death; this world of endless change, disappointment and pain. The Lord of Heaven be merciful to you on your journey . . .

(*The room disappears. Böcklin's painting, "The Island of the Dead," appears in the background, and from the island comes music, soft, calm, and gently melancholy.*)

Designer: Eric Jungerman
Compositor: TriStar Graphics
Printer: Vail-Ballou Press, Inc.
Binder: Vail-Ballou Press, Inc.
Text: 10/12 Electra
Display: Phototypositor Nova Augustea,
machine-set Electra